A PLACE TO GO
A PLACE TO GROW

Simple Things That Make a Difference for At-Risk Kids

LOU DANTZLER, founder of the
Challengers Boys & Girls Club

With Kathleen Felesina • Foreword by Magic Johnson

RODALE

Printed in the United States of America
Rodale Inc. makes every effort to use acid-free ∞, recycled paper ♲.

Book design by Anthony Serge
Photographs courtesy of Lou Dantzler

Library of Congress Cataloging-in-Publication Data

Dantzler, Lou.
    A place to go, a place to grow : simple things that make a difference for at-risk kids /
Lou Dantzler with Kathleen Felesina.
        p. cm.
    Includes index.
    ISBN-13 978-1-59486-418-6 hardcover
    ISBN-10 1-59486-418-7 hardcover
    1. Dantzler, Lou. 2. Challengers Boys & Girls Club. 3. Children—California—Los
Angeles—Societies and clubs—Case studies. 4. Children with social disabilities—
Services for—California—Los Angeles—Case studies. I. Felesina, Kathleen. II. Title.
HS3256.2.D36A3 2006
369.4—dc22   2006002344

Distributed to the book trade by Holtzbrinck Publishers

2   4   6   8   10   9   7   5   3   1   hardcover

To my mother, Narvis,
the original Challenger

GEORGE BUSH

September 12, 2005

Dear Lou,

I am thrilled that you are sharing with the world your inspiring story of courage and compassion. Having had the privilege to know you and to see firsthand the good work you are doing at Challengers Boys & Girls Club, I am delighted that countless others will now have the oportunity to read about a true American hero, Lou Dantzler.

Barbara and I look forward to reading *A Place to Go, A Place to Grow*, and we salute you and all the volunteers at Challengers Boys & Girls Club who give so much of themselves so that less fortunate youngsters have an opportunity to excel and succeed. You are a genuine Point of Light, and you exemplify what is best about our great country—serving others.

Congratulations, Lou. Barbara and I send you our warmest personal regards.

Sincerely,

G. Bush

Mr. Lou Dantzler
Founder, President and Chief Executive Officer
Challengers Boys & Girls Club
5029 S. Vermont Avenue
Los Angeles, CA 90037-2907

Contents

Foreword

By Magic Johnson

The first few months after I moved to Los Angeles in the summer of 1979, I was pretty lonely. I had just left all my friends and family in Michigan and moved halfway across the country to the land of swimming pools, movie stars, and endless freeways—and I didn't know a single soul. I know it may sound unbelievable, but here I was, living my dream of playing for the Lakers, one of the best teams in the NBA, making more money than I had ever wished for, and yet, for a while, I was miserable.

Until one day, the mayor of Los Angeles, Tom Bradley, offered to show me around. He spoke of one place and one man in particular with such pride and enthusiasm that I couldn't wait to see what he was getting all worked up about.

So you can imagine my thoughts as we left the manicured, palm-lined streets Los Angeles is famous for and made our way farther and farther south on busy, congested Vermont Avenue, where some of the cars had more colors of paint than a peacock (as did the walls of most of the stores, thanks to the graffiti), and we turned into a dusty parking lot in front of a plain, blue and white building. I couldn't help but wonder if we made a wrong turn somewhere. I mean, didn't the mayor say we were going to a wonderful place to meet some wonderful people?

I kept my thoughts to myself as Mayor Bradley led me past a leaning, rickety basketball hoop toward a large door at the side of the building. Before we had the chance to open it, however, the door burst open and out walked an energetic, barrel-chested man with one of the most electric smiles I've ever seen.

As Mayor Bradley made the introductions, Lou Dantzler shook my hand warmly and made me feel as welcomed and comfortable as if I were in my mother's kitchen.

"Great to meet you, man!" he said in his unmistakable booming voice. "I'm so *glad* you came down here to see us. We're all really excited to have you here!"

And with that we walked into what he proudly called the gymnasium—packed to the rafters with what seemed like thousands of kids of all ages—which to me looked more like a warehouse, with its painted concrete walls and cracked linoleum floor. Yet to Lou and these kids, this was paradise.

Lou then showed me around the Club—which, shabby though it may have been, was nonetheless spotless—and, with that infectious, positive manner of his, described everything as if this place were the Taj Mahal. As we moved through the Club, I watched how he interacted with the kids and noticed the special relationship he had with each of them, and how eager they all were to please him. Just a simple gesture or a few positive words from him seemed to be all they needed.

I couldn't shake the feeling he reminded me of someone, though I couldn't put my finger on who. He had an easy laugh and an upbeat attitude, yet I also witnessed how strict he could be when someone got out of hand, which is easy when there are several hundred teenagers running around. Well, they weren't actually running, come to think of it. I guess what impressed me the most was how well-behaved those kids were, how they sat where they were told to sit and listened when someone else was talking. They behaved just as I was raised to behave by my strict and loving parents. And then it hit me—Lou reminded me of my parents: his carefree smile and enthusiastic nature was just like my mother, and his strict discipline and take-no-excuses demeanor was just like my father. My dad was my hero, and as I looked around at these kids I realized that Lou was the father and hero to all these hundreds of kids from a forgotten part of Los Angeles.

For the first time in weeks, I didn't feel lonely.

That day became the first of countless visits I made to the Club, and the check I wrote to Lou that day was the first of many checks that I happily wrote because I knew that whatever dollar I was giving to him was being stretched and molded and twisted and coaxed every which way in order to make it go as far as possible for those kids, just like my dad did for me and my eight brothers and sisters when I was young.

I grew up in the kind of African-American family that people today worry is disappearing: a happy, close-knit family with two parents and time for the whole family to be together. Sadly, the way of life I had growing up was alien to many children of South Central, but I breathed a little easier knowing Lou was there to be the father to them all and help guide them to become good, caring, hardworking adults. He was there every day providing protection, safety, and education, all in a place where they learn values, have goals, and look to the future. It's more than just a safe haven.

Now, more than 25 years after my first visit, to see this Club today, what Lou has built for these kids, is truly amazing. The radio station, the tennis courts, the library, the McDonald's training center, the dental clinic, everything. The experience these kids are getting is what's been missing in our community for too long.

I've long believed that the reason inner city people can't compete is because we don't have the resources and opportunities that some of the better-off communities have. Take Challengers' radio and television station. Before Lou built it, how was a kid from South Central supposed to get the kind of exposure to something like that which could potentially lead to a lucrative career? Now any Club member can learn how to shoot and edit video or see what it's like to program a radio show—valuable job skills that are in big demand in Los Angeles.

The determination and will it took to make that happen in the face of so many obstacles—lack of interest in the area, lack of funding, crime, riots—I could definitely appreciate. It's similar to what I experienced when I announced I was going to build a state-of-the-art movie theatre complex in the heart of South Central. *You're crazy to waste your money building something so nice in that area,* I heard. *Within a year it will be covered with graffiti,* some said. Well, here we are 10 years later and the Magic Johnson Theatres are still as beautiful as the day we opened, the staff is just as welcoming and friendly, and business couldn't be better. In fact, its success has encouraged other developers to make investments in the area.

I look at Challengers as being similar to my theatres. Just like the multi-plex, at Challengers visitors are always very impressed by the cleanliness, the friendliness of the staff, and the quality of services it provides, not to mention the incredibly high standards those kids are expected to live up to, which they do. There's no question that we had to bring those kinds of standards to our community, to help its children understand that when they grow up, this is what society is going to be expecting of them.

Soon after my first visit to Challengers, I began to meet more people in Los Angeles, make friends, and become more at ease living here. Now I can't imagine living anywhere else. What I also can't imagine is what this community would be like without Lou Dantzler.

What's being accomplished at Challengers is not done by a committee of planners, PhDs, and politicians; rather, it reflects the vision and dedication of one simple man who, though his own life was marred by tragedy and obstacles, used his ambition and will to succeed not to enrich himself, but to uplift an entire community. Lou believes, as I do, that these young people in South Central want to learn and stay out of trouble, but they need somewhere safe to go. They need a place to go, a place to grow.

Acknowledgments

When I took twelve boys in the back of my pickup truck to the park all those years ago to keep them out of trouble and give them something positive to do, I could never have imagined that almost forty years later, I would end up making a difference in the lives of more than thirty thousand boys and girls. But I didn't do it all by myself.

There have been many angels who have helped me over the years and I have been blessed with their support and wisdom; some are mentioned in this book, and those who aren't I would like to acknowledge, like the people from the early days who, along with my cousin, Willie, and my sisters, Annie, Sarah and Sallie, and my brother, Arthur, helped steer me on the right path: John Thompson, Freemon Thomas, Jonathan Hanton, Thelma Green and James Owens; people who supported me with friendship like Walter Christopher, George May, Ted Bolden, and Ed and Gracie O'Neal; those who helped me start this club, such as Howard Banks, Sharon Ireland, Al Carson, Toby Walker, Carl Moser, Paul Nathanson, Gene Mulkey, the von der Ahe Family, Roland Baker, Dr. Richard Diehl, Curtis Knox, Priscilla Ferguson, Catherine Williams, Doris Hodge, Charles and Deann Brooks, Bob Barker, and Mayor Tom Bradley; people who helped me take the Club to the next level, like Warren Lanier, Maury Wills, Fred Williamson, Don Newcomb, the Los Angeles Dodgers organization, Larry McCormick, Brad Pye, Richard Roundtree, Sidney Poitier, Richard Pryor, Magic Johnson, Lon Rosen, James Worthy, the Los Angeles Lakers organization, Mark Scoggins,

Ken Fearn, Rodney Peete, Helen Washington, Michael Tennenbaum, Bob Gay, Peter Ueberroth, Bruce Hagerty, Bernard Parks, Dennis Holt, Jim Hill, Steve Downing, Richard Dean Anderson, Alley Mills, Lou Gossett, Jr., Ed Lara, Laura Peterson, Jim Shepherd, B.C. McCabe, Lisa Firestone, Win Rhodes-Bea, and Arlo Sorensen.

Support came from all areas, from people like Scott LaChasse, Irma Smith, Roger Smith, Leroy Chase, John Destoute, James Stranton, Jim Richardson, Barbara Stricker, John Schroeder, Richard Jones, Yolanda Nunn, Mike Bruce, L.A. City Council Members Gilbert Lindsey, Rita Walters and Jan Perry, Mayor James Hahn, LAPD Chief William Bratton, Sgt. Mahoney, Dr. Reggie Bennett, Dorothy Banks, James Williams, Howard Schaffer, Wesley, Marilyn and Keith Askins, Murue Floyd, Lurna Nash, Diane, Danny and Lisa Chatman, Jim Kunkel, Dick Burton, Jarvis Johnson, Scott Cunningham, April Janney, Wade Killefer, Ken Crowe, Dr. Charles Belcher, Richard Franklin, Barbara Walker, Dr. Robert Bachelis, John McLocklin, Sam Porter, Bill Bourgeois, John Crayton, Ralph Dow, John Miller, Samuel Williams, Gilbert Williams, Marilyn Owens, Roy Roberts, Lee Mitchell, Paul Carson, Bishop William Lerue Dillard, Jeff Gadlin, Ron Turner, Ed Kirby, Dr. Frederick Rutherford, Yvonne Jackson, Sharon Hemphill, Dave Clark, Denzel Washington, Steve Harvey, Shaquille O'Neal, Orson Bean, Bill Davila, Dr. Louis Sullivan, Sam Taylor, Raphael Henderson, Lee Mitchell, Lindsay Hughes, Bessie Atkins, Lou Johnson, Al Downing, Ivy Maynier, Bill Elkins, Nate Wilson, Mayor Richard Riordan, Rep. Jack Kemp, (R-NY), Secretary of State Colin Powell, and President George H. W. Bush.

As well, there are many people at the Boys and Girls Clubs of America who have helped me climb the ladder of success and I credit them with helping me realize my vision: Judith Pickens, Jim Cox, Lincoln Ellis, Alan Young, Robert Monk, Al Secrist, Pelton Stewart, Jim Canfield, Roxanne Spillett, Tom Garth, Evan McElroy, Steve Salem, and especially Robbie Callaway, my friend, mentor, and staunchest supporter. I will always remember what you did for me.

And let's not forget all the original members of the Club who were there as we found our way in the early days, including those first twelve boys I took to the park—my brother-in-law Michael Talley, Terry Smith, Terry Baker, David Dukes, Milton Collins, and his cousin, Ronald, my son, Mark, and the five Robinson boys (Eddie, Dwayne, Ernie, Ronnie, and Marlo)—all who formed those first branches on the tree that became Challengers. The many who came after them, such as Kenny, Keith and Sylvester Rodgers, Eric Davis, Ronnie Rogers, Wendell "Rock" Williams, Jerome Taylor, Carl Reed and his brothers and sisters, Kelvin Smith, the Sly sisters, the Powell Brothers (Theadry III, Lheadry, Louadry and Deadry), John Singleton, and Terry Bemore, to name a few, strengthened those branches and helped our tree grow.

Writing a memoir is something I would have never considered, but now that it's done, I am so grateful I did, and I have my co-author, Kathleen Felesina, to thank for pushing me to do it. Kathleen brought with her some wonderful angels of her own who helped us realize our vision and have given both of us invaluable advice and support throughout: namely Terry Curtin, Kristin and Neil Spanier, Matt Johnson, Meg Grant, Barbera Thornhill-Wilson, and especially Michael and Janet Feeley, who introduced us to Sharlene Martin, our amazing literary agent, who makes miracles of her own happen every day, and Suzanne Wickam-Beaird, whose instincts and support we couldn't have done without. I would also like to thank our publisher, Rodale, and the two editors who believed in me and brought their incredible talents to this project: Lisa Considine and Leah Flickinger. I am so thankful for their support, wisdom and expert guidance. I would also like to thank Kathleen's husband, Peter, and children, Daniel and Zoe, for letting Kathleen spend so much time with us in South Central; their support and understanding were invaluable.

But, most of all, I would like to thank my family, Ruby, Mark, and Corey, who allowed me to take precious time away from them so I could build this Club and make a better community for us to live in. They are my most profound blessing and without them there would be no Challengers.

The South Central Stare

What shall it avail our nation if we can send a man to the moon but we cannot cure the sickness of our cities?

—McCone Commission Report of the Watts Riot

Driving through my neighborhood, you have to watch for bikes. The streets, wide, flat, and straight, are set in an orderly grid, but even so, you have to keep a close eye out for the boys riding around, sometimes in lazy circles or figure eights, other times at breakneck speed, standing up, pumping on those pedals, bodies crouched forward. They pay no attention to passing cars, but if they do look at you, the expression you see isn't gleeful or eager. Instead, your glance is met by that singular look that is the hallmark of this particular neighborhood: a rock-hard stare through hooded eyes, muscles of the face frozen in a lifeless expression. It's the type of glare that looks right through you: the South Central stare.

In this neighborhood, a child on a bicycle isn't a symbol of carefree summer days spent exploring. These kids aren't riding over to a friend's house to read comic books in the tree house and play fetch with the dog. Here, these kids on bikes are sentries, lookouts, call them what you will; they are gang members—or wannabes, anyway—being paid to scout for police while their homies conduct business hidden from sight in nearby houses, apartments, cars, or alleyways. They weave arrogantly through streets crowded with mothers holding toddlers with one hand and disposable diapers in the other; old, grizzled men clinging to shopping carts overflowing with other people's garbage; and cars that range from aged, limping rust-mobiles to crisp black-and-whites that trail behind shiny, tricked-out cars with blackened windows and the ever-present *thump-thump-thump* of a booming bass that beats a rhythm into your chest.

These are the kids who, though not yet teenagers, can often make more in one day as lookouts than their parents can at their low-wage jobs. I remember one kid who told me, "My momma don't even make $100 a day. If the cops come, all I gotta do is whistle or ride down there to tell them, and I get my money." So you see them riding around all day; no school for them. In this neighborhood, where most of the dogs run neglected in feral packs, these kids on bikes are on the bottom rung of gang life, trying to work their way up.

But as I drove to work on April 29, 1992, it was too early for these kids to be out. No one buys drugs at 7:00 a.m., the time I usually get to work, so I enjoyed the relative peace as I turned off Vermont Avenue onto 51st Street and stopped at the locked chain-link fence. Reaching for my jumble of keys, I opened the lock, slid the gate open wide, and drove across the parking lot to my usual parking spot next to the basketball court.

I got out of my car, absentmindedly squinted around the perimeter of the place, and looked up at the large, neat white building with blue trim and a sign that said in big blue letters: CHALLENGERS BOYS & GIRLS CLUB. I began my day.

~

Twenty-four hours later, as I drove down those very same streets, ones I had driven for almost twenty-five years, nothing looked familiar. The route I had long ago established to wend my way through South Central Los Angeles was as foreign to me as if I had been driving through the streets of war-torn Beirut.

Yesterday seemed like years ago. I drove slowly, not because there was anyone on the streets at this hour but because of what lay before me.

Shards of broken glass carpeted the streets; rubble from what looked like cinderblocks or concrete made them an obstacle course; smoke and ash filtered up from ruined buildings, intermittently clouding my view; cars and overturned shopping carts competed for space haphazardly in the streets and in garbage-strewn lots.

As I approached the intersection of Vermont and Vernon avenues, I noticed the smoldering ruins of the large shopping center on my right and the decimated pawnshop across the street. I took a deep breath, which was hard with all the smoke that still hung in the air, and exhaled slowly.

The destruction from the first night of what was to become the worst riot in our country's history was blocking my path. The day before, a non-black jury acquitted four white Los Angeles police officers of beating black motorist Rodney King. The verdict, read at three o'clock the previous afternoon, seemingly caught most of Los Angeles County by surprise, especially its police department. Because the beating had been captured on videotape and was shown endlessly on TV, many thought that a finding of the officers' guilt in using excessive force was a foregone conclusion, so the subsequent not-guilty verdicts stunned most of this region of almost nine million people.

The verdict, however, didn't surprise many of the almost three-quarters of a million people in the community of South Central Los Angeles, more than half of whom were African American. Many in the area did react, though, and did so violently, setting off a night of mayhem that saw the LAPD—thanks to comprehensive, live television news coverage— beat a hasty retreat from an intersection ruled by an angry black mob set on venting their pent-up rage on unsuspecting nonblack motorists and storeowners. When the police left, the gangs took over. Then the fires and the looting, the shootings and the beatings, began.

My hands gripped the steering wheel with impatience. I'd been glued to the television the night before, hoping to catch a glimpse—amidst the horrifying images of a city exploding—of this particular block to see if the building was still standing, the place that housed the organization I had founded more than two decades earlier in the aftermath of another wave of deadly riots, also sparked by police tensions, that had wreaked unbelievable havoc on this very same community.

I started Challengers Boys & Girls Club in the back of my pickup truck in 1968 with twelve fatherless boys, kids from my neighborhood who said they'd never been to the park and were afraid to go because of all the drugs and crime. I thought that was so sad—shouldn't every child be able to play in the park? So I said I would take them one Saturday to play some sports.

Since then, I have made it my mission to wipe the South Central stares off the faces of the children of this community and replace them with the smiles and laughter and curiosity they each have a right to. But it was and is a constant struggle.

Gang life, the offspring of decades of poverty, racial tension, and despair, had become synonymous with South Central Los Angeles. When I started working with the kids of this area in the late 1960s, I focused mainly on keeping them out of gangs so they wouldn't get into drugs, crime, and juvenile hall; now the club staff was working twice as hard just to keep them alive. Our club is located on the front lines of gang warfare—Vermont Avenue—the unofficial dividing line between the east and west sides of South Central Los Angeles. The Crips and the Bloods each set about trying to carve extra little territories out of our increasingly decrepit neighborhood. The *rat-a-tat* of drive-by shootings with automatic weapons was becoming all too familiar to us, as was the almost never-ending presence of police helicopters circling overhead like noisy vultures. Members of our club had been killed by gang gunfire. One house, barely a stone's throw from our playground—home to both gang members and club members—sported numerous bullet holes, ever-present reminders of the violence right outside our doors. For us, unfortunately, the sight of squad cars screeching to a stop in front of that house and others nearby was commonplace.

However, those problems were nothing compared to this, I thought sadly as I navigated around an abandoned, smoking car. I'd watched in horror the night before as members of the Eight Trey Gangster Crips flashed their gang signs on live TV after they had beaten a poor, defenseless truck driver in the middle of the intersection of Florence and Normandie, about a mile away from our club. I saw members of rival Bloods gangs rip the bars off liquor store windows and smash their way in, grabbing all they could carry. "Everything's free," one shouted happily for the TV cameras.

For so many years, I had dedicated myself to trying to keep the kids of this community out of gangs by providing positive alternatives to the streets. And here these hoodlums were, further terrorizing these streets and the many innocent people who were unlucky enough to live here. The police seemed powerless to stop them. What if they burned my building, too? What then?

Finally, I could see it. Even on ordinary days, our building is hard to miss. The 20,000-square-foot facility stands a good 25 feet tall, with a sign extending almost another 20. Rarely did anything in South Central reach more than two stories high. On a clear day, you can see about 40 square miles of flat expanse from the hills of Ladera Heights west of us. Not a single skyscraper or tower breaks the horizon. It's as if an invisible hand holds everything down, keeping us all in our place. Our building is the exception, though not by our design—it was donated to us. The 40-foot-high sign, which now said "Challengers," once drew people to the grocery store it once was. I hoped it was now a beacon of another kind.

I pulled in the driveway and unlocked the gate in the chain-link fence, which was undisturbed. I squinted through the smoke and made my way over to the building. Preparing myself for the worst, I was stunned and relieved to discover that it looked exactly as I had left it. Miraculously, it was completely untouched.

I said a silent prayer of thanks as I opened the front door and was greeted—and comforted—by the silence of the cool, dark, empty gym.

Just then I heard the sound of a car in the parking lot. My heart jumped. Peeking through a crack in the door, I saw an unmarked police cruiser rolling slowly through and pulling up next to my car. I let out a breath. It was Lt. Bruce Hagerty, head of detectives for the LAPD's 77th Street Division—our precinct—and our board's president. As he got out of the car, I noticed that, like me, the first thing he did was scan the building as best he could through the smoke and haze to see if any damage had been done. A mixture of anxiety, anger, frustration, and fatigue played across his face, which was drawn and pale. This had been hard on all of us.

Bruce is an honest, hardworking, smart, dedicated man who really cares about this community. He cares so much, in fact, that several years earlier, he stopped by the club one day, introduced himself, and said he had heard about what we were doing and wanted to help any way he could. He wanted to make a difference in children's lives. That was all I needed to hear before I put him to work.

"Bruce!" I called out. "Over here!"

His head snapped in my direction, but not before I noticed his body stiffen and his hand reflexively go to his holster. God, we were all jittery.

"Hey, Lou," he said, his face relaxing once he saw it was me. We embraced for a long time. "Are you okay? How are you doing?"

"Oh, man," I whispered. Seeing Bruce's emotions brought mine right to the surface. I was still in a state of shock and disbelief, stunned that such violence could erupt again, especially after all we went through during the 1965 Watts Riot, and now my sadness and anger were coming forth as well. But more than anything, I was thankful—thankful that our club had been spared.

Bruce and I took a walk around the club, both of us still amazed that nothing had happened to it. There wasn't a scratch. On the other side of Vermont, not forty feet away, a row of shops half a block long was still smoldering, completely destroyed.

"Look, they even burned down the church," I remarked to Bruce as we looked at the space across the street from us, where a church had stood not twelve hours earlier, juxtaposed between a beauty parlor and a liquor store. "How could anyone burn down a church?"

"I'm telling you, it's crazy," Bruce said quietly.

It was obvious how much he took all this to heart. But even though he had been up all night working to quell unprecedented amounts of violence, even before going home to see his own family, he came by the club to check on us. I'll never forget that.

"So, you gonna keep the club closed today, Lou?"

"Yeah, I think that's best. I don't want anyone out on the streets today. It was bad enough last night, all of us trying to get these kids home safely in the vans after all the violence started. No, I think I'll keep it closed today and tomorrow, just in case. Then it will be the weekend, and by Monday, hopefully things will be back to normal."

We kept talking for a few moments as the city gradually began to awaken. People slowly emerged from their homes, some stepping gingerly outside, afraid of what they were going to see. Others were more bold.

As Bruce and I talked, I noticed a couple of neighborhood teenagers wearing local colors standing in someone's front yard about a hundred yards from us. Bruce, who was still in uniform, followed my gaze, and I saw his body tense. I recognized the boys, though I didn't know their names. They weren't members of the club. Rather, they were members of their own set, the dominant gang in the area surrounding our club. As I looked over, I caught the eye of one of them, who gave me a brief nod.

A car slowly rolled up to where they were standing and stopped. The driver was Carl Reed, my program director, who got out and went over to talk to them. Though tall, barrel-chested, and more than a match for the teens, I could see Bruce was again on high alert as we watched the three of them shake hands and begin a conversation filled with plenty of gesturing and tough-guy body language. Carl pointed to our building and seemed to be asking about it. The youths simply shook their heads. This seemed to satisfy him, and he started in our direction.

When he got close enough, Bruce grabbed him in a tight bear hug. "Hey, Carl," he said softly, "How's it going?"

I could see the emotion on Carl's face as he turned to me.

"Hey, Lou," he said as we hugged. "You doin' okay?"

"Yeah, man. I'm just glad this place is still standing."

"I know, I know. I can't tell you how relieved I was to see you standing here when I drove up. When I saw those two guys over there, checkin' out the place, I went over to see what was up, and you know what they told me? They said, 'Tell Lou not to worry about Challengers. Go on home. We've put the word out that this place is not to be touched.' Uh-huh; they'll make sure nothing will happen here."

"Well, those are the guys with the power to back those words up," Bruce observed wryly, "so I guess it's okay if I go. That's one less thing for me to worry about."

Soon after Bruce left, I went back inside, where the phone was ringing. It was Laura Peterson, another one of our board members, seeing how we were. Parents called, too, asking what they should do with their kids. "Keep them home," I said, hoping they would listen. Other board members and supporters began calling, too, thanking God once they heard we were all right.

Once I heard that the school district was closing the schools and people were being advised to stay home, I realized I might as well get out of there, too. The wail of sirens was beginning to increase, as were the sounds of more and more angry voices in the streets.

Like most of America over the next few days, I remained glued to my television set, monitoring the destruction, violence, and death toll of what was being alternately called an uprising, a rebellion, or a riot, depending on who was talking. When I saw Rodney King make his tearful plea, "Can't we all just get along?" I thought, "Amen, brother."

Despite what Carl had told me about what the gang members said, I was still uneasy. During those tense few days, I kept in close telephone contact with several people in the neighborhood, checking to make sure they were okay as well as checking on the club. Catherine Williams, one of my strongest supporters in the community, lived just a block and a half away on 49th, and my brother-in-law Michael lived on the other side of Vermont, near Hoover.

"Our power's been out off and on for days," said Michael, "and it seems like everything around here is all burned out, but I just got back from the club, and everything's fine, Lou." I breathed a sigh of relief.

He told me how, when he ventured out when things got calm and he ran into someone from the neighborhood—members of the club as well as gang members—they inevitably said, "Don't worry about the club; we won't let anyone touch it."

While part of me couldn't believe that gangsters were sparing us, another part of me wasn't surprised. I mean, we never had any problems with gangs here, despite being located in one of the worst gang territories in the city. Over the years, some of our members had been active gang members, often from opposing gangs, yet we never had any of that spill onto our property, even during some of our most heated ballgames. Even gang members could see that I was trying to help this community, I guess. Some of the gangsters even had their own kids in the club, or sisters or nephews or whatever. They wanted to give their loved ones a chance to escape the life they led, and they knew we were the answer.

So even though I was sickened by all the destruction and violence surrounding me, I couldn't help but feel heartened by the support the neighborhood showed the club. It gave me hope for our community, that the violence would soon end and we could get back to work.

By Monday, my hopes were realized as things calmed down enough for the schools to begin opening again, for the mayor and governor to lift the dusk-to-dawn curfew, and for the federal troops that had been called in to restore order to board their tanks and return home.

Soon the children began trickling back to our club, some excitedly talking about the previous days' events, others quieter than normal. It was going to take some of them a long time to feel safe again, I thought.

That afternoon, Laura Peterson came by to check on us and told me she had heard that President Bush was going to come to tour the "riot zone," as some were now calling it, that Friday, May 8.

"It's too bad," she said. "He'll probably go to the typical places and talk to the same politicians, look things over, and then leave. Same spiel, no action. He probably won't even get a chance to talk to people like you who could really do a lot to improve things here. That's who he needs to talk to!"

Well, I didn't know about that; I'm sure he had people who knew more about saving cities than I did. I was just a sharecropper's son from South Carolina with a high school education. All I knew was saving kids from the streets, and I knew that now they needed me more than ever. So I went back to work without another thought of the president of the United States coming to my neighborhood, other than hoping that when he did come, he didn't tie up traffic too much.

The next day, I got a call from Robbie Callaway, vice president of government relations for the Boys & Girls Clubs of America. Robbie and I had a great relationship; he was always there to support me.

"You sitting down, Lou?" he said.

"Sure. What's up?"

"I just got a call from the White House, and they heard about your club, how it was one of the only places for blocks that wasn't touched by the riots, and they want President Bush to come there and make a speech, live on TV, from Challengers."

"You're kidding!" I was stunned.

"No, I'm not. He's coming on Friday, and he wants to meet you. Think you can fit him in?" he laughed.

"I'll try my best," I chuckled, hanging up. "Damn!" I thought. "The president is coming. I've gotta make some calls."

As I reached for the phone, something made me stop and look at my hands. I paused and held them up in front of me, turning them over. The palms were smooth now, no calluses, and the tangle of tiny scars that used to crisscross the backs of them had long since faded. I stretched out my long fingers. The nails were clipped neatly, not cracked and split as they used to be, caked with dirt. These same hands that used to chop cotton, split wood, and pick endless rows of string beans and corn in the blistering South Carolina heat were going to shake the hand of the President of the United States. And all because of a job I'd been doing every day for decades. Unbelievable.

2

Twice as Much Love

But as much discipline as there was in our house, there was twice as much love.

—Lou Dantzler

I can still remember looking up and seeing them waving us in. We were pretty far down in the fields, my sisters and I, picking butter beans and peas for Mr. Hildebrand. My basket wasn't quite as full as my sisters'; they were older than I and could pick faster and carry more. I was just seven years old.

It was awfully unusual—unheard of, really—to have the white folks wave you in from the fields in the middle of the day. When there were crops to harvest, you went out and picked from sunup to sundown; you had no choice. The plantation owner said you had to, and since we were living on his property, we did what he said.

It was April 1944, and we had just finished planting the cotton a few weeks earlier. The day was hot and humid, a typical spring day in South Carolina. There wasn't the usual threat of a thundershower, though we would have welcomed it. Rain meant we had to go to school, walking the whole five miles in the rain and mud, but it was better than picking.

No rain on this day, though. It was late morning, and the sun, rapidly approaching its peak directly above our heads, had long eaten away any traces of early morning dew. The crops were dry now, the once-soggy earth beneath our feet baking. A characteristically clammy haze hung in the air, capturing and holding the aroma of warm beans, wilting leaves, and sweat.

No sooner had my sisters begun murmuring about why we were being beckoned than we saw someone heading our way.

"Here comes Mr. Adam," my sister Annie Mae said to us apprehensively as she put down her basket and straightened up. Mr. Adam was a sharecropper like our daddy, with land next to ours, and we knew that for him to take time out in the middle of the day to come get us, the news must not be good.

"It must be Daddy," sighed Sallie as we followed Mr. Adam back to our house.

Our daddy had been sick for a while, and in fact, a couple weeks earlier, he had had a stroke or an attack of some sort on the court steps in St. Matthews, a small town adjacent to Cameron, which was the closest town to our place, about eight miles away. However, sick as he was, we were still not prepared for the sight that greeted us as we walked up the steps of our front porch and through the door into our simple wood frame home.

Our daddy was dead.

Back then in the South, especially with black folks, when people died, you washed them and laid them out in the house to spend their last night at home, until the hearse came the next day. So there was Daddy, who once loomed so tall over all of us and whose deep, booming baritone used to echo across the fields, laid out in a casket in front of our fireplace. I was scared to death.

I wasn't the only one. Five of us slept in one bed that night—me, Sallie, Annie, my other sister, Sarah, and my mother. I can't remember where my older brother Arthur, whom we called Junior, slept. Probably in his own bed. He was seventeen at the time, and if he was scared, he didn't let on. It's possible my twelve-year-old cousin, Willie, sat up with him and the body, the two of them tensing up with every creak and rustle, just as we did. I don't think any of us slept that night.

Arthur Dantzler Sr. was a farmer. He had been a farmer for all of his fifty-eight years. Even though we were only sharecroppers, we were considered a fairly prosperous black family in Cameron. We never had any money, but we had all we needed because what we needed, we grew. It was a sort of luxurious poverty.

Sharecropping is an institution that goes back as long as crops have been cultivated. A landowner let you use a certain amount of his acreage to raise your own crops; he supplied the seed, fertilizer, and so forth in exchange for you working a portion of his land in addition to yours. For this privilege, he got a "share"—usually half—of your harvest. The catch was that since you didn't see any windfall from your crop until you sold it at the end of the harvest, you had no money during the year to buy necessities. So the landowner extended you credit for those things and often rented you a house on his plantation as well, with the costs being deducted from your share at settling time.

Since the farmer kept the books and set the prices for everything, and also had the credit account at the local store where you bought your food and clothes, you had to take him at his word that the amount he said you owed him was correct. It was common for landowners to "cook the books" in their favor. Many sharecroppers had just a few years' education, if any, so they couldn't contest the figures and often found themselves still owing money after a full year's work, a debt that would carry over to the next year. This would go on year after year, with the sharecropper never seeing any profit and continuing to be tethered to the landowner by debt. Sometimes a sharecropper worked up the courage to dispute the accounting, but there was little he could do to protest except pack up his family and belongings and move to another plantation where he could find a better deal and hopefully a more honest landowner who would agree to buy him out of his old debts. If he couldn't, and he still owed the landowner, he usually packed up in the middle of the night, hoping to avoid jail or worse. It was not unusual for some families to move every other year.

In this environment, we were considered relatively fortunate. My father had always been a strong, good farmer with a particular talent for coaxing the sweetest fruits from the orchards and the highest yields from the fields. Our share on the plantation was large enough to provide well for all of us; we had acres and acres. We had peach trees, plum trees, pecan trees. We grew wheat for flour; we grew sweet potatoes, rice, beans, cabbage, carrots, collard greens, peas, and corn. We had chickens for eggs, a cow for milk, pigs for meat, and a mule or two to help us plow. People used to say my father had the richest land in South Carolina, and some were jealous of us. It was true that we had so much to harvest in the fall that my daddy even had to hire a few day laborers. I remember once or twice going to town with him on his mule-pulled wagon and picking them up.

Our house was pretty big then, too, by sharecropper standards. It had to be. You see, I was the youngest of twenty-two children. My parents, Arthur and Narvis Dantzler, had both been married and widowed before they met. My mother had four children before she married my father in the mid-1920s. My father had had four or five children with his first wife and then several more with a common-law wife before he met my mother, married her, and settled on Mr. Hildebrand's plantation to raise the five children they had together: Arthur Jr., Annie Mae, Sallie, Sarah, and me, Lucious Emmanuel.

By all accounts, I was a surprise to my parents when I came; my mother, who was forty at the time and starting to go through the change, had thought she was finished bearing children after she had Sarah three years earlier. However, it soon became apparent to my older siblings that I was cherished by both my parents. "That's my baby!" my sister Annie still remembers my mother admonishing all of them. "Don't touch my baby." She said it long after I left babyhood behind. I got a lot of attention.

Even so, my siblings and I got along really well and were very close.

After chores and picking were done, there were always games to play: checkers with bottle caps as pieces, or our version of jacks, with a rock and peach pits. Though we didn't see my father's older children very often—many of them lived in North Carolina and had their own families—my mother's older children were part of our daily lives, especially while my father was alive and we had the big house.

It was a typical sharecropper's house, though larger than most. Four bedrooms, a living room, a dining room, and a kitchen off the back part of the house, dominated by a large wood-burning stove. No indoor plumbing or electricity, though. Or glass in the windows, for that matter, just wooden shutters we would close tightly in the winter to keep the bitter wind out and throw open wide on sticky summer nights in hopes of catching a breeze. For us kids, having no glass in the windows had its advantages. When we washed dishes, guess where the water went—out the window. We had no drains or plumbing, so we just threw the water outside. We had to be careful no one was walking underneath, though!

Since the house was set up high on a block foundation to keep the critters and water out, it wasn't unusual to peer through the floorboards and see a chicken or a possum scurrying around on the ground underneath. We put cheap wallpaper on the unfinished walls in place of plaster, as the graying, splintered clapboards that served as the outer walls of the house were the interior walls as well. The reddish rust of the tin roof was the only color houses like ours had. Rarely did you see a tenant farmer's or sharecropper's house painted. That was for the landowners and townsfolk. Our house bore the distinctive gray tone of weathered pine that had never been painted, but we hardly took notice. Almost everyone we knew in Calhoun County—well, sharecroppers like us anyway—had houses like ours. We didn't know anything different.

There was a deep front porch the length of the house where, on hot summer evenings, the adults would sit in chairs and talk while we children scattered here and there through the shadows, catching snippets of their conversations. Much of what they said was boring old farm stuff—the price of cotton, what the almanac said the weather was going to be for the harvest, what was happening at church—but sometimes my parents and other adults from around the area would gather and tell stories of the old days or gossip.

"Mind your business, boy!" my father's voice would boom if he caught us listening in. Sometimes he'd make a move, half getting out of his chair, stamping one foot on the porch as if he were going to take after us, and we'd hustle out of there, back into the shadows with the fireflies and crickets, while the older folks chuckled in low voices.

Every so often, the adults would pretend they didn't know we were listening and embark on a ghost story about eerie jack-o'-lanterns or the bogeyman in the woods that stole children who didn't listen to their parents. Or they would talk about some distant cousin who stared into the fire too long and got hypnotized by the flames and carried off. It was silly stuff that scared the daylights out of us, but that was part of the fun. We didn't have TV; we had the folks telling stories on the front porch.

People were always coming over to our house to sit with my mother and father. My mother was an excellent cook and generous, too. She was always giving extra food to our friends or making them a little apron or something else to take home. "Here, take these potatoes and the rest of this chicken," she'd say, even if we didn't have enough for ourselves. Everyone loved Narvis.

And she kept a clean house. "Wash your feet!" she always said to us, because we were barefoot all the time. "Don't track the dirt in the house." And we listened to her. Even though she was a tiny little thing, no more than five feet two, she commanded respect from all of us. You didn't argue with Momma.

I don't remember very much about my father, other than that he was an imposing man with a manner and voice that made people listen. My mother used to say about him, "Other men, they just wear britches, but your father, he was a *man*."

Our favorite time of the year was settlement time, when Daddy would go to Mr. Hildebrand and settle the accounts. From what I could tell, Mr. Hildebrand was a fair landowner, and if he "cooked the books," he didn't do it egregiously; he treated my father fairly. I think he understood that my father and his children were hard workers and that with my father's natural knack as a farmer, his tending to Mr. Hildebrand's acres improved his farm, so in turn it seemed he gave my father a fair shake.

Settlement usually came in December, after all the crops had come in and been harvested and the cotton had been weighed and ginned. For us kids, a lot more rode on Daddy's settlement than just whether we would face a year in debt. Since settlement came around Christmastime, we knew that if we'd had a bad year, we'd have to make do with the holes in our shoes for another year and settle for sardine cans as playthings instead of a wooden truck or other store-bought toys.

However, the few times I'm able to remember, Daddy came home after settlement, sat us children down at the dining table, and handed out coins.

"Here," he'd say, giving Annie or Arthur a pile of coins. It was the money they'd earned helping in the fields. We each got our little pile, depending upon how much we had worked. Mine was always smaller, but I still got something. Enough to buy five gumballs for a penny or a 10-cent comic book at the drugstore, or to see the picture show over at the movie house in nearby Elloree. Once we got our share, we couldn't wait to go to town!

Saturday for a farm boy is the day you look forward to all week, especially if you've got a few coins in your pocket to buy an ice cream cone or a lollipop to suck on as you walk up and down Main Street. We usually only worked a half day on Saturday, which meant we had the afternoon and evening to ourselves.

A pack of cinnamon rolls was 6 cents. A fish sandwich was 10 cents. A Pepsi—during the war for some reason, black folks weren't allowed to drink Coke (my sister Sarah to this day will still not drink Coke)—was only 6 cents. At the barbecue in Elloree, you could have a full meal for 25 cents. "If you had a quarter, you could *eat*," my sister Annie always said. Other than the drugstore and the movie house, though, we never had any particular destination; we simply walked back and forth—cruising without a car. Everyone came to town on Saturdays.

Sundays were a different story. Like many of the families in our community, ours was a God-fearing one. I can't recall ever missing a Sunday service at Brown Chapel African Methodist Episcopal Church. Those were the days when people truly didn't work on Sundays because they expected to spend most of the day at church. Children were no exception; Sunday school was a must. My mother was especially devout. She read the Bible almost every day and taught us life's lessons by quoting scripture. Her favorite was John 3:16, "For God loved the world in this way: He gave His only Son, so that everyone who believes in Him will not perish but have eternal life."

My mother also had a children's Bible book with pictures in it that she often showed me. There was one story in particular I saw over and over, and it always stuck with me. There were pictures of two boys who grew up in the same house until they were twelve years old or so. They did all the same things and were given the same things. However, one brother began to get a little wild and started drinking and smoking and not listening to his parents. His life didn't turn out well. The other boy went the straight road, listened to his parents, and ended up being successful. I wanted to be that guy, the good guy.

That doesn't mean I couldn't be a little devil, though. Just ask my sister Sarah why she doesn't have eyebrows anymore. One day, she was tending to something near the fireplace in our house when something came over me—my mother thinks it was the Devil, of course—and I just pushed her into the fireplace! Junior had to pull her out, and he and Sallie had to put out the fire in her clothes.

My mother's reaction wasn't a surprise: "Lucious, go out and cut me a switch!" There were some periods when I had to cut a switch almost every day. My mother didn't fool around when it came to discipline.

"Uh-uh, Lucious! I said cut me a *switch*! Not a twig," she scolded if I tried to make it easy on myself by getting a little tiny branch. No, Momma wasn't kidding. And if the switch broke while she was beating my backside, I had to go get another one so she could finish the job.

Once I was punished, Momma often hugged me and talked to me about what I did wrong and why I shouldn't do it again. She never held on to her anger for long, and neither did we.

Much of what happened after they came and took my father away in the hearse was a blur. It wasn't as if we had the luxury of sitting around and mourning. Springtime for a farmer leaves time for only one thing: farming. As sick as he was, I don't know how my father managed to plant the cotton before he died, but soon the little green sprouts were popping up all over the plowed earth. Plums and peaches were blossoming. Corn was shooting up, and the carrots were ready to be pulled. By early summer, the work clearly overwhelmed us. It was more than a grieving forty-seven-year-old widow and her five kids could handle. But we managed the best we could. One of Daddy's older sons, George, came down from Winston-Salem to help out for a while, and his brother Jimmy from Durham came too for a bit, but they both had families to support, so they couldn't stay long.

Farming cotton, especially as many acres as we had to till, wasn't easy for a group of children to do. There's constant plowing and tending throughout the summer. Weeds usually began to sprout in June, and we had to constantly hoe and chop, all day. Chopping cotton was just as hard and back-breaking and boring as harvesting in the fall, when you have only a certain window of time to pick all the bolls from the stalks before the rains come. Add to that the fact that all our other crops needed tending as well; corn withered on the stalks, and overripe peaches and plums dangled heavily on their branches for a few days before surrendering to gravity and then rotting on the marshy ground below. Gone were the days when we'd go with Daddy to sell overflowing baskets of summer-ripe fruit in Columbia or nearby Orangeburg. We did the best we could, but we couldn't keep up. There were the pigs, cows, and chickens to feed, and Momma had her job cooking and cleaning for Mr. Hildebrand to take up her time.

Nevertheless, when harvest came, we all picked. My sisters taught me how to take a piece of cotton and wrap it around my ears to keep the gnats and sweat out. Though I was smaller than the rest and couldn't pick as fast, one thing I did have going for me was my small fingers—if I was careful, I could pluck the cotton without getting pricked by the cockleburs on the stalks. Plus, cotton is waist-high to a man, so I was still short enough to take refuge in its shade while I picked.

As far as the eye could see, there was cotton, planted right up to the edge of the trees, right up to the edge of our house. Each row of cotton looked endless, and the nine-foot-long cotton sack over my shoulder seemed bottomless as I stuffed boll after boll of cotton into it. A bale of cotton at that time was worth about $150, give or take, depending on the markets. A good crop could produce a bale an acre. We started early in the morning while the dew still clung to the stalks and bolls; we loved it when the cotton was damp because it weighed more and we made more money. For the first hour or so, before the sun got too high and baked everything, the cotton was soft and gentle in our hands. After that, we just did the best we could to avoid the burs, which drew blood, and the snakes and other critters hiding in the dense maze of stalks, because they bit.

A twelve-foot sack like the adults used could hold about 60 pounds of cotton. Most grown men could pick between 200 and 300 pounds a day, but I don't think I ever filled up my nine-foot bag in one day during that harvest. At certain periods during the day, we unloaded our sacks for weighing and then piled our cotton onto Mr. Hildebrand's truck so he could take it to the gin in the evening. The gin, a giant, corrugated-tin building that sat idle for most of the year, was right outside of Cameron. During picking season, it must have run all day and night.

Somehow we managed to get through the harvest. I can't remember if we got all the cotton or left some clinging to the stalks, which would soon dry up and free the cotton to be blown by the winter winds through the plowed-up fields before settling in the furrows and rotted logs like dirty snow. I'm sure at some point, my mother must have despaired at the thought that the once-fertile land my father had tended so painstakingly all those years was now becoming fallow. She never showed it to any of us, though.

We couldn't help but notice our lives had changed, though, and not for the better. Settlement time came, and I could tell there would be no store-bought presents that year for Christmas, no piles of coins to jingle in our pockets as we rode the wagon into town. Junior took the mule and wagon when he went to work on another farm.

When Mr. Adam offered to take over our acres, I'm sure my mother was relieved. But that meant we had to leave our house. Soon we found a place to live and work at Mr. Bill Spires's farm. Momma's sister Edna and her husband were sharecropping for Mr. Spires, and Momma arranged to take on an acre or so as well as work in the Spires house, cooking and cleaning in exchange for a place to live.

Our new place was one of three houses in a row situated right along State Route 176, which was still a dirt road at the time. Our house, with only two bedrooms and built in the same rickety fashion as our other home, was between the other two. Though it was a step down from our old place, at least we had family near us. On one side of us were my Aunt Edna and her husband, and on the other side were their older son, Junior, and his family.

Another advantage was that our new house was closer to school. We had to walk only about three miles one way to Brown Chapel school. Though walking all that way was at times a chore, it could be fun, too. All the kids from the neighboring farms gathered along the way, and we walked in a big group. We rushed through morning chores and wolfed down breakfast because we didn't want to be late when our friends came calling outside. We walked along Hokes Gin Road and Harvest Drive, though at the time they were little more than dirt paths with no names, and we often stopped on the small bridge over Flea Bite Creek to skip a few stones over the slow-moving water.

On those mornings when our chores took longer or we spent more time picking before school and had to skip breakfast, we surreptitiously scooped up some pecans from the ground in front of one of the white folks' houses, hoping they wouldn't catch us and sic their dog on us. "Get away from my house, boy!" they yelled if they caught one of us. Sometimes what they had to say was worse.

And what the white folks said, their kids said, too. The sound of a school bus grinding down our dirt roads was often enough to get us to scramble off into the woods and hide in the thick of the Spanish moss and undergrowth, waiting for the dust to settle before we ventured out again. If the bus, which was for whites only, came along and we were out in the open field and had nowhere to hide, we were subjected to the ridicule and taunts of the white farmer kids laughing at us for having to walk to our dilapidated little segregated school. We considered it a good day if they didn't throw things at us from the windows as they sped past.

Even so, for the most part, we liked going to school, which was a four-room structure next door to Brown Chapel AME Church. There weren't more than a hundred kids in the whole place, kindergarten through eighth grade. But we knew everyone, we were all in the same circumstances—sharecroppers' kids—and the teachers were kind, if strict. My third grade teacher, Miss Rice, really cared about us. I still remember sitting in her classroom, seven or eight kids to a desk, as she taught us how to spell and read. She was nice, but we made sure we learned our lessons and did our homework because no one wanted to be embarrassed if she called them up in front of the class.

A lot of kids I knew didn't go to school until twelve o'clock because they had crops to pick in the morning. Or some families rotated which kids went to school and which stayed home to work. We didn't know any different; that was the way it was. We all had to take a break from school completely when the cotton came in, because we had to pick from sunup to sundown.

During that time, I went into the field at 5:30 a.m. and worked until the sun went down behind the trees. And I *worked!*—whatever had to be done. When you live on a farm like that and there's no father, the oldest boy at home becomes the man of the house. I had to help support my mother, who had resorted to bringing home scraps from Mr. Spires's kitchen to help supplement our table.

"Promotion is in danger if student cannot attend school regularly."

That's what my teacher, Mr. Green, noted on my tenth-grade report card, which I had to take home for my mother to sign. I was pretty nervous; I hated to show my mother that I was in danger of failing anything. She always had such belief in me.

"School is very important, Lucious," she always said. "You must do well in school."

Though she had only a third-grade education herself, my mother knew the value of knowing how to read and "figure numbers." While my father was alive, she worked in Mr. Hildebrand's house mainly so she could put John, her oldest son by her first husband, through college and graduate school. She was so proud when he got his master's degree and became a school principal.

She had the same ambitions for me. I had always been fairly good in school, and I liked it, for the most part, when I was allowed to go. But when crops were coming in or planting had to be done, the landowner would come get you, and you didn't have a choice. He would come to the house and say, "I need the nigger boy to work tomorrow," and that was that.

By this time, I was about fifteen and in high school at St. John's across town. This new school was quite a shock to me; there were more than two hundred kids there, from all over Calhoun County. This was right before the Brown *v.* Board of Education decision, and schools were still segregated, but there were other types of black kids at this school now. City kids. Kids like Freemon Thomas, whose father owned his own land and had a car. Freemon didn't have to walk to school like me, or wear the same clothes every day and wash them out in the pot in the front yard at night to have them ready for the next day. Freemon had money for lunch. He didn't have to put cardboard in his shoes to make them last through the winter, and he had store-bought drawers, not old flour sacks like my mother sewed up for me. To me, it looked like Freemon had it all.

Including girls. Boy, did I really start to notice the girls!

I had always been somewhat of a quiet kid at school, though that didn't mean I didn't horse around like the other guys, doing things like swinging like Tarzan from the vines on the trees behind the school before class. But I was shy in new situations, and this school was so different—we had to change classrooms, and there was this whole new set of rules. I don't think I talked to anyone at St. John's for at least the first month. It didn't help either that my attendance at school was dismal.

By this time, it was basically just my mother and me in the house. A year after Daddy died, Annie, who was then fifteen, married a boy from a nearby plantation because he joined the military, and with his steady salary, she could get off the farm. She moved to New York. Sallie and Sarah got married, too; Sarah was just fourteen when she got pregnant and married one of the local boys. Both sisters stayed in Calhoun County for a while but worked on other farms, so there was just me to help Momma. I worked all I could.

There was also another reason why I was working so much, hiring myself out to be a day laborer for Mr. Eldon Higler and Mr. Spires and others. I wanted a car: a 1946 Ford.

With my growing interest in girls and a social life, I could see very quickly that guys like Freemon Thomas had all the advantages when it came to girls. How could I take a girl out on a date and expect her to walk for miles down a dirt road with me to Elloree or Cameron? No, she would definitely prefer to go out with someone who had a car and who could take her into nearby St. Matthews or even Orangeburg, where there was much more going on.

Dating aside, I just wanted a car. I craved the freedom it would bring, the prestige. I could go somewhere in an instant and not have to trudge along some dirty road and jump off the side when the white tourists drove through on their way to Myrtle Beach or Charleston. Every teenage boy wants a car.

But where to get the $300 or $400 to purchase the old jalopy? Well, Mr. Spires had offered to lend me the money. On the face of it, it sounds like he was just being a nice guy, and it was common for landowners to lend money to their laborers, especially those who were young, strong, hard workers like myself. Actually, though, it was just another way for them to tether you to their farm; once you owed them that much money, it was doubtful you'd ever come out from under. Pretty soon, you'd get married and move into one of his houses, and the cycle would start again with another generation. Yeah, Bill Spires would have loved to lend me that money.

I can't quite remember her exact words, but my mother made it very plain that she wanted me out of this sharecropper life. If I did what it took to buy that car, I'd have no hope of ever getting out. I had to finish school, she said. The only one of her nine children to have finished school so far was her son John. Junior had long since dropped out and was now in New York, along with Annie. Sarah and Sallie had followed them up North after several years of seesawing back and forth between their own share-croppers' shacks and our mother's, recovering from the beatings their husbands inflicted. Now my mother was raising their young children while they tried to make a new life in Brooklyn with no education and only farming skills.

"You can't let that happen to you, Lucious," she would sigh. My mother cared so much for her children, and I know how much it must have grieved her to see them have it so hard. Junior was in the early stages of alcoholism at this point, and she even had to sacrifice a precious $20 once to go to New York and rescue him from the street.

I didn't want to let my mother down. I decided I was going to graduate, with honors.

That decision was a turning point for me. Because my mother cared enough and was strong enough to stand up to my objections, I took the more difficult road and finished school. It would have been nicer for her, to be sure, if I had taken Mr. Spires up on his offer. She could have ridden to town for her groceries, not walked. She could have depended on me to be around to help support her and the grandchildren she was now raising, as I could have eventually started farming a bigger plot of land and made more money so she could retire. But Momma sacrificed for me. No, I was not going to let her down.

3

He Taught Us to Be Men

A father who was strong enough to provide for his family, tough enough to endure sacrifice and hardships without complaint, and wise enough to show us that respect—for him, ourselves, and each other—was something of supreme importance, something that no one could take away from us.

—Lou Dantzler

There weren't many opportunities for young black males to escape plantation life in the South in the first half of the twentieth century. Back then, in my area, if you wanted to get off the farm, there was the saw mill, the cotton gin, or the meatpacking plant in Orangeburg, if you had a connection to any of those places.

The only other option, which gained in popularity in the 1940s, especially during World War II, was joining the military. If you're going to be out in the mud and heat doing someone else's dirty work, you might as well earn fair pay for it, many young black men reasoned. At least it got you off the farm.

In the early 1950s, my cousin Willie, who lived in the house next door to ours and was the closest thing to a big brother I had, enlisted and went to fight in Korea. I was about thirteen at the time. I felt his absence keenly; even though we were five years apart in age, we were close, and I was left with no one to talk to about my burgeoning adolescence. I have many great memories of going over to my aunt and uncle's house after dinner and listening to their radio with Willie. One nice feature of living on Mr.

Spires's place was that we had electricity (though still no indoor plumbing). I can see us sitting there, Willie and me, letting our imaginations go free, transported out of days of never-ending work into the adventures of Hopalong Cassidy or Shotgun Kelly. Or sitting transfixed by a baseball game, picturing the feats of Jackie Robinson. Though we had our own radio by the time Willie left, it wasn't the same.

When he came back in 1954, I was ecstatic. I remember coming in from the fields one evening and my mother running out to the front porch to meet me. "Lucious! Son home, Son home!" she called (Son was what we called Willie at the time). "Go next door and see him." I leapt off the porch stairs and ran over.

I knocked on the door and heard Aunt Edna say, "Son, it's Brown. Brown's here to see you!" (Brown is what they used to call me).

Willie came to the door, and I think he was expecting the little guy I was when he left four years earlier, because the first thing he said was, "Who's that? Is that you, Brown? Lordy, look at you! Look how big you are!" I was taller than he was, a little over six feet.

As a kid, I had always been interested in sports, and I idolized Willie, who was so good in baseball he was recruited to play for a semi-pro team in Orangeburg. I tried to do everything he did, emulating his batting stance and catching balls as he practiced his pitching and fielding.

When he was in the service, my friends and I began taking ball games more seriously, however meager the playing surface. Basketball was played outdoors on the dirt, with a pot on a tree for a basket. Baseball was played between two houses, with one of them serving as the backstop—we didn't have to worry about breaking any windows because we had none. I also played basketball at Brown Chapel after school, and I got into it in earnest when I was at St. John's. Even though I was shy, the fact that I had athletic ability helped me feel more comfortable, and eventually I started to make friends with some of the guys on my team, including Jonathan Hanton and Freemon Thomas.

Freemon was a gregarious, good-looking guy who had a bit of the devil in him. Jonathan was from my area, but he, like Freemon, was a little better off because his father was still around, and his family had a car. But they never made me feel bad about my situation, and the three of us soon became close. We had a great time playing ball and cruising around together.

By the time Willie came home, I had already played a few seasons of baseball and had a certain flair for pitching.

"Damn, Brown! Where'd you learn to throw like that?" he said when he saw some of us goofing around in the fields one day. We were a bit rag-tag at this point—we used old sugar sacks for mitts and empty fertilizer bags filled with sand for bases—and things weren't well organized; we just played to play.

"Looky here, Brown, you got yourself quite an arm! Let me show you somethin'," and with that, Willie took me under his wing. After being in the military for four years, he had a little money saved and ended up spending a lot of it on me and my friends. He organized us into a team, bought us uniforms and equipment, took us into town for sodas—we felt like kings.

Day after day, after we were done with our work and chores, Willie worked with us. I could throw, but it was Willie who taught me how to pitch. He always wanted me to pitch to the batter's head to intimidate the other team, but I never had the nerve for that. I did have a good breaking-out curve, though, and I could throw a good fastball.

One day, Willie decided we were going to play the team from Elloree. Those city guys were considered pretty good, definitely better than us. They used to beat everyone in Calhoun County, and it wouldn't surprise me if they did the same in Orangeburg. But Willie psyched us up and convinced us we had a shot.

At first, we were a little intimidated, especially with all their trash talk about us being country farm boys. But as soon as I started pitching to their side, they quieted down. I don't know what came over me that day, but I shut that team down! Pitch after pitch, their best hitters were popping up or striking out. One inning, I pitched nine strikes! Nine innings later, I had pitched a complete shutout.

I can't tell you what that did to my self-confidence. My whole life up to that point, I had had such a bad inferiority complex; I used to hold my head down because not only was I black but I was very dark, just like my Daddy, and I was just a sharecropper. I know it was just a game and all, but the fact that I had beaten all those city boys mattered to me. Sports are very important to kids who don't have much else, and to be seen as being good at something my peers put so much importance on, well, that gave me quite a boost.

Having Willie's attention too at this time helped me immeasurably. He not only took me and some of my friends under his wing to teach us baseball, he also tried to teach us the facts of life: how to be with a woman, how to go on a date, how to get off the farm.

I was so grateful for what he did; it really changed my life. Willie believed that the sharecropper's life was a dead-end road, and he did everything he could to open my eyes to that and encourage me to develop other skills.

I know Willie would have loved it if I had become a professional athlete. It was a dream he had for himself as well. But we lived in a different time. The doors weren't open to us, and we didn't dare try to push our way in. When you are brought up to believe certain things aren't for you, that there are certain careers and places to live that are barred to you, you believe it, even if you don't agree with it. I mean, Jackie Robinson was in New York, not South Carolina. Even Jackie had to go to the back of the bus when he was in training camp in Florida. We didn't have the confidence to think we could compete on that level anyway.

Even going to college back then was no guarantee of a better life for us. There was a saying at the time that the only thing a college-educated black person could hope to do was preach or teach. Willie likes to say we just were born twenty years too early.

～

Much has been written and discussed over the years about racism in the Jim Crow South. Looking back, it seems unbelievable that eating out meant getting food at the back door of a restaurant or that going to a show meant sitting in the sweltering balcony even when there were plenty of seats in the cooler part of the theater below. We couldn't even try on clothes in a store; our parents used to trace our feet at home and then go into town and get our shoes. But at the time, we didn't know any differently. We knew where our place was. It was understood that you addressed white folks as "Mr." and "Miss" and "Sir" and "Ma'am," while they always used our first names. We were brought up to never challenge the word of a white person, no matter what their age—"When you're white, you're right," we always said—and we knew that no matter how friendly a white person could be to you, there was never a true friendship, since friendship is based upon equality and respect. A friend would throw his front door wide open to greet you, not make you skulk around and enter through the back. America's founding fathers may have found certain truths to be self-evident, but we didn't. All men weren't created equal.

That isn't to say that we didn't get along with white folks. Mr. Eldon Higler, a large landowner near us, was always very encouraging to me; he complimented me on my abilities, seemed to appreciate my hard work, and paid me fairly. His encouragement really gave me a lot of inspiration. I worked for him as a day laborer; we didn't live on his place. It wasn't a situation where I would work and sweat for him all year and then be cheated at the end of the year; he wouldn't do that. So I saw that not all white people were bad.

Then there was Bill Spires's son, Bud, who was a friend of Willie's. Bud was a good kid, and his friendship with Willie was based on their mutual appreciation for and obsession with baseball.

One time, a white boy said to Bud, "Why you playing with them?" referring to Willie and me, the implication being that Bud was not being with his own kind the way he should. Whites even made it hard on each other.

Luckily for us, Bud, who heard comments like this all the time, didn't succumb to peer pressure. Quite the opposite, in fact. You see, he saved Willie's life.

When Willie was seventeen, he was working as a driver and doing chores around the house for a local white landowner and his wife. He helped in the yard, drove the owner's truck to the gin or the market, brought in the mail, whatever.

One day, Willie's boss, Mr. Jack, asked him to go along to town to help sell his produce, but his wife told him she needed Willie home to help with some yard work. Soon after Willie got to work on some weeding, he heard Mr. Jack's wife call from inside the house, "Son, bring me the paper, will you?"

"Yes, Miss Ruth," he said as he ran to get it. When he hustled into the room, he stopped dead in his tracks. There she was, lying on the couch with just her bra and panties on, just as relaxed as could be.

As fast as he could, Willie turned around, backed into the room, laid the paper on the table next to the couch, and fled.

"Son," she drawled, "are you looking at me?"

"Oh, no, Miss Ruth! No, ma'am!" he stammered as he ran out of the house.

A few days later, when Mr. Jack was out in the fields, Willie was feeding the dog out front. Miss Ruth went up onto the porch, sat down on the steps, and pulled her dress up to her thighs, exposing herself. Again, Willie turned around right away and made an excuse to go around the other side of the house. He didn't want any part of this bored white woman playing games with him and then, if she was caught by her husband, blaming it all on him.

A few weeks later, Willie was driving Mr. Jack's truck to town with some produce to sell. As he passed by Mr. Spires's place, he saw Bud and his mother, Daisy, out on the veranda. "Afternoon, Miss Daisy!" Willie called. Bud wanted a ride into town, so he got in the truck with Willie.

After Willie got to town and began unloading the produce, a white guy Bud knew came by and said he needed to borrow the truck because he wanted to take it to Mr. Jack and get some money that Mr. Jack owed him. Willie said all right. You didn't question white folks.

A while later, Mr. Jack heard from a neighbor that Miss Ruth was fooling around with someone in his truck by the highway. As he was going to investigate, he saw Miss Daisy, who told him that she saw Willie driving the truck. Mr. Jack sped off in a cloud of dust.

I was oblivious to all this until that evening, when Mr. Jack came to Aunt Edna's house with a bunch of his friends, who started tearing up the place looking for Willie. Willie had a baseball game that night in Orangeburg and had caught the bus from Cameron, where he had been selling Mr. Jack's produce all afternoon. He had no other transportation since the white man took Mr. Jack's truck.

Soon the Spires family came by to see what all the commotion was about. We all stood frozen, listening to Mr. Jack curse Willie, tear up his bed, and talk about skinning him alive and stringing him up if he caught him. When Mr. Spires asked him what it was about, Mr. Jack told him about his wife and what Miss Daisy said about Willie driving the truck.

"Is that true, Daisy?" he asked.

"That's what I saw," she said.

That's when Bud Spires finally spoke up. "No, Daddy, no! It wasn't Son. I was with him. He lent the truck to Rue, who said he needed to find Mr. Jack. Willie wasn't with Miss Ruth."

Everyone became quiet and listened to Bud's earnest defense of Willie. When he was finished, even Miss Daisy believed him, which was a good thing, because Mr. Jack and Mr. Spires and many of the other landowners in the county were rumored to be members of the Ku Klux Klan, or at least sympathetic, and when they said they were going to string someone up, they meant it.

A year earlier, in 1949, there had been a large KKK rally in Orangeburg, less than a dozen miles away, accompanied by a mass ride through Calhoun County. We stayed inside our homes that weekend and for many thereafter; no trips to town for us unless it was absolutely necessary, since we didn't want to take any chances. As nice as some white folks tried to be, you knew most would do anything to preserve their way of life. All it took was one misunderstanding like what happened with Willie, and your life would be over.

Because Mr. Spires was a rich white man, he was able to protect Willie. Mr. Jack wouldn't dare challenge the word of Bill Spires's son. So he and his band of troublemakers soon left, though they were still muttering under their breath. I don't know if Mr. Jack ever really believed Bud's story, but he had no choice but to leave. The next morning, Willie's dad got him up at five o'clock, and before he told him anything, he sent him to talk to Mr. Spires. Willie didn't know what to think, especially when Mr. Spires's first words to him were, "Son, something happened last night, and I'm glad you wasn't home, 'cause they woulda killed ya!"

"Let me tell you one damn thing," he continued as Willie stood there, speechless, "I know it didn't happen, but let me tell you, you don't play with white women in South Carolina, you hear?"

Willie was dumbfounded and managed a few "Yes sirs" and "No sirs" as Mr. Spires went on: "Now I took care of it; no one's going to mess with you now, go back home. But don't forget what I said."

Willie was terrified. He stumbled home, thanking God for sparing him. And then he thought about it for a while and became angry. He didn't do anything wrong! Why should he be frightened? He then realized he didn't want to deal with this life, this constant fear, anymore. He was becoming ever more downhearted and discouraged about his limited opportunities and the lingering threat that white rule imposed on his everyday life. He knew he needed to get out of Cameron, away from the farm. So he joined the Army.

When he came back, all those years later, he had a mission. He decided to teach me how to become a man, the right kind of man, who had the strength and courage to leave this downtrodden, go-nowhere life and not have to deal with what he went through. What he learned in the Army about life, he brought home to me and my friends. He taught us how to be men.

And I just soaked it up. I reveled in having an older man tell me things, listen to me, and help me out. Not that I didn't get plenty of attention and love from my mother; it's just that it's hard to talk about girls or sports with your mom. There are some things only another man will understand. And Willie was so patient and caring. He spent so much of his money on me, I could never repay him. And the advice he gave me about treating women with respect, I'll never forget.

I think one of the first dates I went on was a double date with Willie. There was this girl in my high school that I liked, Rebecca, whom I wanted to ask out. She had an older sister, so I thought maybe Willie could ask her out and we could make it a foursome. That way, I wouldn't have to talk so much.

We went to one of the local juke joints in Elloree, one of those places where there was a little jukebox at your table and you put coins in and listened to the Duke, Basie, the Five Royales, Eddie Vinson, Little Willie John, Louis Jordan, or a new group called the Famous Flames, fronted by an audacious screamer named James Brown. All the great music you could move to, snap to, tap your feet to, dance to, sing to; all the music that would soon put the beat in what was to become rock 'n' roll. Well, I never had much money to speak of, but Willie, he pulled out what seemed like a huge wad of money and said, "Okay, y'all, anything you want, it's on me." Damn! That's my cousin! We spent a lot of evenings over the next few months at the juke joints and piccolo joints around the county, listening to music, singing, dancing, whatever. Rebecca and I became serious, and so did Willie and Liz, Rebecca's sister.

However, with his military savings dwindling and his fear of being sucked back into farm life increasing, Willie soon made plans to leave. He found a job as a driver at a summer camp in upstate New York and was planning to leave in mid-June. He heard that they were looking for kitchen help and busboys, so he asked me if I wanted to come along.

I didn't need much prodding. Just a few weeks earlier, we had been in town on a Saturday night, walking down the street as usual, when the sudden sounds of shouts and screeching tires caused us to jerk our heads around. We saw several pickup trucks full of men wearing white sheets, arms raised, fists pumping, and shouting as they sped down the main street of Elloree. We didn't stick around to hear what they were shouting about; we knew. We took off running for the woods in an instant, crouching behind pines and oaks in the muddy forest as we prayed they wouldn't find us, only to creep home on back roads hours later in our stained, ruined clothes. This was one of the few times I was thankful for the inky darkness of the country night sky, so black that you couldn't see your hand in front of your face. We made it home safely.

By the time Willie decided to leave, my mother and I no longer farmed any land of our own. Because I was strong, I could make more money—as much as $2 a day sometimes—hiring myself out as a day laborer. I did everything. I drove a tractor for Mr. Bill Spires and picked cotton—I could pick upwards of 250 pounds a day. Back then, cotton was about 45 cents a pound. That meant whoever I was picking for made over $100 a day from me—and I made $2. So the thought of going with Willie for the summer sounded great. Anything to get out of chopping cotton. And the pay at the camp was pretty good—about $300 for two months' work, room and board included—almost as much as I could make in a whole year in South Carolina. That was *money!* I couldn't pack fast enough. My mother wished me well. She understood my need to get away.

That summer was a revelation to me.

Tucked way up in the trees near Hancock, New York, was Camp Pinecone, a camp for Jewish city kids. I never knew places like this existed, where you spent your days canoeing on a lake and hiking or fishing just for sport, not for dinner like we did when we caught catfish and eel and ring-eye in the muddy holes and creeks around Cameron.

And the people talked so funny! One day, the wife of the owner, a Jewish woman, came in and said something I couldn't understand. I had to ask her to repeat it three times before I finally said, "Yes, ma'am." Then I said to one of the cooks nearby, "What did she say?" and he said, "She was reminding you to make sure to put bread out for lunch." I thought she had said something like, "Take my head and give it a punch." Good thing I asked.

But other than that, the job was great. Washing dishes and busing tables was a cakewalk compared to farming. We even had breaks during the day and got off as soon as the dinner dishes were done. That's when Willie and I would fool around on the court, playing basketball. One evening, a few of the counselors, white college boys, said, "You guys want to play us?" We said, "Sure," so we played a little two on two and beat them. Then we played with two other guys and beat them, too, so they went to get these other guys who were supposedly the best players in the camp. After we beat *them*, they said, "Hey, there's another camp over the hill. Why don't we get a team together and go play their team?"

So we did. Me, Willie, and all these white college boys. Willie would drive it in to the basket, hit the guard, turn around, and throw it over the guard's head to me, and I would come in and dunk it in the basket, time after time. Man, we played some ball!

It was so much fun, playing with those guys, being treated with respect.

Northern white boys didn't have the same hang-ups about being with black kids as Southerners did. We talked and laughed and had no problems at all, no attitudes. This really opened my eyes.

After the summer, Willie decided to stay in New York. Sam, one of the counselors, got him a job driving a truck in the Bronx for his dad's company. I would have loved to go with Willie, but I knew I had to go home to finish my senior year of high school—and graduate.

⤐

I was so proud to be one of only twelve kids to graduate that year. But you couldn't find anyone prouder than Momma, especially when she learned that I was salutatorian—second in my class. I had gone from Cs and Ds my sophomore year to As and Bs my senior year. I really worked hard at school, all the while working full time. I managed it by getting up at 5:00 a.m., going out into the fields, coming back home at 7:30 or 8:00, washing up, and going to school, then coming home at 3:00 and working until sundown. After that, I did my homework.

After graduation, I went to Camp Pinecone again that summer. The money I made at camp that year was going to be for college. My mother had made a plan with my half-brother John that I would live with him in Sumter, a few hours north of us, and attend Morris College. Even though I was aching to stay in New York with Willie and my sisters, I did as my mother asked and went to Morris.

4

Picturing It

I just loved the way Spencer Tracy took all those boys and got them together to do something positive. He was strong but kind. He cared enough to help those poor kids change their lives for the better.

—LOU DANTZLER ON *BOYS TOWN*

It took only one of semester of college before I decided it wasn't for me.

My brother John had decided that since I liked science so much in high school, I should study chemistry, with the idea that I could become a pharmacist. I respected him and thought he knew best, so I did what he said.

However, it didn't take long for me to realize that studying chemistry didn't interest me. John kept insisting this was the right plan, and with the weight of not wanting to let my mother down, I kept my misgivings to myself until finally, in February, right after spring semester began, I took off. I took the bus back to Cameron and told my mother what I wanted to do. I wanted to go to New York. She knew there was no stopping me, so she gave me the $20 for a ticket, packed me a box of food, and sent me on my way.

In those days, in the 1940s and '50s, it seemed like everyone I knew from the South had a dream to get off the farm and go to New York. New York was the Holy Land, it was Mecca. The land of Harlem and 125th Street. In New York, there was no dirt anywhere, just concrete. I was tired of dirt.

You could take buses and trains everywhere; you didn't have to walk. There were stores where you could buy anything you wanted and restaurants where you could eat at any table just like everyone else. Movie houses had five shows for 45 cents, and you could sit anywhere you pleased. It sounded like paradise.

❧

My sister Annie found a room for me right next to her place in Brooklyn. It was basically a closet off a hallway, and the rent was $7 a week. But since it was right next to hers, I could use her bathroom, and she cooked for me, so it all worked just fine.

In the evenings, there were the clubs. The Apollo, the Baby Grand—man! We saw all the live shows: The Drifters, the Moonglows, James Brown, all those groups from back in the day. For $1.65, you'd see a great show. And even though the city had some gangs and crime back then, it was safe to walk the streets.

I was on the cusp of nineteen and having the time of my life. Annie got me a job in the laundry where she worked, and I made $1 an hour. Forty dollars a week! For working 8 to 5! I had cash in my pocket; I felt like a king. I bought some new clothes, went out at night, had me a great time. I even had some money left over to send home to my mother, who was now off the farm, living in an apartment in Orangeburg, and working in a corner grocery store. I sent her $4 or $5 a week, and to her, it was like $50.

By far my favorite thing, though, was the movies. I spent almost all my free time there. Though I did go to the clubs now and then with Willie and Annie and some others, I never drank or partied like they did. In fact, to this day, I've never tasted a beer, smoked a cigarette, or tried any type of drugs. I knew who I wanted to be.

So as I said, movies were my main passion. Air-conditioned theaters—how great is that? For a dollar, you could buy your ticket and candy and popcorn and sit there all day, in any seat you wanted, and no one would bother you. I liked westerns a lot, cowboys and Indians. I also watched *Boys Town,* one of my particular favorites, many times.

I kept seeing examples of how I wanted to live and conduct myself. Back then, there was no violence or sex or cursing on TV or in the movies. On television, the father came home at the end of the day and listened to your problems. In the movies, the sheriff in town always chased out the bad guys. Even though all those people were white, the movies and TV shows I saw gave me an idea of how I wanted to treat people and how I wanted to be treated.

It wasn't long before I began to think about my future. Working in a laundry and spending my free time at the movies was fine for a kid of eighteen or nineteen, but I knew it wasn't going to get me very far. I had to do something else.

⟨⟩

During that summer, I often passed by the recruiting offices for the armed services. They had colorful posters up in the windows, depicting soldiers in full regalia in various heroic poses. I liked the looks of those uniforms.

I remembered how Willie came back from Korea with a pocket full of money and a mind full of confidence. We had talked a bit about his experiences in Korea and what it was like to fight in the trenches, and I decided to forgo the Army. I had had enough mud and dirt on the farm. The Air Force, with its airplanes and aircraft carriers, looked like the way to go. Airmen didn't have to fight in foxholes.

So that fall I signed up for the Air Force. I didn't tell anyone of my decision until one or two days before I was scheduled to ship out: November 19, 1956.

When I shed my civilian life, I shed my Southern past as well. Joining the military from Brooklyn was different from joining from South Carolina. For the first time in my life, I didn't have to worry about the pervasive Southern racist attitude following me like a menacing shadow.

On the troop train from New York to basic training camp in San Antonio, I left behind the insecure, inferior sharecropper's son. I could be whoever I wanted to be.

The first thing I did was to introduce myself to everyone as "Lou." I never liked the name Lucious—"*Lush*-ious" the kids in Cameron used to tease; it represented all I was getting away from. The second thing I did was tell everyone I was from Brooklyn. I was done having people think I was an ignorant farm boy just because I was from the South.

By the time I entered the military, segregation was over, at least officially, but there were still reminders, mostly just an attitude here and there. On the surface, we were all integrated—even the troop train we took to Texas and the bus to the base had everyone thrown in together. I pretended to take it all in stride—even the red-faced drill sergeant screaming at me seconds after I stepped off the bus—but inside, I was shaking.

My first morning of basic, I literally sprang out of bed when those lights came on at 4:30 a.m., got dressed as fast as I could, fell in, and headed over to chow. The chow line was great. I had never seen so much food in one place in my life: ham, eggs, oatmeal, bacon, sausage, potatoes, and bread *all for one meal*.

Our basic training lasted four weeks, and except for the fact that I was petrified of my drill sergeant, it was pretty good. I was already physically fit, so the drills and runs didn't bother me. Apparently they felt I had an aptitude for communications, because after basic, I was off to the Air Force base in Cheyenne, Wyoming, to train in communications. It was Christmas Eve, 1956.

Talk about culture shock. We stepped off that bus in the middle of the night in Cheyenne, and I felt like the air was being sucked out of my lungs, it was so cold. Though I had spent one winter in New York, and the winters in South Carolina weren't balmy by any means, winter in Wyoming was like nothing I'd ever experienced. The snow in Cheyenne, unlike the slushy, slippery mess I was used to in New York, was knee deep, and with the wind, it formed even deeper drifts. Our government-issue parkas felt like breezy linen shirts in that fierce, blistering wind. This was something else.

A day or two after we settled in, the sergeant called for me. I racked my brain to think what I could have done.

"Private Dantzler, I've been watching you these past few days," he began.

Uh-oh. Here it comes, I thought.

"And I like the way you carry yourself," he continued. "Clean, orderly. And you're a big guy, too, the biggest in the outfit, I'd say." I had no idea where he was going with this.

"I'm going to make you barracks chief. That means you're in charge of the duty roster for the barracks, you set the schedule of the fire guard, make sure the barracks is clean, and make sure the unit learns the drills, stuff like that. Think you can handle that?"

For a moment, I was stunned, though I still managed to cough out a "Yes, Sergeant!" before I was dismissed. I was amazed. Never before had I been put in charge of anything, let alone a large bunch of white guys. Therefore, I was determined to be the best barracks chief there was. First thing I did was recruit myself an assistant, one of my friends, who also happened to be one of the only three black guys in the unit. Together we assigned the duties for the barracks, the most dreaded one being fire guard. The fire guard had to spend the night making sure the fire in the barracks always remained stoked. This was something I had done for many winters myself on the farm, and now, as chief, I was able to delegate that task to someone else. I also assigned who cleaned the latrines as well as other barracks duties. You could make friends or enemies really fast with that kind of authority.

There were reasons the sergeant appointed me to be chief, the main one being that no one would dare mess with someone my size—and they didn't. I played up my badass side a bit, too. These guys had no way of knowing I was just an insecure farm kid from the South who had never thrown a punch in my life, but I could talk the talk when I needed to, and it was my job to motivate them to do their duties and learn their drills, otherwise I'd get *my* ass chewed out.

I never did get my ass chewed, though. I made it my mission to keep my unit on top of those drills and make sure that the latrines were clean, the snow was shoveled, and we marched in formation. This was my first taste of respect and authority, and I liked it. I learned that in order to get people to follow you, you had to have their respect, and you earned their respect by being tough but also fair. You didn't earn it by trying to be friends with everyone; sometimes you had to make unpopular decisions to serve the greater good and make sure the people affected by those decisions knew they were part of that greater good.

Soon my training was over, and I was sent to my permanent assignment: the Pentagon. I couldn't believe it. Intelligence communications at the Strategic Air Command, which meant I sent out messages on top-secret teletype machines. I had my own quarters on the base and could walk to work. Everyone treated me with respect. I met so many nice people, too—in the service, you become just like brothers. When I got leave on the weekends, I took the train up to New York and had a friend or two go with me. I was getting three meals a day, had a clean place to live, worked an eight-hour shift, and had time off to myself. Yeah, much better than chopping cotton!

I was also able to help out my mother, which made me happy. I made her a Class-2 Allotment, which meant part of my military pay was sent to her every month. I went to visit her from time to time in her little place in Orangeburg. It broke my heart to see her living in such a deplorable place. The man who rented the rooms to her was the equivalent of a slumlord, and her apartment was no better than our shack on Mr. Spires's place. I wished I could do more for her, but she couldn't live with me on the base.

As usual, she never complained, and in fact always lifted my spirits when she talked of how proud she was of me. Her son, her baby, working at the Pentagon, in an office, with security clearance!

Then, in 1959, after about two years of working at the Pentagon, things changed. I was sent overseas to Saudi Arabia. It was my first time on an airplane.

~

If I thought Wyoming in the winter was a shock, it was nothing compared to the Middle East all year round. It confronts you the minute you step off the plane.

Now, I was used to heat; I grew up in the South. I was used to sweating even before I finished breakfast, used to praying for the sun to slip behind the trees so I could take refuge in the hazy shadows at twilight. But Saudi was something else altogether.

First of all, there were few, if any, trees, for the sun to slip behind. There was no Spanish moss dangling lazily from a shady oak or gum tree; no wildflowers and grasses cushioning your bare feet as you walked, smelling that delicious, pungent green smell. I was used to color as far as the eye could see: the greens of the trees and grasses contrasting with the red earth beneath our feet, the wildflowers and tree blossoms dotting the horizon, the billowy white of an endless cotton field. Not in Saudi. Everything there was shades of beige—the sand, the sky, the buildings, the clothing we wore.

And the heat! That arid, acrid, unrelenting, oven-baked desert heat, which seared your lungs if you took too deep a breath. The ground conducted the sun's rays, holding in the heat and radiating it out, right through the soles of your boots. The sun was so bright, and its blinding intensity was amplified by the whiteness of the sand. This wasn't an oasis of palm trees as in some tale out of *Arabian Nights*. We had cinderblock barracks and oleander bushes, whose spiky leaves and tiny flowers were deadly if eaten.

Even so, I looked upon my posting as an adventure. I knew some of the guys there already and met more at the PX and the service club. It was a pretty tight-knit group, this band of Americans so far from home. I went to the service club quite a bit, and there I met three guys, Jimmy, Ray, and Simms, who each had a passion for music.

I shared that passion. Ever since my days in the juke joints of Cameron and the nightclubs of Harlem, I had always been into music. A lot of the money I earned at the laundry in Brooklyn went to buy albums by Fats Domino, James Brown, and the great doo-woppers of the time. I played their songs over and over, copying their style, singing in the bathroom to get that echo.

One night at the service club, Jimmy, Ray, Simms, and I were goofing around, singing a Drifters song. I sang in the church choir growing up, as had those guys, so we knew about four-part harmony. Easily, we all fell into our parts, harmonizing perfectly. When we finished that song, we went on to another and then another, all night long. Pretty soon, a group had gathered around us, and we really got into it. After a while, someone said, "Man, you guys should sing on the base's television show!"

That was all the encouragement we needed. The four of us got together and practiced whenever we could. We bought tailored dark suits with matching narrow ties and white shirts. The Sheiks, we called ourselves.

The armed forces took great care in making sure their soldiers stationed overseas had as many of the comforts of home as possible. We bought American products in the PX, had a library with all the latest books and magazines, and ate our hotdogs and apple pie at the mess hall. The USO gave us good old red, white, and blue entertainment, broadcast from the base's closed-circuit television station. In Saudi, a woman named Miss de La Rue had a sort of musical variety show going on at this station—a little south-of-the-border, Carmen Miranda–type thing—and she let us come on her show. Pretty soon, it became a regular thing, and we expanded our repertoire into backing her up on the bongos and maracas. After a while, we began touring all the bases in the Middle East—Lebanon, Ethiopia, places I had never even heard of—to perform our act.

In addition to singing, I was using my athletic ability again. Soon after I arrived, I was recruited to play in the Air Force's Arabian Basketball Conference, which had teams with names like the Flyers and the Rockets. I played for the Flyers. Being part of that gave me even more opportunities to travel about the region and meet new people. Some of the people in the Middle East thought we were the Harlem Globetrotters! My confidence grew and grew. I was no longer Lush-ious Dantzler, barefoot kid from the sticks. I was Airman Second Class Lou Dantzler, traveling around the world and decoding top-secret messages for the Air Force.

After thirteen months in the Middle East, I was transferred back to the States, this time to March Air Force Base in Riverside, California. I had always wanted to see California.

At March, I roomed with a guy named Ted Bolden, who was from Compton, a predominantly black city about sixty miles to the west of our base. We became good friends fairly quickly. Ted, who was married, asked me to come home with him one weekend in August of 1960. We had big plans to go tear up the town. Ted's wife, however, had other ideas.

"I don't get to see you but once a month, and you're gonna just drop in on your way out to party? Uh-uh! I don't think so; you gonna stay with me," she told him. "We're going bowling." Then she looked at me. "Dantzler, you wanna meet a friend of mine? Let me call her and see if she wants to go bowling with us."

I said fine; anything to keep the peace. I told her, though, that I was engaged, so this wasn't going to be a date or anything. Before I had shipped out to Saudi, I had asked a girl I had met in D.C. to marry me. However, the distance hadn't done too much for our relationship, especially now that she was in New York and I was in California.

After Ted's wife hung up the phone, she said, "Let's get going." Next thing I knew, we were driving over to nearby Watts, to the Jordan Downs housing project, and when we got there, out walked this little slip of a girl, not more than 100 pounds, with the most beautiful skin and a smile that lit up her whole face. Ruby Talley. I don't think she was more than twenty at the time.

I found out later that Ruby really didn't want to come on this setup either. She already had a boyfriend and wasn't interested in meeting anyone. But Ted's wife insisted. "Ruby, I keep asking you to go out with us, and you never come," she had said on the phone. "If you don't go out with us tonight, I won't be friends with you anymore." So Ruby came. She didn't pay too much attention to me, however. Ted's cousin came with us, too, and she talked mostly with him. I wasn't bothered, really. I had someone in New York anyway.

After bowling, we drove down to Central Avenue near 12th Street, which was at the time the Harlem of Los Angeles, with its thriving African American life. There were literally dozens of nightclubs to choose from: the Jungle Room, the Down Beat Club, the Last Word, the Dunbar Grill, the Ritz Club, the Parisian Room, Ivy's Chicken Shack, and the Plantation Club, among others. Music and dancing, this is what I came for.

In the car on the way over, I told a silly joke that broke the ice with Ruby, and from there we were off. She liked to dance as much as I did, and we certainly tore it up that night. Since we were both involved with other people, we just remained friends, but that didn't stop me from calling her. I had a buddy at the base who worked the switchboard, and I could call anyone I wanted all over the country for free. I called Ruby the most, though. We talked and talked. She even comforted me when I found out that fall through a mutual friend that my fiancée was four months pregnant—and I hadn't seen her in six months. That was the end of that.

By December, Ruby had broken up with her boyfriend as well, which was one of the reasons I was especially looking forward to the party Ted and his wife were giving for New Year's Eve. Our first kiss was that night.

We became engaged in April (I was a fast worker). Ted threw us an engagement party, and Ruby organized a going-away party for me in May. I was getting out of the service and going back to New York, but not before we set a wedding date: October 6, 1961. Since we planned to settle in New York, I thought I'd go back there and get us a place to live. I contacted Camp Pinecone and worked there again that summer, figuring it was the fastest way to make a few hundred bucks to get us set up. Then, after we got married in California, Ruby and I moved to Brooklyn.

5

When Chickens Had Nothing But Backs and Feet

Trust in God, believe in God, and He will show the way. My faith in God has always given me the ability to look at the big picture. You need to have faith in something.

—LOU DANTZLER

To this day, my sisters still tease me about how I used to treat their kids. Remember, my mother took care of Sarah's and Sallie's kids off and on for most of their childhoods. When those kids were younger, I was still at home and responsible for them when Momma wasn't around.

"Lucious, make sure the house is clean when I get home," she'd say on her way to work. I knew I'd be the one to get my butt whipped if there was any dirt tracked in that house, so I'd get the kids to help me mop the floor, dust the tables, do the dishes, whatever. Then, when the house was clean, I'd make them sit on the edge of the bed and not move, just so they wouldn't mess anything up before Momma came home. And those kids listened; I didn't fool around. Yet they looked up to me, too, I think, because even though I gave them a hard time about keeping the house clean, I also spent lots of time playing with them and taking care of them. I think I was a positive role model for Michael, George, Bobby, and William—all Sallie's boys—because three of them went into the service and did well.

Now, with Ruby and me living in New York, I was doing the same for

Arthur's kids (we no longer called him Junior). I cut their hair, and we played stickball or basketball together on the weekends and had a great time. Arthur had four kids, three boys and a girl. They all looked up to me, and I thought I had a responsibility to show them that life could be different from what they saw around them. I set an example for them to follow, too: I didn't smoke or drink. I spent time with them, sitting down with them after our ballgames and talking to them and listening to them and trying to give them direction.

Unfortunately, by this time, in the early 1960s, the neighborhood in which we lived was rapidly declining. Poverty, delinquency, crime, hopelessness, addiction—all were bombarding the children of Brooklyn, especially the black children. Ruby and I looked around and decided this was not the place we wanted to raise the child that was growing inside her. Eight months after we moved to Brooklyn, we left and moved back to Los Angeles.

We arrived late one Friday evening in June 1962. Ruby was at the beginning of her eighth month of pregnancy. By Sunday, we found a place to live, a little one-bedroom apartment for $80 a month. It seemed funny to me to be living in a part of town known as Country Club Park. I later found out the area had been named due to its proximity to the Wilshire Country Club, a traditional, white, conservative golf club near the old-money area of Hancock Park.

Los Angeles was quite a change for me. Living in New York, I had become accustomed to the concrete grids and sparse, fenced-in greenery of that cramped, congested city. L.A. was different. With its wide streets, palm trees, and neat little houses, each with its own patch of lawn, this city represented for me the perfect blend of the rural life of my youth and the energy of city life.

We moved our meager belongings into our new place, and I set about finding myself a job. Los Angeles was known at the time as one of the chief migration points for blacks wanting to escape the still-oppressive South. The lure of nice weather and what was believed to be unlimited opportunity for jobs brought black families by the hundreds of thousands from the 1940s through the 1960s. During that time, the black population of Watts increased eight times over as countless families left the farms of Texas, Louisiana, and Mississippi and headed west to fill jobs in the shipyards, railroads, and assembly lines.

Once they reached L.A., however, many found they were confronted by the same racist attitudes they had left in the South. Los Angeles was still a very segregated city. There were severe housing restrictions that gave property owners the right to refuse to rent or sell to people of color, especially if the owner felt it would reduce property values. "Redlining" was common: Banks declared certain areas of the city off-limits to blacks and refused to lend them money to purchase homes there.

Most found they had no choice but to settle in the area referred to by whites at the time as Mudtown—Watts and South Central Los Angeles. The migration to this area was so pronounced that after the war, the federal government erected several housing projects for the growing population. Nickerson Gardens, Imperial Court, Hacienda Village—clusters of two-story apartment houses built on what used to be sugar beet fields—were christened with optimistic, utopian names. Before long, however, the complexes became overcrowded. More than a third of the total population of Watts lived in public housing projects, such as the Jordan Downs project where Ruby grew up. They were a far cry from the paradise their names promised, but many people who were used to sharecroppers' shotgun shacks or the rat-infested, high-rise tenement apartments of other big-city ghettos felt lucky to live there all the same.

As for us, I felt Ruby and I were lucky to have found the place on Country Club Drive, which was about seven or eight miles northwest of Watts. The neighborhood was mixed and fairly quiet.

The Monday morning after we arrived, I set out with a newspaper and coins for the bus. I had to find a job. I decided not to listen to the discouraging reports of limited opportunities for blacks in Los Angeles. I was young and strong, had a high school education, and had been in the Air Force—I was sure I would find something soon enough.

And I did. I found a job right away in a warehouse of a company called Sidney Newhoff, in the industrial area near downtown, which paid $46 a week. Ruby wasn't working—she was too close to her due date—so my $46 a week was our whole income, and half of that went for rent. Needless to say, money was tight. Even spending 40 cents for the trolley downtown and back was stretching things. But I wasn't discouraged. I didn't sit around and bemoan the situation. I just tried to figure out what I needed to do next.

I've always had a lot of energy; I've always liked that sweaty feeling, the deep-down-in-your-muscles ache you get after a hard day's work. I remember being in the cotton fields and getting so much satisfaction from looking down a finished row of cotton, knowing that it all went into my sack because of my hard work and sweat. At the end of the day at Newhoff, which was easy by comparison to field work, I came home at 5:00 p.m. with energy to burn.

One day, I started sweeping the sidewalk in front of our apartment building. When that was done, I went to work weeding the tiny flower beds on the front lawn. In the middle of this, the owner of the building came over and asked what I was doing. He was a really nice guy, and when I told him I liked doing this type of thing, we struck a deal: I would act as the manager/handyman for the place for a reduction in rent—by half. Man, did that help!

And it came just in time. When I went to work one Thursday in early August, I was told that I had been laid off. I went home that night and told Ruby, who was set to deliver our baby any day. One thing about Ruby that I've always loved is that she's always had belief in me and never let anything get her down. If she was upset or scared about this new development, she didn't burden me with it. I think she just knew that something would happen for me.

Let's put it this way: I didn't let any grass grow under my feet! I got up the next day, August 3, shined my shoes, put on my suit, and went down to the Hall of Administration, where they had the employment bulletin board. I must have walked and talked for ten straight hours that day, trying to get a job. I knew something was going to break for me; I just knew it.

That evening, I came home to an empty apartment. Where was Ruby? I wondered. Maybe she had gone over to her mother's. I called over there, and Ruby's sister, Alice, said Ruby was in the hospital. She was in labor. I think I ran all the way to the hospital, a good two miles away.

That day, our son Mark was born.

If my feet touched the ground, I didn't feel it. A son! A beautiful, healthy baby boy, born in a clean, modern city hospital with doctors and nurses to help with the delivery, not in a three-room shack with a midwife in attendance and everyone waiting on the front porch. I was on cloud nine.

I soon realized, however, that we had nothing in the apartment for the baby, and I had little in my pocket with which to do anything about it.

I went back to the apartment after Ruby and the baby fell asleep at the hospital. I called a couple of my friends from the Air Force who now lived nearby, George May and Walter Christopher, and told them the news. They said, "That's great, man; congratulations! Let's go celebrate!" Which we did, at the local Sav-On drugstore, where we pooled our money—I think we had about $41 between the three of us—and went shopping for the baby. Bassinet, diapers, formula, bottles—we had so much fun.

Yes, I was out of a job, but I was happy. I had a son, and I had friends who pulled together and helped me out in my time of need, just the way it used to be in our little community in the South. Back then, when anyone we knew needed help, all the neighbors got together and did something, with my mother first in line. Even when we had nothing, she was giving what little we had to others. There was a time I thought chickens didn't have anything but backs and feet, because that's all we could afford to buy. She'd make a stew out of those parts and give a portion of it to one of our neighbors who'd fallen on hard times. There was never a shortage of people having hard times.

And now it was me who was having a rough patch, and these guys were helping me out and having fun with it. I didn't stop to think, "Man, I lost my job and I'm all depressed, and now I should start drinking." No, I thought, "Just trust in God, believe in God, and He will show the way." I really believe that. My faith in God has always given me the ability to look at the big picture, and it certainly helped then. You need to have faith in something.

On Monday, while I was hitting the streets looking for work, I stopped by Sidney Newhoff to tell the guys my wife just had a boy. I didn't bear any grudges; they were all good guys, and business was business. When I saw my supervisor and told him I had a boy, he congratulated me. As he was shaking my hand, he said, "Lou, you want to come back to work?" They knew I was a good worker and that whatever they paid me, they'd get the most for their money. They could depend on me to get the job done. So, just like that, I had my old job back. By the time I left there two years later, I had doubled my salary to $80 a week.

From that point on, things started moving. Because money was so tight, Ruby had to go back to work. She had taken a leave of absence—unpaid, since there was no such thing as maternity leave back then—but it was over. Her mother cared for Mark.

In the meantime, I was looking for more ways to earn money. I had always done things on the side—for example, when I was in the Air Force. I made extra money by ironing the officers' shirts—and I was eager to start a business or something of my own.

At this point in my life, I had ambition but not too much direction. The communications and typing skills I acquired in the Air Force qualified me for mostly clerical work, and one of the reasons I hadn't reenlisted was because I was tired of working at a desk all day. I had no desire to spend my life at a desk. I liked being out of doors; I liked being with people, especially kids; and I liked being creative. I had taken a photography course while I was in the military and thought about starting a photography studio. With my interest in music, I toyed with the idea of starting a record shop. Ruby said that since I was so good with kids, maybe I should go to college and become a teacher, like a high school coach or something, but although I liked coaching and working with kids, the thought of spending four years in a classroom filled me with dread.

I liked to learn and could apply myself when I needed to, such as when I had hit the books and made salutatorian in high school or passed my communications training in Cheyenne the first time around. But I never really responded to the structure of a classroom and a teacher telling me what to do—I found that out when I was at Morris College. I preferred to learn by doing.

Take learning to drive, for example. I had driven tractors in South Carolina; Mr. Eldon Higler had taught me. For me, driving a car was the natural next step. I studied the book from the DMV, then went in on a Friday and took the test, and by that afternoon, I had my license. The next step was to buy a car. I had my eye on a particular 1957 Pontiac that I saw at Majestic Motors on Crenshaw Boulevard. Ruby and I arranged a $1,000 loan through the telephone company credit union, and I went into Majestic and slapped down the full $855 cash and drove home. What a feeling! This was definitely better than that 1946 Ford I had thought of buying back in the South. Here I was, just ten years later, a man with a wife and child, a job, and beholden to no one. Oh, I am certainly glad I listened to my mother! With that car, I felt free, independent, adult. I think I almost rubbed the paint off by polishing it every week, I was so proud.

What I lacked in direction, however, I made up for in drive and ingenuity. Since we were now saving all we could to buy a house, I cut corners wherever I could. When I took my car in to get the brakes serviced, I watched what the mechanic did, and the next time, I did it myself. I changed the oil, changed the plugs, you name it. I also became quite adept at cutting hair. When we were in Brooklyn, I had cut all my nieces' and nephews' hair, so here in L.A., I did my own and some of my friends'. I even thought at one point of starting my own hair salon, but Ruby put a stop to that right away! "Uh-uh! No way. I'm not gonna have you in a salon all day touching ladies' hair," she said.

I instead started a handyman business on the weekends. I organized some friends of mine and bought tools and gardening equipment, and soon we had a few jobs, mostly cutting lawns and painting. Eventually, I thought, we could buy rundown properties, fix them up ourselves, and sell them for a profit.

At this point, I had lots of free time during the day. In 1964, I quit Newhoff and got a job with the Los Angeles School District as a janitor. The pay and benefits were better, and the hours—graveyard shift—meant that I had plenty of time during the day to pursue my gardening business.

After a while, the handyman business I had wanted to build with my friends had fizzled out. They didn't really buy into my dream. That was okay; we parted friends, and I took the lawn service part of the business, along with the equipment and customers, with me. I had twenty-seven lawns to cut, each for $10 a month. Pretty soon, I decided I needed a truck to carry all the equipment around, so I bought a blue Ford pickup.

Then Ruby and I began looking for a house. We were ecstatic when, in early 1965, we found a cute, two-bedroom Spanish bungalow with a spacious yard on Sixth Avenue, near the Crenshaw area of South Central, for $19,000. The street was wide and sunny, with those beautiful California palm trees lining it all the way down. There were hardworking families like us nearby, and kids riding their bikes on the sidewalks. For us, this was a dream come true.

My contentment was tempered, however, by the harsh realities I was beginning to see in other parts of our community.

❧

From what I had seen of Watts, where Ruby's parents and younger brother still lived, it was becoming as depressing as what Ruby and I tried to leave behind in Brooklyn. One-parent households were becoming the rule, not the exception.

Classrooms there were cramped, the average fifth-grader couldn't read, and two-thirds of kids who entered the seventh grade dropped out before finishing high school. Crime was rampant; local police reported nearly fifty arrests a day.

The average age of a Watts resident at the time was sixteen. Many of the kids who had long since dropped out of school spent their time hanging out on street corners, looking for kicks—anything to alleviate the boredom and frustration of ghetto life. Perhaps one in ten of these kids would ever see the beaches Los Angeles was known for; for many, the only trip they would take outside their neighborhood would be the bus ride to jail. I faced the same sense of hopelessness and despair that I experienced when I was growing up and I had joined the military to escape. Things were different now, though—who wanted to go to Vietnam?

One of the biggest problems was that those kids had nothing to do. Well, nothing positive to do, anyway. The world of summer camps, summer jobs, and Boy Scouts was miles away on the west side of town. "You never see a green Boy Scout uniform on our side of town," observed Kenny Rodgers, a friend of Ruby's brother, Michael, who also lived in the Jordan Downs project. "That's sissy stuff. Little League is okay. If you can hit a ball, you're all right." But if you couldn't? Plus, you needed committed fathers to be Little League coaches and Boy Scout troop leaders, and the neighborhood had far too few of those. For many youths in Watts, summer meant 20-ounce bottles of malt liquor, hanging out on the corner with their friends, listening to their transistor radios, and watching life go by.

Luckily, Ruby and I were pretty removed from these situations. Even though the area in which we lived was considered part of the forty-square-mile South Central L.A. district, we were in the western part of it, near the Crenshaw district, where many middle-class black families were. In the heart of this district was Crenshaw Plaza, one of the first shopping malls in America, built in the 1940s. We had a grocery store, a butcher, everything we needed nearby. We didn't have to take the bus and change two or three times to find a decent supermarket with decent prices, as many of our Watts neighbors did. We were working hard and doing what we could to live our American Dream.

That's why the events that occurred during a sticky August heat wave in that summer of 1965—events that alternately made Ruby and me angry, frightened, bitter, shocked, and saddened—ultimately just left us heartbroken.

Arriving home late one evening from work, I was too tired to notice the smell of smoke and the far-off wail of sirens miles to the south of our house. In our neighborhood, everything was quiet, as usual. However, the next morning, August 12, I awoke to a different world.

The night before, a routine drunk driving arrest near Watts turned into a bloody, fiery clash between the LAPD and the young residents of the neighborhood of 116th Street and Avalon Boulevard, just outside of Watts. It lasted into the early hours of the morning, and when it was over, nineteen policemen and sixteen civilians had been injured by rocks, bottles, and nightsticks. Cars were overturned and torched; white motorists caught in the area on their way home were dragged from their cars and beaten. Fifty vehicles, including two fire trucks, were burned. At first, police officers made futile attempts to quell the escalating disturbance, but soon someone decided their presence was only serving to fuel the hostility, and they left, abandoning the law-abiding people of the neighborhood.

It was no surprise to any of the black population of Los Angeles that there was a clash with the police. Though the LAPD had a reputation, furthered by television shows like *Dragnet,* of being one of the most professional, well-ordered forces in the nation, what wasn't so apparent was that the police department was largely a whites-only organization. This was at a time when Los Angeles had the biggest population of African Americans of any city in the western United States. White police officers and poor, urban youths had little tolerance for one another.

The next few nights, the only light in that area was from burning buildings. Streetlights had been broken, shot out, or toppled. The streets were covered with shards of broken glass from store windows and liquor bottles. Scraps of metal from abandoned cars and chunks of concrete from bus benches prevented passage of vehicles on Avalon and Imperial. Police used their cars to erect makeshift barricades and crouched behind them between efforts to make arrests. It was a battle zone, a real no-man's land.

By this time, the riot reached beyond those few blocks north of Watts, spreading to about twenty square blocks of Watts and South Central L.A. Nearly 1,000 police were on hand, but again they were overrun, useless. There was hope that by Friday, August 13, the mayhem would begin to cool down. As the sun rose, however, nearly seventy-five stores in the area were smoldering ruins.

Molotov cocktails were stockpiled, as were other weapons and ammunition, the latter by both blacks and whites. The few black business owners in the area put "black-owned" signs on their doors, which helped them on Thursday but by Friday were ignored. By 9:00 a.m., in broad daylight, packs of youths and young adults roamed the streets of Watts, leaving destruction in their wake.

The rioters and looters had a rallying cry: "Burn, baby, burn!" We heard that over and over during the next few days. Ruby and I anxiously noted the violence as it progressed onto nearby Crenshaw Boulevard. We couldn't help checking the night sky, which had taken on a bright orange glow, from time to time, and we jumped in alarm at every sound. We stayed inside as much as we could, for safety's sake but also because of the acrid, choking smoke that kept billowing our way. We tensed with every siren and checked on sleeping Mark more than usual.

While I understood the rage that engulfed the people of our community—much like the rage that had driven other urban blacks to participate in lesser riots the previous year in New York, New Jersey, and Pennsylvania—I drew the line at the wholesale thuggery happening around us. I had always been a big supporter of Martin Luther King Jr.'s philosophy of peaceful resistance. Violence simply begat more violence. Once the fires cooled down and the glass was swept up, where were the law-abiding families of this community supposed to go for their goods and services? What if you didn't have a car to drive into nearby Compton or Inglewood or even Crenshaw? The whole situation broke my heart.

Judging from what I saw on TV that Friday, the situation was far from being under control. "Turn left or get shot," warned a hand-lettered sign at the top of one street near the area.

Then the tanks rolled in.

My 4 1/2 years in the service were spent in peacetime, so I had never faced a true battlefield situation. When I was discharged, I figured I had dodged that bullet—I would never have to encounter an armed conflict, and for that I was grateful. So the sight of armed tanks rolling into the streets just miles from my home came as quite a shock. Ten thousand National Guardsmen were called in Friday evening to help the police quell the disturbance and restore peace. They had their battle helmets, their flak jackets, their bayonets, and their machine guns, and they set up barricades and roadblocks around the perimeter of the "battle zone."

Gradually, as the world looked on from their living rooms in horror, the violence decreased, and by Monday evening, the streets were relatively peaceful. On Tuesday, August 17, California's governor declared the riot under control and ended the curfew. Slowly, the National Guard units began pulling out one by one. The riot—or disturbance, uprising, or rebellion—was over.

I'm not sure where the expression "We won the battle but lost the war" originated, but I think it is the perfect phrase to describe what happened to the communities of Watts and South Central Los Angeles in the months, years, and decades after those bloody, awful six days in August of 1965.

When the smoke cleared, the glass and other debris were swept off the streets, a few businesses tentatively began to resume operations, and many people in the community rejoiced. The violence had finally focused the world's attention on their situation. Even Martin Luther King Jr. came to the area, though he soon curtailed a proposed tour of the riot zone after he was heckled and told that many area residents weren't sympathetic to his movement's peaceful ideology. Indeed, the rage and fury that had erupted seemed to embolden some people. The white folks are listening, they reasoned. We won!

It was true in a sense. The rioting, which was then considered the largest and most violent such occurrence since the draft riots during the Civil War, did attract worldwide attention and bring some desperately needed federal disaster efforts into the area—including a blue-ribbon panel, the McCone Commission, which was put together to study the reasons for the Watts Riot and determine what remedies were needed to prevent something like it from ever happening again. But it also seemed to confirm what so many whites had believed about blacks in general: that we were violent, lawless thugs who deserved to be locked up.

Unfortunately, as we can now see, the war was just beginning. While individual criminals were prosecuted, the bigger issues of urban poverty and inequality in housing, schooling, and jobs went unattended to. We may have won our civil rights, but the law and the practice of the law are two different things; changing the patterns and attitudes that took generations to develop was not going to happen overnight.

Soon after the riot, white working- and middle-class families by the scores began a mass exodus from the heretofore racially mixed, peaceful neighborhoods of Crenshaw, West Adams, and Harvard Square, moving to newer housing tracts in the San Fernando and San Gabriel valleys. Businesses shuttered or destroyed during the riot moved elsewhere. Pepperdine University, a prestigious university that had its main campus in South Central, relocated west to a bluff overlooking the Pacific Ocean in Malibu. Gradually, shopping centers began to sport more and more empty spaces, like missing teeth in an old man's smile. Stores, such as the Vons supermarket on 51st Street and Vermont Avenue, closed their doors for good, leaving their once-bustling buildings vacant, magnets for street crime and vagrants.

With so many young people on the streets with nothing to do, it was no wonder they got into trouble. "Idle hands are the Devil's workshop" was one of my mother's favorite expressions, and like so much that my mother taught me, it proved to be true. If those kids had something positive to do—whether a job where they could start to develop life skills or an organized recreation program so they could get down to the business of just being kids—most wouldn't have time to get into trouble. But how and where could that happen?

As summer receded into fall, things gradually returned to normal for us, at least superficially. Ruby and I were both working hard to build our life together. We began to talk about having a little brother or sister for Mark.

By 1967, I was working as a janitor at Gage Junior High School. I liked the job, I worked with great guys like Howard Banks and Ed O'Neal, and the hours meant I could spend time with my family and devote myself to my other interests. The lawn business was thriving; I had customers all over the area. I was getting to know a lot of people, and Sunday barbecues were frequent at our house. In addition to the lawn business, I was nurturing a little freelance photography business, shooting mainly weddings and birthdays. Someone had also turned me on to selling Amway products. I didn't go at this too hard and sold mostly to people I knew, but it was some nice, steady income. I was still cutting hair, too; all the kids in the neighborhood came by on Saturday afternoons after I had done my lawns. We'd sit in the kitchen and laugh and talk, and I'd try to make sure all the hair was swept up before Ruby got home from shopping.

Five jobs. It sounds like a lot, but I was never an oh-it's-my-day-off-so-I'm-gonna-sleep-all-day-and-watch-TV kind of guy. I liked projects, and I liked to keep busy.

My lawn business was especially satisfying. It was always gratifying to see a neatly trimmed green patch surrounded by nicely sculpted hibiscus or camellia bushes, with not a weed in sight, and know that when I had pulled up that day, the grass was poking up unevenly and threatening to overtake the sidewalk, dandelions and crabgrass were beginning to choke the flowerbeds, and the driveway sported a thin carpet of leaves. Not anymore. I edged those lawns as if I had an invisible ruler guiding me. I attacked the weeds with my hoe, and my blower took care of any stray leaves that found their way onto my customers' yards.

Boy, how great it would have been to have some of these tools when I lived in Cameron, I thought. I mean, did you ever sweep dirt? My mother was a stickler for cleanliness and order, and her yard was no exception. We snapped branches from the mulberry bush in our front yard and bound them to a whittled piece of pine—that was our broom. That's what I used to keep our yard spotless.

Occasionally, I would stop and marvel that I had spent the last dozen years escaping those chores, and here I was choosing to do them all over again. The difference this time, though, was that I was getting paid for it, and I was my own boss. What I made, I kept.

Even with all the work I had, I still had enough time for my family, which was the most important thing. Mark, a sweet, quiet five-year-old, sometimes went with me when I went to do lawns. Afterward, we would head over to see Ruby's parents, who had finally gotten out of the projects and bought a house in Compton, and visit her brother, Michael.

Michael was much younger than Ruby. Much like me, he was born late in his parents' life, around the time they thought they were going to start having grandchildren.

I remember when I first met him, when he was about seven years old. Ruby and I had just started getting serious, and I thought he was a cute kid. I played with him sometimes while I waited for Ruby to get ready. He was very bright and always eager for my attention, which at times proved to be really annoying. Michael always had a sixth sense for when I was about to lean over to kiss Ruby, because he would inevitably jump on us or something, destroying the mood.

But I didn't mind too much. I understood. His father, a welder at the docks in San Pedro during the day and a horn player at night in a club in Watts, was approaching his late fifties and didn't have the energy to handle a seven-year-old boy. His mother worked as a housekeeper in Beverly Hills, so she was often exhausted at the end of the day, too.

So I always had a special affection for Michael. After we moved back to Los Angeles, especially after we bought our house, I tried to spend time with him at least once a week. Just as I used to do with my nieces and nephews, I played ball with him, cut his hair, took him out for ice cream or to a movie, whatever. Sometimes I let him invite some of his friends along. We had some nice times. He was good with Mark, too, and sometimes baby-sat if we wanted an evening out.

By 1968, my marriage to Ruby had settled into a nice groove. Even though our personalities are a bit different at times—Ruby is what she likes to call a B personality, meaning she likes to take things slow, sleep in, and linger, as opposed to my fervent, constant A-type energy—our marriage was strong and happy. I had made the decision early in life that whoever I married, I was going to treat her with respect and caring. I had seen so much verbal abuse and domestic violence visited upon my three sisters—once, Annie's husband took after her with a knife and slashed her face and throat, leaving scars she still bears to this day—that I vowed to never raise a hand to my wife. If I got mad, which wasn't very often, we worked it out some other way.

That year, we were elated to learn that Ruby was pregnant again and due in November. The only thing that tempered our happiness was the fact that my mother would never get to see our new child. Narvis Fogle Thompson Dantzler succumbed to what we think was cancer in late 1967. She was 70 years old.

I had gone back on my own to see her that year, and as usual, her smile of pride when I walked into the room filled me up. I had always hoped that I could bring her out to live with us in Los Angeles, but by the time we got settled enough to send for her, she was already ill and didn't want to leave the place that was the only home she'd ever known.

Born in 1897, my mother entered this world in a time when most white people believed people of color were property. She lived long enough to see our race achieve equal status under the law, to live free of the fear of being strung up on a whim, and to see people of all colors share the same drinking water. Not that any of this came in time to elevate her life, but I vowed that I would do everything in my power to improve things for my family and, in my own small way, my community.

6

Taking the First Step

It saddened me to see how so many of these kids' lives lacked laughter. Kids should be laughing and relaxed, not worried if they turn a corner they're gonna get jumped.

—Lou Dantzler

One of the best parts of my lawn business was seeing the children. As I moved from neighborhood to neighborhood, loading and unloading, clipping and edging, mowing and blowing, I looked forward to seeing the boys, maybe two or three, sometimes more, who shadowed me while I worked, asking me loads of questions about my equipment and begging for rides in my truck.

It made me recall my days as a youngster in the South, riding around in the back of someone else's truck with the wind on my face, that sense of freedom and the feeling of speed hollowing the pit of my stomach. Man, I loved any opportunity to get in the back of a truck, even though it was usually when a white man drove me to work. That was okay; those few minutes bouncing along in the sunshine were worth it.

I understood how those kids in the neighborhood felt. Sometimes, if I had some time, I let one or two of them hop in the back for a spin around the block. I'd speed up and then slow down on purpose, just to listen to their squeals. I loved looking in the rearview mirror and seeing those smiling faces, listening to their excited chatter, "What's he doin'? Is he gonna stop? Whoooooaaaaa…"

They were fascinated with my lawn equipment, especially my leaf blower. They'd line up for a chance to crank that baby up and watch the leaves fly. "My turn! Now it's my turn," they'd shout, jumping up and down. It didn't matter what their age—most were between eight and fourteen, I think—they all liked to use it.

Three years after the disastrous violence in 1965, it was summer again, school had just let out, and there were more kids on the streets than ever. Boys mostly, though a girl or two would venture off her shady porch and talk to me from time to time. But the boys, they were the ones who really liked seeing my blue truck pull up. They would run out to meet me, jockeying for the chance to help me unload something.

"You here *again?*" I'd say to them in a teasing tone, and they'd laugh. I found it so sad that the highlight of their day, a beautiful summer day, was the guy coming to cut their mom's lawn. Most of my customers were single mothers, women who didn't have men around to do yard work.

"Why aren't you at the park?" I asked a couple of the kids one day. "Don't you want to play ball with your friends or something?"

"Yeah, we like ball," one murmured, head down, kicking an invisible rock on the sidewalk. "But the park's too far to walk."

"My mom won't take me to the park," piped up the other, "ever since she saw those drug dealers on the basketball courts."

"Yeah," said the first kid, who was about ten or eleven, "the last time we went and started playing, they came by and said it was their court and we had to get off. And then they took my ball." He looked like he was about to cry. I felt that way, too.

It broke my heart to think that these kids, who weren't yet even out of childhood, had to deal with those kinds of adult issues. Instead of worrying about a flat tire on their bike or getting home in time for dinner, these kids were grappling with life-and-death situations on a daily basis. Heartbreaking.

By June, Ruby had made it through her bout of morning sickness, but she was still tired all the time, so I tried to give her breaks on the weekends as much as I could. I would take Mark, who was six, with me down to Compton to visit Michael. We'd play some ball on his street or go see a movie.

One Saturday, I came home a little early after cutting lawns. I was planning to take Mark and Michael out for the day, and I wanted to get going. I wanted to get unloaded and cleaned up quickly to be ready when Ruby came home from the store with Mark. I had to go to the bathroom, so instead of unloading my truck in the driveway as I usually did, I simply pulled up in front of the house and went to the front door, figuring I'd unload the truck in a minute. As I unlocked the front door and went inside, I heard something at the back of the house.

"Ruby?" I yelled. I didn't see her car in the driveway; I didn't think she was home. No answer.

"Who's there?" I yelled. After a few seconds of silence, I heard some scrambling toward the kitchen and the screen door opening. I raced back there just in time to see a little kid bolting out the back.

It was Donald*, the eleven-year-old from next door. He had broken into our house.

"What are you doing, boy?" I yelled as I grabbed him by the collar and he dropped what he was carrying. I marched him home to talk to his mother.

I couldn't believe it. This was Donald, the same kid who, since we had moved in three years earlier, had always been a fun-loving if mischievous little guy and who was also very particular about how I cut his hair. His mother was a nice, quiet lady. His father, though, was a merchant marine

*Name has been changed.

and was gone at sea for months at a time. It seemed evident now that Donald was becoming more than his mom could handle by herself. His easy smile didn't come so easily anymore, and his interests seemed to be moving away from reading comic books and riding bicycles to "hanging out." You didn't need a road map to read the signs.

It wasn't only Donald I was worried about.

Across the street was his best friend, Milton Collins, a nice, funny, bright kid. He and Donald were tight. I was worried. If Donald was breaking into houses, how long would it be before peer pressure brought Milton into it, too? As I was finding out, in our community, it often was only a matter of time.

I then thought about all those kids on my lawn route who had nothing constructive to do and no positive male role models to show them how to be men, either. I knew that they needed to take all that youthful, hormonal, adolescent energy and put it toward something, and in the absence of something positive, I feared what they would choose.

I also thought about Michael, my brother-in-law. He was coming up on fifteen soon, and he had an intensity and a smart mouth I knew were going to get him in trouble. I didn't think he had any real ambitions to do anything serious, but often just talking tough was enough to invite trouble. The problem was, he was on the small side and really sensitive; I knew he wouldn't hold his own for long in his neighborhood without some help.

I had a talk with Donald's mother. She was at the end of her rope, in tears. She didn't know how to handle him, he was just so strong-willed, and he wouldn't listen to her.

I told her I'd talk to him. I had an idea.

"Hey, man," I said to Donald as I went back to his room. He had his head turned away, thinking I was going to yell at him some more or hit him or something. "I'm gonna take Michael and Mark to the park in the truck in a few minutes, just to shoot some baskets or play some baseball. Wanna come?"

"Huh? Yeah!" That got his attention.

I called Michael. "Hey, I've invited Donald to come along with us, and I'm thinking of asking Milton, too. That okay?"

"Fine with me," he said. Michael knew Donald and Milton already from hanging out at our house so much.

"Do you want to see if your friend Terry wants to come?" I asked him.

"Which one, Terry Smith or Terry Baker?" Michael asked.

"Ask them both."

Next, I went across the street to see Milton. The smile on his face was ear to ear. "Can I ask my cousin Ronald to come along, too?" he wondered. I said sure. Then his younger sister, Valerie, piped in.

"Hey, can I go, too?" she asked.

"No, baby dolly," I said with a chuckle. "It's just for boys."

"Oh!" she scowled, "That's not fair!"

I then called my friend George May, whom I'd known since we were in the Air Force together and who was so helpful to me the night Mark was born. George was seeing a woman who had five teenage sons. I thought with those guys along, we'd have enough to make a team. George was thrilled. Corinne, the boys' mother, had her hands full with them and was glad to get them out of her hair for a while.

When I counted up all the kids I had invited, it added up to twelve. "Hmmm," I thought, "how am I gonna fit twelve boys in the back of this truck so they don't all fall out?" Then, as I was unpacking my lawn equipment and hosing out the truck, my eyes fell upon the new redwood picnic table in our backyard, six feet long with two benches. The benches fit perfectly in the bed of the truck. The older kids could sit on the benches and the younger ones, like Mark, could sit on the floor of the bed and be sheltered by the older kids' legs.

It worked perfectly, and the kids clambered in. The laughing and joshing and whistling and singing didn't stop the whole way to Centinela Park, in nearby Inglewood.

That day was perfect. The weather, typical for early summer in Los Angeles, was mild—around the mid-70s.

We pulled up to the park sometime after lunch, and the kids jumped out of the truck as if their legs were spring-loaded. Centinela Park is a skinny, mile-long patch of green and shade about two miles from my house, directly across from the cemetery on Florence Avenue and in the flight path of Los Angeles International Airport. It is one of the few parks in the area and has gentle hills of grass and large, shady sycamore, magnolia, and jacaranda trees. It also has exactly what we had come for: two baseball diamonds and two concrete basketball courts. None of us had ever been there before.

We unloaded some equipment—balls, bats, gloves, the cooler where I was chilling the gallon of milk I took from our fridge—and set about doing some warmup calisthenics. Mainly, I was just going by memories of boot camp: doing pushups and jumping jacks, running laps, stuff like that. The difference this time around was that there wasn't any cursing from a drill sergeant. No, it was much different. I joked with the boys and cajoled them the whole time, inventing pushup contests, for instance, so that even some of the less athletic ones were working up a sweat and enjoying it.

Then we set out to play some ball. Suddenly, I was transported back to the mid-1950s and the endless summer evenings of baseball with Willie coaching us and cheering us on. And now here I was, a man of thirty-one, doing the same thing for these kids.

It was a tossup as to who enjoyed it more—me or them. I got right in the thick of things, playing a heated defense during basketball, pitching breaking balls and fastballs during baseball. I wasn't easy on the kids; I didn't baby them and lob slow pitches right over the plate or let them steal the ball from me during a fast break. I demanded more from them. We weren't there just to fool around; I wanted them to really get competitive and raise their levels a bit, which I knew from my own experience would build their confidence. There was frustration for sure, but then again, there was nothing like the look of pride on a boy's face when he executed a perfect layup or connected with one of my pitches and sent it sailing over my head. "Hey, look! I hit one of Lou's fastballs!" someone would yell to his buddies as he rounded the bases. Their victories were so much sweeter.

I wanted them to feel the same sense of pride and confidence I felt when I took what Willie taught me about throwing a fastball and used it to defeat a better team. I hoped they would derive the same satisfaction I had from pushing their bodies to the limit to see what they were capable of doing and mastering something they never realized they could do. I knew firsthand that in order for these boys to think about the possibilities of their future, to get them to see beyond the street corner, building their confidence and stimulating their imaginations was the key.

We eventually took a break in late afternoon, sweaty, tired, and happy. The exhausted, contented looks on those boys' faces made me recall my favorite time of day when I was a child: early twilight. The time when the shadows became longer, the sun dipped behind the pines, and the blistering heat began to fade to just plain hot. I'd look up and see the smoke coming from the chimneys and realize supper was near. The long day was ending. I'd hurry to finish my row or fill my sack, whatever I needed to do to get in for supper. Then we'd all sit and pray together and laugh and talk and relax.

It was so nice to have that sense of togetherness and family. That was really fantastic to me. As a kid in South Carolina, I thought the whole world was like that. As an adult, though, I knew differently.

We flopped under one of the bigger trees near the basketball courts and enjoyed the small snack of milk and cookies I had brought from home. *Ruby's gonna kill me when she finds out I took the milk she just bought this morning,* I thought. Looking around, though, I realized that whatever trouble I'd be in with Ruby was worth the looks on those relaxed, joyful, eager young faces. Even Donald was giggling about something.

"So what do you guys think," I said after a while. "Did you have fun?"

"Oh, yeah!" was the resounding reply.

"That's great!" I laughed. "Do you want to do it again in a couple weeks?"

Their eyes got wide and their mouths made little Os of excitement as they looked at each other and then chorused, "Sure, man!" "You bet!" "I'll be here for sure!" "Great idea, Lou!"

"Hey, can I ask my friend to come?" someone said. Another boy asked, "Yeah, how about my neighbor?"

"Sure, whoever you want." Another chorus of cheers and clapping.

Then they settled down, and we just started talking. About what they wanted to be when they grew up, about problems some were having in school or with their parents, and especially about girls.

Most of these boys either didn't have fathers they knew, or if they did, they weren't around much, like Donald's dad, or were older, like Michael's. They didn't have anyone to talk to about girls. Needless to say, I could relate, thinking about my teenage days on the farm. I remember the first girl I liked—I think I was eleven or twelve at the time; I didn't know what to say to her or how to act. So I just stood beside her, and that's how I showed her I liked her. Coralee Jamieson. Then we talked a little bit, and she gave me her handkerchief. I kept that handkerchief and washed it every day. Until Willie came along, that was as much as I knew to do.

I knew the boys sitting in front of me were also experiencing some of the same feelings, and they didn't have anyone to shepherd them through the facts of life. I also knew from experience how important it was to have someone you could trust to talk to. So we started talking. These boys, who had never gathered as a group before then, really opened up and shared their feelings, their fears. We all bonded that day, and there was a sincere sense of trust and friendship developing. Instead of me just telling them "how it is," we all took turns discussing life and the confusing problems particular to a teenage boy.

What I mainly found was that these kids definitely had something to say, but they didn't have anyone to listen to them. That day, we got down to the raw feelings: what they felt about things in the world, at home, at school, on the streets, you name it. The older ones tried to give advice to the younger ones. Above all, they listened to what I had to say, and it was truly gratifying to see it sink in. I really felt that I was getting through. I could tell how much of a difference it made when someone took the time to really talk to the kids.

Twilight was turning to darkness. We packed up our things and scrambled back into the truck. Mark sat up front with me, his head soon cradled in my lap as he slept while I dropped everyone off. Everyone was tired and happy. I think the happiest person that day, though, was me.

Two weeks later, I got up early; I had told the boys I'd pick them up by eight o'clock. I had done double duty all week on my lawns so I'd have the whole day free. I loaded up Michael, who had slept over the night before, and Milton and Donald and a couple of their friends and headed over to pick up Corinne's five boys. As I pulled up, I noticed they had a couple of friends with them. Same thing when I picked up the two Terrys. This was getting to be a tight squeeze, I thought as we tried to cram almost twenty boys into the truck. I had to make two trips. I left Michael and one of the Terrys in charge at the park while I went back and picked up the rest of the group. This is great, I thought. We'll have bigger teams.

That second Saturday was even better than the first. Centinela Park had a fountain that shot water in the air, and we must have spent hours having water fights. We explored the rest of the park, too. At the far end were a few tennis courts, though no one was playing. Then we walked along the perimeter toward the east and discovered an amphitheater. There was so much clowning and hamming going on that several of the boys had to be dragged off the stage. We looked through the chain-link fence at the park's sparkling blue pool, which was off-limits to us because we weren't residents of the city of Inglewood. Those kids stared so longingly at that pool after getting sweaty playing ball. Many of them had never even been in a pool, and I made a note to myself that one of these days, we were going to find a place to go swimming.

By the third Saturday, it was clear that this was where these guys needed to be. "You know," I told them that day as we sat talking, "we could do this on a regular basis, make it into a club or something. We could have shirts, have dues, and have a name." They liked the sound of that.

"What do you think we should call ourselves?" I asked them.

Everyone had an idea. "The Tigers! The Hellcats!"

"How about the Challengers?" came a familiar voice to my left. It was Michael. "From the comic book, 'Challengers of the Unknown.'" Michael, like many of his friends, was a comic book fanatic.

Oh, the guys liked that one! We voted, and we became the Challengers Boys Club. Any boy between the ages of six (Mark's age at the time) and eighteen (the oldest of the group) could join. Dues, 15 cents every two weeks, enough to cover the milk and cookies.

And so it began. That Monday, the kids went to school and told their friends about their adventures at the park as Challengers. Michael told his best friend, Kenny Rodgers, who, along with his twin brother, Keith, and little brother Silvester (Tooney), decided he wanted to come along next time and check this out.

Kenny grew up near Michael in Jordan Downs and moved to Compton right around the time Michael and his parents did, on the eve of the Watts Riot. Kenny's father was a former baseball player from the Negro Leagues. He played for the Baltimore Giants and had been inducted into the Negro League Hall of Fame. Kenny and his brothers had played baseball practically before they could walk. They liked it, too, until they got a little older and their father began to get thrown out of their games for trash-talking his own sons, drinking, and getting into fights. Soon, baseball was no longer fun for them, so they quit. Whatever interest their father had in his sons vanished.

When I met Kenny, he was fourteen, like Michael. Despite what was going on at home, Kenny was a bright, funny, enthusiastic kid, and so were his brothers. With the Rodgers boys with us, I now had about two dozen kids coming to the park with me.

A month later, that number doubled.

I knew that by the time I ferried four dozen kids to the park, there wouldn't be enough time to play, so I asked George May to help me out and pick up a bunch. Then I called Ed O'Neal, who also worked with me at the school district, to do the same. They jumped right in. The next time, when we had even more boys, I asked another co-worker and friend, Howard Banks, to help out.

By now, the kids who had gone a few times knew the drill. I'd drive by their house, stop, and toot the horn a couple times. If they were coming that day, they were supposed to hustle out to the truck. There were times I'd see a kid struggling to get his pants on and get out the door, and I'd pretend to take off and see him book it down the street after the truck. I'd stop, he'd climb in, and we'd all have a good laugh. Sometimes I'd give them a jolt on purpose just to hear their squeals.

By far their favorite route was going down what we called the Arlington Double. Arlington was a street near where I used to live on Country Club. It ran north-south, right through the historic West Adams district, where there were many large, turn-of-the-century Craftsman and Victorian homes.

Corrine and her five boys lived in one of those homes, situated on top of a hill. Now, South Central is mostly flat, about 95 percent. It isn't until you go west on Slauson toward Ladera Heights and Baldwin Hills that you reach any sort of elevation—except on this little ridge in West Adams, just south of the Santa Monica Freeway. It was probably the only hill in South Central. I'd load the kids in the truck, turn south on Arlington, hit the dip in the road at the Adams intersection, and then gun the engine a little bit, just enough to send us sailing down the hill, where the shocks would bounce us up and down at the bottom. To us, it was Disneyland.

"Are we gonna do the double, Papa Lou?" (Papa Lou was what the kids started calling me during one of our first trips to the park.) "Can we do the double today?" It's amazing how little things like that were enough in those days to make a child's day. They definitely made mine.

7

Cracking the Shell

Most kids in my neighborhood had never been more than four blocks from home. I wanted to take them to places where they could open up and take a good look at a different view.

—Lou Dantzler

By the end of July, the trips to the park were no longer just a casual thing. Getting all those kids there was a job in itself.

I arranged my lawn service work for alternate Saturdays so I could have the others free for the club. By now, we were collecting kids from neighborhoods all over the place, including most of the kids I met through my lawn service who were once afraid to go to the park. We had no set boundaries; we picked up boys from Compton and Watts in the southern part of the city, the Crenshaw district to the west, and the West Adams district to the north, in addition to all the neighborhoods in and around the heart of South Central Los Angeles.

Now that I had my friends to help, I needed to get organized. All the kids had to have their parents fill out enrollment forms. I spent Friday nights on the phone, finding out who was coming the next day and then mapping things out for the drivers. We had everything from old station wagons to a little Volkswagen Bug to ferry those kids! I divided the pickups into territories, depending on where the kids lived, and assigned drivers to them.

After a few weeks, I decided we should explore a little more than just

Centinela Park. Griffith Park, about eight or ten miles north of us, is huge and hilly, with trails for hiking, an equestrian center, the famous observatory, and, on the other side of the hill, the Los Angeles Zoo. We had to check that place out.

Of the almost 100 boys we took there that day, I think maybe 10 had been there before. To the others, it was like discovering paradise. My main concern was that we would lose someone in the dense eucalyptus and pine trees, so we split up into groups, with one adult for about fifteen kids, and set off. We must have covered every inch of the place that day. Of course, we had to play hide and seek and every kind of tag you could imagine. In the afternoon after lunch, we organized a few touch football games on the grass, too.

Lunchtime was one of my favorite times. To me, food always tastes better when you eat it outside in the fresh air. We gathered in a big group, and the kids began unpacking whatever they had brought in their bags. Inevitably, a kid or two forgot his lunch. No problem; he soon had more food than he knew what to do with. It was so gratifying to see how those kids dug around in their bags and produced something for their friends or split a sandwich or banana in half. They bartered, of course—food changed hands faster than goods in a Middle Eastern bazaar.

Around four o'clock, I gathered everyone up—this is where inheriting my father's booming voice really came in handy!—and we collapsed in the shade for what we were now beginning to call our Rap Session. Though it was hard, with all the boys we had now, to re-create the sense of closeness we had experienced those first few weeks, we still had some amazing rap sessions, where kids talked and shared their feelings. We split into groups, each with an adult as a leader; the grownups all tried to be there for the boys, listen to them, give advice, and, above all, show them positive role models who looked like them and whom they could relate to. We all learned a lot from each other.

My big goal for that summer of 1968 was to organize a trip to the beach. We lived not twelve miles from some of the most famed and beautiful shores in the country, yet few of us had ever been west of the 405 Freeway, five miles away.

I knew that part of building character and confidence in young adults has to do with exposing them to things they didn't normally have a chance to experience. So much of my own life and views had changed once I got out of the South and went to New York, and I knew that many of these kids needed to escape the invisible barriers of the few blocks they hung around.

There's a bit of contention about what constitutes South Central Los Angeles, which in the 1930s and '40s was basically the area surrounding South Central Avenue. I've always defined it by the roadways Los Angeles is so famous for: its freeways. The 110 Harbor Freeway, which runs north-south, provides a rough eastern border, as Crenshaw Boulevard does to the west. The northern border is the Santa Monica Freeway, Interstate 10, which traverses the United States from sea to shining sea. The southern border is Imperial Highway, which runs through Watts and Compton.

Most if not all of the kids in Challengers had never set foot outside those borders. Parents who were lucky enough to have cars spent their weekends running errands or relaxing from a hard week. Going to the beach, the playground for white Los Angeles, with its surfboards and Beach Boys, was like going to another country.

I wanted the Challengers to see that other country, and we did. I got a friend from the school district to "lend" us a school bus, and he volunteered to drive us up to Malibu. We set off west on the Santa Monica Freeway and watched out our windows as the scenery gradually evolved from square, flat apartment complexes and warehouses to lush green landscaping, large homes, and the rolling hills of the west side. In another few minutes, the freeway narrowed from four lanes to two, and soon—whoosh!—we entered the McClure tunnel, which marked the end of the freeway.

Before our eyes had even had time to adjust to the dark, out we shot at the other end into the bright sunshine and beaches. Just like that, another world. Driving up the famed Pacific Coast Highway, with the ocean on our left and the beautiful Santa Monica mountain range on our right, we truly did feel like we were in a different world, farther than just a dozen miles from home.

During our foray into Malibu, we discovered the gentle, sloping Santa Monica mountains, with their great hiking trails and campgrounds. One weekend in August, we organized an overnight camping trip, complete with sleeping bags, ghost stories, toasted marshmallows, and hot chocolate. The campsite itself was nothing more than a huge patch of dirt, but we didn't care. It was the first time many of the kids had ever seen the stars; the cloudy haze and bright lights of Los Angeles often shrouded even a full moon.

Before we set up camp, I took everyone for a nature walk. With heads down and arms folded, many were unsure of themselves at first and found it hard to shed their tough-guy personas, built through years on the streets. There in the woods, they had no idea what to do! So I asked them to close their eyes and tell me what they heard. At first, no one said a thing. Then, after a few moments, one of the kids gasped in wonder, "Papa Lou, I hear a bird!"

"I can hear the wind blowing in the trees," another cried proudly. Soon most of the kids were chattering in wonder, enjoying the soothing forest sounds and cool, fresh air.

Now, we know that all kids, no matter where they're from, tune things out. But for these kids, the sounds they tune out in their daily lives are the sounds of people fighting, sirens screaming, and shots being fired. They tune these things out to protect themselves. Many of the kids on the trip that day had never seen a pinecone before, or a stream. When we arrived at the campsite, they put up that angry, hard shell, but after we were there a while, they transformed into kids—the goofy, silly, fun-loving kids they had a right to be. It was wonderful to see.

George, Howard, and Ed, as well as a couple of other parent volunteers, came along to help out. To keep everyone safe and to make sure no one wandered off and got lost in the dark, we parked our cars in a rectangle around our campsite, turned on the headlights so we could see, and played the radios for entertainment. Everyone had a ball.

Even though we had dozens of kids of all ages running around, it developed into a sort of organized chaos. In addition to the parent volunteers, I got some of the older kids to act as junior counselors to help out with the younger children, which gave them a sense of responsibility.

I had had it in my mind for a while that the club should have shirts with a logo to identify us when we were out at the parks and to give members a sense of ownership and belonging. After doodling for a few weeks, Terry Smith, who revealed himself to be a creative artist, came up with a simple design that everyone liked: a white background with a large orange sun in the upper left corner and a tree in the lower right one. From the bottom left corner up to the top right corner stretched the club name "Challengers," with the tail of the letter C underlining the whole word. The letters arced across the shirtfront, the tail of the C with them, like a wave.

The symbols of the sun and the tree went back to a discussion I had with the kids in those first few weeks. "The sun is a powerful source of energy," I told them. "It nourishes the trees and gives them strength to grow, to establish strong roots and produce lots of branches. You," I said, pointing to the twenty or so kids seated in a circle around me, "are the roots of the tree. I am like the sun, helping you grow, become strong, develop branches. The branches are the other children coming up after you that you pass this strength and wisdom on to. The stronger you are, the more branches you can make, and the bigger and healthier the tree will become."

I was really proud of those shirts. Because money was always tight, I decided that instead of paying a T-shirt shop to silkscreen them for us, I would do it myself. The school district had silkscreening equipment for its shop classes. I struck up a conversation one day with the shop teacher, and he let me watch the kids in his class make some shirts. It didn't look too hard, I thought. That night, I rushed through my janitorial duties at the school and brought in about eight dozen white T-shirts I had bought that day on sale at Sears. After a few tries, I managed to get the results I was looking for with three colors: orange for the sun, green for the tree, and blue for the letters. It looked sharp.

The last weekend in August, I handed out the shirts to coincide with our club's first Sports Day, held at Centinela Park. The kids couldn't wait to get those shirts on! Now we looked like something!

That first Sports Day was something, too. I organized all sorts of games for the kids to compete in: flag football, relay races, tug-of-war, sack races, you name it—all the games I'd seen the rich campers play at Camp Pinecone. Some of the parents came out with picnics to watch and had a great time. I even decided to have a Challengers Most Valuable Player award, and the kids were very competitive about this, knowing that whoever won would be the first MVP ever. No one was keener on winning that award than Michael.

Michael loved Challengers. He never missed a Saturday, and neither did many of his friends, like Milton, the Rodgers brothers, and the two Terrys. Michael was one of the junior counselors, and he felt an intense sense of ownership of this organization, thriving in its camaraderie. Unfortunately, though, he still had his smart mouth.

Michael was a talented athlete, so I made him quarterback of one of the flag football teams. He was really showing off in the game, too, pumping his fist in the air as he hit Milton with one pass after the other. Then, in the third quarter, one of the referees, a parent volunteer, made a call Michael didn't like, and they started to get into it so I took him out of the game. Being relegated to the sidelines didn't stop him from talking trash. He was a real bad sport that day.

When Michael's team won, I could tell he could already feel that MVP ribbon hanging around his neck. Here he was, Lou's nephew, the first Challengers MVP. You could see how cocky he was just by the way he walked.

I didn't see the look on his face when I announced Milton Collins as the first Challengers Sports Day Most Valuable Player, but I did see him kick a can and stomp off a few moments later. After a while, I went over to where he was sitting on a table and said, "So you're pretty upset, huh?"

And he started in. I let him rant for a minute or two before I cut him off. "Now, you listen," I said, in probably not the nicest tone. "You're a smart kid, a talented kid, but your mouth is gonna get you in a whole lotta trouble, you understand? You better tone it down! You're all mouth, but what do you have to back it up? You're small, and I know you're not as tough as you think you are. You're gonna get yourself hurt."

Michael didn't say anything, but I could tell he was listening. His pride wouldn't let him acknowledge me, though. I didn't mind. It was much better to have him learn this lesson by playing an innocent game of football in the park than by getting shot at after mouthing off to the wrong person in his neighborhood, something that was happening more frequently to many kids his age.

~⋙~

In early November, our second son, Corey, was born. Mark was a big brother and proud of it, especially when we let him have the honor of naming his new little brother. Ruby was home, taking another leave of absence from work. I took Mark with me from time to time on Challenger outings, but because he was still a bit younger than the rest of the members, he didn't go every Saturday.

If I thought the enthusiasm for the club would cool once the kids started school in September, I was seriously—and happily—mistaken. By then, we were drawing kids from all over. One of my lawn service customers, Florene Jones, a single mother who lived on the corner of 60th and Vermont, was so pleased with what the club had done for her boys that she told a friend of hers, a Los Angeles County social worker named Al Carson. He came by one day and saw what I was doing, and we had a nice talk. He liked the fact that my main goal was helping boys before they had a chance to become juvenile delinquents. He wondered if I would take some of the kids he was involved with in the Department of Public Social Services system—foster care kids. I said sure.

I'm not going to say it was always easy. Some of those kids were already in some kind of trouble with the law and often had abusive home lives, but I could tell that when they were with us, at the very least, they enjoyed themselves. Most had never had anyone in their lives pay attention to them, make them feel special, or expect anything of them, let alone make them live up to any sort of standard of behavior. I am convinced that the reason I became the man I had become—a caring, honest, hardworking husband and father—was that my mother stood firm on what she expected of me and made me adhere to her standards of good character. It wasn't easy, but she never let me slide, even when it would have been nicer for her, such as when I wanted to drop out of high school to make more money.

I tried my best to get this message across to all these kids. Go to school, have respect for yourself and others, don't get into drugs, be honest—just your basic Golden Rule–type stuff, but South Central–style. I didn't have any book telling me what to say to them; I just used my gut feelings most of the time, and I think because I did, they could tell it was sincere, and they listened.

The saddest part was that some of what I had to say was really basic, yet this was the first time many of the boys had heard anything like it. Take hygiene, for instance. I could tell when I saw some kids on Saturday that they hadn't bathed or brushed their teeth for several days. I tried to make a joke out of it—"Hey, watch that breath of yours, man!"—so I wouldn't humiliate anyone, but I could tell there were some kids who were just plain being neglected. The bright side, though, was that some of the feedback I got from some of the parents showed that I was getting through.

"For months, I'd been yelling at that boy to brush his teeth in the morning," said a mother to me one day. "Now he not only brushes twice a day and showers, he washes his own shirt out on Friday nights before he comes to the club on Saturdays!"

"Yeah, I told these guys that they couldn't come with dirty shirts and dirty faces," I laughed.

"Well, thank you, because for once, he's really listening! He said, 'Oh, Mr. Lou said if I didn't wash my shirt I couldn't go to Griffith Park,' so there he was, doing it himself! Amazing! What's your secret?"

I was asked that a lot. I didn't have any secret. I just spent time with them, built up trust and caring, and then required them to live up to certain basic standards, otherwise they couldn't come anymore. I never forced them to do anything; it was always their choice. If they wanted to be a part of what we were doing, they had to play my way. If not, they were free to do something somewhere else.

And we did have some kids who fell away. Donald was one of the first, unfortunately, then one or two of Corinne's five boys. They were older; milk and cookies in the park didn't hold the same appeal as the action on the streets. I think maybe if I had gotten to them when they were younger, I might have had more of an impact. Donald needed a strong father figure more than one day every other week to help him change his outlook.

I realized that's what all the kids needed, more than just fun and games and a little leadership twice a month; they needed a place to be able to go every day, a place where they could just be kids, safe from the deplorable and dangerous influences that were spreading through our neighborhoods like a disease.

But how could I accomplish that? I had enough trouble trying to hold together this little operation as it was. The dues, which were now a quarter, covered the cost of the snacks, nothing else. If a kid couldn't pay, we didn't make a big deal of it. The 25 cents was really meant to give the kids a sense of ownership, to help them feel as if they belonged to something.

To sponsor special trips like those to the zoo or to buy gas for the borrowed bus, some of the parents began to have little fund-raisers. One of the mothers had a Tupperware party and donated all the proceeds from her sales to the club. Another time, a bunch of the parents got together and had a "Waistline Party," where the guests' waists were measured at the door, and they paid a penny per inch to get in. There were other things like that, but to get enough to afford an everyday club? We'd have to sell a truckload of Tupperware.

I kept the idea of a full-time club at the back of my mind, but I never had too much time to really consider it. By early 1970, I was becoming more and more involved with the club's members in ways beyond what we were doing on alternate Saturdays.

I was helping out some of the children who were having a hard time in school. I talked to their teachers to try and see what the problem was and helped the mothers (most often it was just the mother) work out the problem. Some of the women worked full time and couldn't make it down to the school to have meetings with their children's teachers, so I went for them. The kids, in turn, knew they could trust me and often told me more about what was going on than they told their mothers, so that helped, too.

Right around this time, Al Carson introduced me to another social worker at social services named Sharon Ireland. She was impressed by how committed I was to the kids, and she liked my philosophy of providing kids with alternatives, something positive to do.

It was right around this time that a member's mother called me in a panic. Her son had run away and had been gone for a couple of days. I started calling around to the kids I knew were his closest friends. Within a few hours, the boy called me, scared and confused. I told him to just come over to my house, and I'd help him figure things out. I called his mother to tell her he was safe and told her I would talk to him. I could hear the relief in her voice.

I had a long talk with that young boy that afternoon. I reassured him that the teenage years are confusing for everyone and told him that drugs and crime, which he had been contemplating, only make things worse. I took him home to his mother. I'm happy to say that even though several of his brothers, who didn't stay in the club, ended up getting into trouble and jail later on, this young man grew up to lead a productive, law-abiding life.

Sharon saw how I handled the crisis and asked if I could help her with some of the foster kids she was working with. Through her, I met a lot of wonderful people who cared enough to take in those neglected children. Soon I began helping Sharon find homes for more of her foster kids, and that made me feel great, knowing the kids were finally going to get some needed attention and a stable home life with decent people.

Sharon and I talked a lot about the club and my vision of what it could be—a place for kids to come and play and be safe as well as a community center of sorts for parents to get to know each other and help each other out, the way it was for us in the South. People in this community didn't know each other from one street to the next, and that just added to their sense of isolation. I knew that if we simply got all of them together, we could build something really positive.

"You know who you should talk to?" Sharon said, "Ruth Murch, of the Los Angeles Regional Volunteer Bureau. She might be able to help you. Let me give her a call."

One day in April of that year, a reporter named Jean Murphy from the *Los Angeles Times* called me. She said that Ruth Murch had told her about all the wonderful things I was doing, so she wanted to talk to me about it and maybe do an article for the Sunday paper.

That was fast, I thought. I'd talked to Ruth only a few weeks before. The interview with the *Times* was just basic; I told the reporter what I was doing, and that was about it. It took about ten or fifteen minutes; no big deal.

That Sunday, Ruby and I looked through the paper, thinking there would be a little paragraph somewhere about Challengers. We were surprised and pleased to see a long, four-column article. It said things like I should be Man of the Year and quoted people saying that I was a "marvelous man." It described our trips to the park and how I sometimes took kids with me to church on Sundays. It even quoted Sharon Ireland saying, "He is one of the most wonderful volunteers I've ever worked with." I was overwhelmed.

Other than being written up in the Air Force newspaper in Saudi Arabia for my exploits on the basketball court, this was the first time I had ever been in the paper. When the reporter had asked where people could contact me if they wanted to help, I gave my home phone number, not thinking anything of it.

That morning, I went down to the store on the corner to buy more copies of the paper because I wanted to send some to my sisters. When I got home, the phone was ringing—some people were calling to help, and others wanted to sign up their kids. Since that day, I don't think the phone has ever stopped ringing.

8

A Helping Hand

I want to show kids that they have a place in this society, regardless of their family background.

—Lou Dantzler

One Saturday, I came home after taking the kids to Griffith Park to find Ruby in the kitchen with a funny look on her face.

"You're not going to believe the phone call I just had," she laughed.

"Why, who was it?"

"It was this guy, let's see…," she said as she picked up a piece of paper from the counter. "His name is Toby Walker."

"Never heard of him."

"I know," she laughed. "He just called because he read the article in the paper about you, and he said he wants to help us. He said, 'What does your husband do? A custodian? No, no. We've got to get that guy out of that job. He should be doing this club full time!' That's what he said."

"What, did he sound crazy?" I laughed.

"I know, I know, it sounds crazy, but he did sound sincere. He sounded real businesslike, too. Maybe you should talk to him, Lou."

"Maybe I'll call him on Monday," I said as I put the message down.

By Monday, I'd forgotten all about that funny phone call. Then, a few weeks later, as I was going through my routine at Gage Junior High, my supervisor came up and told me I had a phone call. I never got calls at work. I hope Ruby's okay, I thought as I raced to answer the phone.

"This is Lou," I began.

"Lou Dantzler?" boomed a voice on the other end. "Hi there, this is Toby Walker! Boy, you are one hard man to track down!"

"Oh, hi there," I said, uncertainly, trying to remember where I'd heard the name before.

"I read the article in the *Times*," Toby went on, "and I'd like to help you out. Can you come to my office tomorrow at around ten?"

"Um, okay. Sure," I think I said, still trying to figure out who this guy was and what he wanted.

"Here, let me give you the address: 9255 Sunset Boulevard in Beverly Hills. D. A. Campbell and Company, on the sixth floor. Got it? See you tomorrow." Click.

Well, that was strange, I thought. Now I knew why Ruby had that funny look on her face after she talked to him. Then I looked at what I had written down. *Beverly Hills!* I'd never been to Beverly Hills, and I wasn't looking forward to going, either. Even though it was only a few miles away, that city of mansions and movie stars was far removed from my life in South Central. What could a guy from Beverly Hills possibly want with me?

The next day, as I parked my car on Doheny Drive near Sunset Boulevard, I took a deep breath as I looked up and saw the tall, shiny office building I was about to enter. Sixth floor, my note said. Waiting at the bank of elevators was a man who looked familiar to me, but I couldn't figure out why until we both stepped into a car and someone said something to him. Then I heard his voice, and I realized, "Oh, man! That's James Garner, the movie star!" Of course, I didn't say anything to him, but I kept sneaking peeks. Wait till I tell Ruby who I saw in Beverly Hills, I thought.

The young white receptionist at D. A. Campbell, which I later found out was an investment banking firm, took my name and politely asked me to wait. So far, so good, I thought as I rubbed my hands together. Boy, am I glad I decided to wear this suit!

"Mr. Dantzler?" a woman called, "I'm Mr. Walker's secretary. Follow me, please."

She took me through a maze of nicely paneled hallways with large mahogany doors and thick, lush carpet. Though the offices weren't exactly quiet—there was a sort of low-frequency murmuring, muted sounds of phones ringing, and muffled typing—I unconsciously walked a little lighter on my feet than usual and didn't say anything to anyone.

We got to the end of one hall and the secretary knocked on a door.

"Mr. Walker?" she said as she opened the door. "Mr. Dantzler is here."

She showed me in and shut the door behind me. Sitting at a large desk with a large picture window behind him was Toby Walker, talking urgently on the phone. He looked up and motioned for me to sit down in one of the chairs in front of his desk. Using the forceful voice I recognized, he was apparently working out a financial deal, because he kept throwing out huge numbers. The first thing I noticed was that he looked a lot different than he sounded on the phone. His voice was so commanding that had I expected someone in his midforties at least, but this guy looked to be about my age, with fair, freckled skin and sandy hair. His youthful appearance was in direct contrast to the way he carried himself, though. He acted and looked like he had all the confidence in the world.

As he talked, I looked out the window behind him and took in the view of the nearby Hollywood Hills and Sunset Strip. Then I looked around his office a bit, and I saw a picture of an attractive young woman, probably his wife, holding two young children. Up on the wall to my right was a framed diploma from Harvard University.

"Lou Dantzler? Toby Walker," he said, offering his hand over the desk. "How are you? Thanks for coming down."

"Oh, no problem," I said, smiling.

"Do you know how long it took me to track you down? I kept calling that number you gave in the article, and it would just ring and ring. I finally got your wife one afternoon. She sounds very nice, by the way."

"Oh, thank you," I said, not knowing what else to say.

"I had my secretary track you down at work—it was in the article."

"Oh, I'm sorry about that," I said.

"No problem," he waved his hand. "Listen, like I said on the phone, I liked what I read in the paper. Tell me a little bit more about what you do."

So I took a deep breath and told him how I got started just taking a few kids to the park to have fun and how it just grew and developed because there were so many young boys without fathers who didn't have anyone around the house to spend time with them.

"I realized a lot of these kids' lives lacked laughter as well as other things that make a boy's life happy, like playing in the park, so I decided to do what I could. I also wanted to show these kids somewhere beyond the four blocks of their neighborhoods. I mean, a lot of these kids live in all-black neighborhoods and go to all-black schools. How are they expected to adapt to the outside world if they never have to deal with people who are different from them? Usually, it's a parent's job to do this sort of thing, but these kids don't have fathers, and the mothers are busy just trying to get by. If the old man leaves home, who do kids have to pattern themselves after? Just the guys in the street, right? Well, there are a lot of negative things in the street.

"I want to get those kids before the street does. I want to instill character in these kids, things like leadership, awareness, and responsibility. I want to show them that it doesn't matter where they come from, they can still dream and achieve great things."

I didn't have any sort of speech prepared, I just spoke from my heart. Toby sat back and listened without too much expression on his face. When I finished, he finally spoke.

"You know, I've been looking for something to get involved in—helping people, you know—for a while now, and maybe I could help you out. What do you need?"

"Well, we've been raising money for various things, like trips to the beach and a camping trip, stuff like that, but we found we can't ask businesses for any real money because we're not a nonprofit organization. And in order to become one, a lawyer told me it will cost $1,000. We don't have that kind of money."

"Umm, I see," Toby said, leaning back in his chair and looking off into space. "Now what would happen if you became incorporated, then what?"

"Well, I'd like to raise money for a clubhouse, one that we could use afternoons and after school as well as weekends. A place where the whole community can come and work together for the kids."

He was quiet for a moment and then said. "You seem really committed to this, but it sounds like a big project. Are you sure this is what you want?"

I didn't really know what he meant by that. I mean, I had been doing it for a year and a half—of course it was what I wanted. Looking back now, thirty-odd years later, I guess I can see how he just wanted to make sure I was in it for the long haul.

"Oh, yes, I'm sure," I said.

"Well," he said, suddenly, "let me see about this. I'll call you in a few days."

And with that, the meeting was over. Okay, I thought, that was a little strange. I left the building thinking I had just wasted an hour of my time. Oh, well, at least I got to see Beverly Hills.

I didn't think too much more about my meeting with Toby because one or two days later, I got a phone call from George Putnam, the news anchorman from the local CBS affiliate. He wanted to do a story on me for his nightly newscast. I was told to come down to the station the following evening and to bring Ruby. We were pretty excited.

The next night, we went there just as they asked. When we arrived, however, Putnam was out to dinner, so we had to wait.

"I've got an idea," his assistant said. "While you're waiting for George to get back, why don't you go over to the next soundstage and watch them tape *Truth or Consequences?* You know, the show with Bob Barker."

Oh, we knew who Bob Barker was! It was exciting to sit there in the audience and watch all the behind-the-scenes stuff. At the end of the first commercial break, Ruby and I were thrilled when he came to stand next to us, and the camera pointed right in our direction. I thought that with him standing so close, maybe I'd get to be on TV.

"And now, ladies and gentlemen," Barker announced when the show resumed, "I have a special treat for you. I have a newspaper clipping here from the *Los Angeles Times,* and it's about a remarkable man. 'A marvelous man,' is how they describe him, and his name is Lou Dantzler."

I heard my name and was stunned. Why was Bob Barker talking about me? Before I had the chance to process this, he leaned toward me with the microphone and said, "Now, I bet you that seated right here is Lou Dantzler.... Yesss! Stand up here, Mr. Dantzler! I'm glad you're here!"

The audience started applauding, and somehow I found the strength to stand up, though my legs felt like they were made of Jell-O.

"Now," Bob Barker went on, "you were told that George Putnam was going to interview you, and then someone said he was held up at a dinner and they brought you in here to wait, right?"

"Uh-huh," is all I managed to say.

"Well, Mr. Putnam is a fine man, and I'm sure he would like to interview you, but he's not going to right now. We arranged all of that to get you down here for *Truth or Consequences!*"

"Oh, man!" I giggled nervously. "Oh, brother!"

"Now," Barker continued to the audience, "this gentleman has been working with boys from ages eight to sixteen, is that right?"

"That's right," I said. It wasn't, but I wasn't going to correct Bob Barker on his own show.

"How long have you been doing this?"

"About a year and a half."

"What he has done," Barker told the audience, "he has done on his own time and with his own money and perhaps a few donations. He has formed a club and chosen boys to join this club who are from fatherless homes, right?" He turned to me, "And from what I understand, you also grew up without a father, so you knew what it was like to be a boy without a father around the house. What are some of the things you do with these boys?"

I think I managed to put together a couple of sentences about what we did. My heart was pounding in my ears so hard it was difficult to think. I had certainly never expected this!

Then he took me onto the stage, and out came Sharon Ireland, Ed O'Neal, and even the principal of Gage Junior High, who said he wished more people were like me. Just when I thought this was over, Barker took a new tack.

"Now I want to bring out some guys who *really* know a lot about this. Boys, come out here and say hello."

The organ music played and the audience applauded as Michael; the two Terrys; and two other members, Eddie Robinson and Scott Cunningham, came onto the stage. Barker started asking them questions, and there was Michael, telling him in a very calm, mature manner all about what we do. It was unbelievable.

"Boy, you must be proud of them," Barker said to me. "They're a fine-looking group of boys, and I think you have every right to be. Now, I understand that one of your problems is getting the boys where you want to go, and you often have to make several trips to the park in your old truck, isn't that right? Well, you won't be using that truck anymore, Mr. Dantzler. Look what we have for you!"

The giant, glittery curtain we had been standing in front of suddenly swept open as the music swelled and the audience cheered. I turned around and saw seven or eight of my boys surrounding a gleaming new gold Pontiac station wagon.

"Oh, man! Is that ours?" I said, dumbfounded.

"That's right," he said. "You could get plenty of boys in there!"

"Oh, yeah," I said. "We can get at least forty in there!" The audience laughed. " 'Cause one of the guys who helps me has a Volkswagen, and he got fifteen in it." More laughs, even from Barker.

"If you can get fifteen in a Volkswagen, you can get a lot more in this! I'm so proud of you...From everything I read in the article and then just meeting you and seeing your attitude, I can see why you've been so successful with these boys. Thank you for being such a fine man!"

The applause sounded like a thunderstorm in my head. I felt close to tears. All I could manage to say was, "Oh, thank you! Thank you so much!"

Later on, I talked to Barker more backstage, and he wanted to do even more for us.

"Is there anything else you need?" he asked. He was so nice and made me feel so comfortable. If I had been asking for a new living room set for myself, I never would have had the courage to talk, but because I was asking for the kids, it was almost as if I were another person. I wasn't the shy, quiet kid from South Carolina. I was much more confident now, confident enough to say, "Well, we need a clubhouse."

Barker said that if I found a place, he'd try to help me get it.

"There's this old abandoned grocery store on 60th and Crenshaw, a big old place with lots of room that would be perfect for us," I said. "It used to be a Safeway store, I think."

He turned to someone next to him and asked, "Do we know anyone who could help with this?" Then he turned to me. "We've got your phone number, and we'll look into this for you. How about that?"

I was really impressed. This was long after the cameras stopped rolling, so I knew he wasn't doing it for the ratings. He was just trying to do what he could to help.

Unfortunately, the company that owned Safeway wasn't interested in donating a building they weren't doing anything with. They wanted to sell it, not give it away. Nonetheless, I was grateful to Bob Barker for trying and for giving us that car.

Oh, were we proud of that car! When we sped down the Arlington Double, the kids loved it even more when their heads hit the ceiling at the bottom of the hill. As for me, I was just so happy that people wanted to do something to help me help these kids who before had no kind of special attention whatsoever. It was really gratifying.

A few days after the show, I was busy washing the new car when the phone rang. Ruby said, "Lou, it's Toby Walker again."

I really hadn't expected to hear from him again. "Hello?" I said.

"Lou, I got you an appointment with a friend of mine who's an attorney. Five-fifty-five South Spring Street. Paul Nathanson at O'Melveny and Myers. Can you meet him Thursday morning?"

"Uh, sure! Thanks, Mr. Walker."

"Sure, no problem. Just tell him what your needs are, and he'll take care of it as a favor. And by the way, Lou, you can call me Toby."

So I put on my suit again, the blue one I had worn to Toby's office, and went downtown to the business district of Los Angeles. I had no idea at the time that O'Melveny and Myers was one of the top law firms in the state, if not the country. And I'm glad I didn't. Just the fact that it was downtown was enough to make me nervous.

What I remember most about that first meeting was how pleasant everyone was and how big the offices were—much bigger than Toby's, and just as luxurious. I asked Sharon Ireland to come with me, just to help me explain things. I also thought someone from the county would give me a little more credibility.

Our meeting was pretty short, but Paul Nathanson couldn't have been more pleasant and accommodating. He was especially excited about Bob Barker and the station wagon. He agreed to handle our nonprofit incorporation for free. We were jubilant.

"See, Lou?" Sharon said as we were leaving, "I knew as soon as the word got out about you that people would line up to help."

And she was right.

The next day, Toby called me again. By this time, I was getting used to his cut-to-the-chase approach. He wanted to know about my meeting at O'Melveny the day before.

"How were you treated?" was the first question he asked.

"Fine," I said, meaning they hadn't kicked us out or anything, if that's what he meant.

"Great. Now, what else do you need?"

I told him about the station wagon and some of the other things that were being donated since people had seen the article. I needed someone to help me with the books, I said. "My wife, Ruby, has been doing it up until now, but she's not a bookkeeper, and I want to make sure we do everything right."

"Indeed," he said. "Let me make some calls, and I'll get back to you." And this time, after he hung up, I believed him.

The next week, he called. "A friend of mine named Carl Moser at Coopers, Ross Brothers, and Montgomery said he'll help you with the books. They're a Big Eight accounting firm, so I know they'll do right by you. Here's his number; he's expecting your call."

I had no idea what he meant by "Big Eight," but I didn't care. I was sure that anything "big" meant "good." By now I knew that if Toby said someone would help, they would help.

Carl Moser was a really great guy. We clicked right away. He heard my whole story and didn't interrupt me or make me feel rushed; as far as I could tell, I was his most important appointment of the day. A real class act.

"Sure, we can do the books for you; no problem," he said. "It won't cost you a thing, and it'll be real easy for us. Don't worry. What else do you need?"

And, as I had with Toby and Bob Barker and everyone else, I told him of our need for a clubhouse. When the Safeway thing didn't pan out, I had begun driving through the neighborhood once again, looking for sites. There were plenty of vacant lots and boarded-up storefronts by this time, businesses that had closed down since the Watts Riot.

One particular place that caught my eye more than any other was the old, abandoned Vons Supermarket on the corner of Vermont Avenue and 51st Street. It was large—at least 20,000 square feet—and had a sizeable parking lot that would be perfect for a playground. After I talked to Carl, I drove down there and took one more look at it. Yes, it definitely had potential. I called Carl back.

"I found this old Vons store on Vermont," I told him.

"Vons, huh? Hmm, I think one of our clients is the Von der Ahe family; they own Vons. Let me check into it and get back to you."

Wow! Things are really moving, I thought. I can't wait to tell the boys. They'll be so excited. But I remembered what had happened with that Safeway, and I didn't get my hopes up. I decided to keep it to myself for the time being.

It was a good thing I did.

9

Making It Our Own

One way to instill a sense of responsibility is to make children a part of the process. If they know they're working toward something, they feel a sense of ownership, of belonging.

—LOU DANTZLER

When I didn't hear from Carl Moser for two months, I really began to get down. Things had been moving along so well, we had momentum, and now, nothing. I went about my days as usual and decided to forget about it.

Two weeks later, in the summer of 1970, I got a call from Carl while I was at work at Gage Junior High.

"Hey, Lou!" he said. "Good news. We got a donation."

"Really? That's great!" I was excited; any donation was always terrific news. "How much is it?" I asked, thinking it was probably at least $1,000, judging by Carl's voice.

"It's for $187,000."

"Come again?" I couldn't believe what he said.

"That's right, *$187,000!* But it's not in cash, mind you. It's in kind."

"In what?" I said, confused.

"That means...well, Lou, the donation is from Vons. They're giving you the building on Vermont. It's worth almost $200,000."

I thought I was going to fall down. I started yelling and pounding on the wall, I was so happy. I hope I thanked Carl, but I don't know because

I don't remember much of the rest of the day. I do remember talking to my friend Howard Banks, telling him the news and asking him if he would cover for me for the rest of my shift. I had to go celebrate. I had to check out our new place.

I couldn't wait to show the kids. I went by that very afternoon and picked up Michael, Kenny Rodgers, Milton Collins, and some of the other guys to go check out our new club.

"Where we going, Lou?" Milton asked as we piled into our new station wagon.

"It's a surprise," I said, barely able to contain my excitement. "You'll see."

I was vaguely aware of their animated chatter in the backseat on the way over, as they speculated about what I could be so excited about.

When we pulled up to the building that took up the whole block on Vermont Avenue between 50th and 51st streets, the chatter stopped.

Decrepit chain-link fencing surrounded the property, with holes in some places and some sections knocked down altogether. Garbage was strewn everywhere: on the sidewalk, in the weed-choked parking lot, piled up against the building. It was a mess.

"What's this, Lou?" asked Michael when we got out of the car. "What are we doing here?"

"This," I said, sweeping my arm past the garbage, the peeling paint, the boarded-up windows and doors, "is ours. It's our new clubhouse."

In unison, all their heads snapped around.

"This big place?" Kenny said. "It's all *ours*?"

"That's right."

"Wowww...."

They shot over to the fence, trying to climb over. I found a large hole over by the entrance, and we all crawled through. We walked around the back and saw that one of the boards that covered a back entrance had been partially pried away. We gingerly stepped through the opening into the dark, dank, smelly old grocery store.

"Whew," Michael said, waving his hand in front of his nose. "It sure stinks in here!"

Did it ever. The building had been closed for more than three years, and in that time a small army of vagrants and animals had made their homes amidst the bare shelves, old checkout counters, and empty freezers. A huge skylight overhead gave us just enough light to see the dirt and garbage. This place was going to need a lot of work, I thought. I wasn't daunted by the prospect, however; I was energized. "You see, over here," I pointed to one corner, "we could have the arts and crafts section. Over there," I pointed to another corner, "could be where we have the woodshop or the photography studio. Over here, we can put up some walls and have a library, and over here, we could get a pool table or something and set up a teen center. Doesn't that sound great?"

They got just as caught up in it as I was. I could tell by their expressions that they were seeing past the broken linoleum floors and the rotting, stained ceiling and seeing the possibilities. They were pumped up.

"When can we move in, Lou?"

I found out later that the reason it took Carl Moser so long to obtain the building was that even though the Vons Corporation wanted to give it to us—in fact, Gene Mulkey, assistant to the chairman of Vons, loved what we were doing and wanted to help—the board was worried about giving it to an organization that was so green, with a leader who was untested. They wanted to make sure that if they gave the building away, it would go to something that was going to be around for a while. So Carl did a little investigating and decided that it would be in our best interests to become affiliated with a more prominent nonprofit organization, one that had a longer track record and could lend us support and credibility. I think he talked to the YMCA and maybe the Boy Scouts, two organizations that were also working in greater Los Angeles, but the talks didn't go far. Then he talked to someone at the Boys Clubs of America.

Al Secrist, assistant regional director of the Boys Clubs, met with Carl and Toby, and they told him what I was doing. They figured that since we already called ourselves the Challengers Boys Club, it would be a natural fit. I didn't know it at the time, but the Boys Clubs were only too happy to help us out since they had been lamenting the fact that there wasn't a Boys Club in South Central, where it was badly needed. The closest Boys Club was in Watts, sixty blocks away from our site on Vermont, and it wasn't large enough to handle the thousands of children in the community who needed its services.

Once the Boys Clubs decided to support us, the Vons board voted to deed the property to them, and they in turn would lease it to us for ten years—for $1.

Carl and Toby explained all this to me in detail, and it made perfect sense to me. Vons didn't know me from Adam, and I had never run a non-profit organization before, or even a small business for that matter, so they needed some assurances. How did they know that I wasn't going to sell the building and leave town or something if they gave the deed to me? I had to prove myself.

My only concern was about becoming affiliated with the Boys Clubs. I had a real feel for these kids and what their needs were, and my program seemed to work. I was afraid their organization was going to come in and tell me to change things, to do it their way, whatever that was.

I needn't have worried. The Boys Clubs of America is an umbrella organization that was overseeing almost 1,000 individual clubs throughout the United States at that time. It provided valuable resources such as organizational and fund-raising training as well as program and tactical support from its regional offices. Its overall mission was to provide safe, positive places for kids, the very same thing I was trying to do. It was a perfect match.

We couldn't become affiliated formally right away, however. There were certain criteria we had to meet with regard to membership, hours of operation, and staffing, as well as fund-raising capabilities. In terms of membership, it was a no-brainer. Once we ripped the boards off the doors and set up shop, we had more kids than we knew what to do with. Staffing was a problem, though; I was it, and I wasn't even being paid. I supervised all the junior counselors and volunteer parents, also unpaid. Because we had no paid staff—and no money to pay them anyway—and most of the adults had other jobs, there was no way we could operate on weekdays as the Boys Clubs would have liked. As for fund-raising, well, I think they had more in mind than the rummage sales and waistline parties we had been having. Getting this building was a blessing, but it also required a different and more serious commitment. No problem, I thought. I'm ready. Where do I sign?

A week or so later, Carl called and said Vons wanted to formally hand over the deed to me—as a representative of the Boys Clubs—at a ceremony at Los Angeles County Supervisor Kenneth Hahn's office. "Can you come down with some of the members?" he asked.

Terry Baker, Terry Smith, Michael, another club regular named Jeff Gadlin, and I all drove downtown to the Hall of Administration, the place I had gone in 1962 to look for a job the day Mark was born. This time, however, was much different. I had been invited.

When we got there, we were whisked into Supervisor Hahn's office, where Carl was already waiting for us with William Von der Ahe, Vons' executive vice president. It was so nice to be able to thank someone from Vons in person.

"You know," Von der Ahe told me, "my family used to live in that neighborhood, on 48th and Vermont. So we're especially glad to see someone like you taking his time to put something back into that community."

I didn't know what to say other than "Thank you."

The next day was Saturday, and we picked up the kids as usual. But instead of heading to the park, we all went down to our new club. As we spilled out of cars and trucks and station wagons, I could hear the gasps and excited chatter from kids and parents alike.

"How big is this place, Lou?" Howard Banks asked me.

"It's almost an acre of land," I told him, "and the building is around 20,000 square feet."

"*20,000 square feet?*" a group of boys shouted when they overheard me. They'd never imagined a place so big. "And it's all ours? Yippeee!!" They started dancing around and singing. Some of the boys were already playing an impromptu game of tag over by the alley behind the property. Oh, yes, this is the place, I thought.

"Okay!" I yelled. "Rap session! Everyone gather around." Quickly, the scattered group of about 100 boys formed a semicircle near where I stood.

"Now listen," I began. "I want you all to know that this is *your* club. Yours. This is going to be a place where you can come any day of the week to hang out and see your friends and play. I know it doesn't look like much now, but just imagine the possibilities! With a little hard work, we can have this place looking good in no time!" A cheer went up when I said that.

"But," I continued after they quieted down, "it's going to take some work. We won't have as much time to go to the park anymore because we'll be working here, you understand? If you don't like that and don't want to be a part of it, that's okay. But those of you who do want to make this place the best club in Los Angeles are welcome to stick around and help. Are you with me?" More cheers. No one left.

I wasn't surprised at their enthusiasm for the cleanup project. Most of us had been together almost two years now, and they knew that I was doing this for them. I wasn't just making them work for nothing. This would be their place, a place in their community that would be safe and offer them a sense of belonging to something positive.

Since that first summer, I had been thinking that we needed a clubhouse. Getting kids out to the parks, mountains, and beaches was still part of the plan, but coordinating all the cars, kids, and drivers every weekend was quite a task. It would be much easier if we had a place to go, and then we could plan day trips from there. Plus, I thought a clubhouse would be nice so we could have games and maybe a basketball court on site, so kids could drop by anytime they wanted to. I wanted them to have a place they could call their own.

⁓

Before we knew it, things started taking shape. Someone knew someone who had a dump truck, and we hauled out two large loads of garbage that first day alone. Toby came down a lot to help out, too. I was really beginning to like him. I didn't know what to make of him at first because his personality was so forthright and upfront; he was a venture capitalist, and that was the way he did business. I had never encountered anyone like him, and I didn't understand him. But now, after all he'd done for us, I really began to see that he was all he said he was. He didn't fool around. When he said he was committed to something, he meant it. And he wasn't the type to just make a few phone calls, either, I was finding out. He was down there with us that day, rolling up his sleeves and getting to work.

I even began to pattern myself after him. Toby was a successful businessman who had clients all over the country, and he often got to the office before the sun came up. His favorite time to call me with ideas or suggestions was at six o'clock in the morning. After the first few times he woke me up, I thought to myself, This successful businessman is at his office in Beverly Hills at six o'clock in the morning, looking for ways to help me out, and here I've got my butt in bed. I've gotta rethink this. From that day on, I started my workdays early, too—around 6:30 or 7:00—and I believe that adopting that work habit of Toby's is one of the things that contributed to my eventual success.

I learned a lot from Toby, most of it by watching him interact with people. When he wanted something, he just asked, straight up. "The worst they can do is say no," he told me.

He also became a trusted friend. Every so often, he would invite me, Ruby, and our kids out to his house in San Marino, a posh suburb of Pasadena, which was about fifteen miles east of the club. The first time we went was for a Fourth of July pool party. We were the only black family there, but Toby and his wife, Barbara, made us feel so at ease and at home that we never felt out of place.

⋙

Inside the building, the only light we had was from the skylight overhead. The power lines to the building had been cut some time back, and from what we could tell, the wiring in the place was in pretty bad shape.

"Let me make some calls," Toby said, referring to our electrical problem, "and see if I can find someone to get us some juice." I knew by now that if Toby said he was going to make a call, things were going to get done. Lo and behold, within a few weeks, he found an electrical contracting company that agreed to get us some power, free of charge. The electricians who came in to do the work liked what we were doing so much that they told their union buddies. Electricians kept coming, one after the other, week after week, until they had redone the wiring and gotten us the power we needed. I'll never forget that.

Our next problem was the ceiling. It was sagging, rat infested, moldy, you name it. It had to go. We got some bids from contractors who said it would cost $5,000 to take it out. I listened to what they had to say, asked some questions about how they planned to remove it, and decided that it wasn't such big deal. The kids and I could do that! So we did it ourselves. We took the ceiling down, and what we could salvage—some of the ceiling tiles, undamaged wood, steel beams—we sold for $3,000 to a scrap yard.

Then people in the neighborhood began to get curious about the caravans of vehicles pulling up to the location every Saturday and spilling out hordes of kids and adults armed with hammers, saws, and ladders.

Curiosity got the better of some of them, and when they came over, we told them what we were doing and asked them to help. Pretty soon, someone would come back with a jar of nails or a can of paint, and an old lady or two from down the street would make a pot of lemonade for us. It was nice.

I was just as happy about the way our kids handled themselves. I told them that this was their club, and they took it to heart. They felt so much pride and ownership in this building, I doubt they would have treated their own homes with as much care. We worked hard and sweated a lot, but rarely did I hear any grumbling. Plus, the improvements they saw as a result of their hard work boosted their enthusiasm and confidence.

One of the biggest problems I faced was what to do with the front doors—two huge glass doors that opened directly onto the sidewalk on Vermont Avenue. I didn't think that we should have our entrance on such a busy street, and Toby agreed with me. There was an entrance the same size around the north side off the parking lot that would serve our purposes much better, but we had to get rid of the front doors. I found someone to buy them from us, and with the proceeds, I arranged to buy some cinderblocks and have someone come in and brick up the opening. The catch was that I had to take the doors out completely before the bricklayer could come in and do his work. In other words, there would be a gaping hole in the building for at least a day and a night.

I figured I needed to spend the night there to keep vandals and vagrants away, and when some of the older kids got wind of this, they asked to join me. A problem had just become an adventure—an indoor campout. We had a blast, telling ghost stories, eating junk food, all the things you would normally do on a campout. I think the kids finally settled down around 2:00 or 3:00 in the morning, but I don't think I ever slept. Every crack and shudder had me bolt upright with my ears pricked. Ultimately, we encountered no trouble, other than my sleeplessness.

By the end of the summer of 1970, the clubhouse was really starting to come together. There still was a lot of work to be done, but at least we could use the place. We decided to have our Third Annual Sports Day at our new club.

If we thought we got attention from the neighborhood before, our boisterous Sports Day left little doubt that we had arrived. Over the summer, some of the families behind us on 50th and 51st streets had come over and asked what we were doing. Once they saw what was going on, many signed their kids up, too. Word was slowly beginning to spread.

After Sports Day, though, it spread like wildfire. People began to leave notes on the door when we weren't there, asking about our program, and kids from the area simply stopped by when they saw our cars pull up.

"Can we join?" they asked.

"Here," I said, giving them an enrollment form, "go give this to your mother or father and have them fill it out, then bring it back. Then you can join." Some of those kids came back with completed forms and dues by the end of the day.

Some neighborhood kids, however, weren't so sure about us.

One day in 1971, while I was cleaning outside the club, I noticed a group of four or five young teens standing across Vermont and looking at us. I could tell they were talking about us because they kept pointing in our direction. I didn't think much of it until I noticed one of them, the smallest one, jam his hands into his pockets and stride purposefully across the street in my direction. This little guy means business, I thought to myself, chuckling.

"Hey, what you guys doing here?" the kid said in a little tough-guy voice. He couldn't have been more than ten or eleven.

"We've got a boys' club here. This is our clubhouse," I said, as I kept scrubbing.

"I thought it was a grocery store," he challenged me.

"Well, it was, but they gave it to us for us to use for the boys' club," I explained to him.

"What's a boys' club?"

"It's a place where boys can come and play and make friends, and sometimes we take field trips to the park and play football or basketball, things like that."

"Can we join?" he asked, gesturing at his friends, who were still watching from across the street.

"Sure can. You just gotta get your parents to fill out this form I have and come back with the 65 cents for dues." I gave him some forms, and he went back across the street. I watched out of the corner of my eye for a few minutes as the little boy explained what I had said to his friends, who looked mostly to be between twelve and fourteen.

One of those boys particularly caught my eye. He sort of stood back from his friends a little, cradling his basketball in a certain casual way, though the way he was standing was anything but easygoing. He stood straight and tall, as if he were on high alert or something. He had an air of being watchful yet reserved, an attitude that pegged him as the leader of this little ragtag bunch. I kept an eye on him as he and his friends ambled north on Vermont, then I went back to work and forgot all about them.

Then, one day a few months later, that same boy came back—same basketball, same attitude, but this time, he was with just one other kid. I noticed him talking to a couple of our members through the fence, and I walked over.

"Hey, there," I said in a friendly way. "How ya doin', man?"

"All right, all right," he answered guardedly. "Y'all gonna play some ball here?"

"Yeah, we'll probably get a game going this afternoon."

"Can we play?" he asked, indicating the friend next to him.

"Sure, once you join the club. Let me get you a membership form," I said as I turned toward the building.

"Got one right here," he said as he pulled a piece of paper out of his pocket. His friend did the same. "And here's the dues." They handed over some coins.

"Great," I said, "come on in. Let me tell you the rules."

That stopped them both in their tracks. "Rules?" they said in unison.

"Uh-huh, rules. We have no fighting here, no bullying or disrespecting of any kind, otherwise I put you out of the club. You're suspended. It's no big deal," I said as I saw them exchange looks. "Just follow my rules, and everything will be okay."

I could tell the first boy didn't like the sound of that, but the fact that he wanted to play ball won out, so he and his friend stayed. I looked down at their enrollment forms. Carl Reed and Jerome Taylor. Carl was the one with the basketball. The forms said both boys lived just on the other side of Vermont, on 50th Street. They were fifteen years old.

10

Can't Run Sitting Down

Don't be afraid to be tough—you're their leader, not their friend. There's a difference between being tough and being cruel, and children will pick up on which way you're being.

—LOU DANTZLER

According to Rock, the demise of the neighborhood surrounding our club on 51st and Vermont began when the city cut down the palm trees lining the streets.

"We had palm trees all along this long street, and it used to be so nice here," he said to me one day. "In the '60s, this was. Then they came and cut all those trees down; I think it was to fry all our brains and make us ignorant, because after that was when things started getting bad."

Wendell Curtis Williams was the kid who crossed the street that day in 1971 to see what I was doing cleaning up an abandoned grocery store. He got the nickname "Rock" soon after he joined the club the following summer. During a scuffle with some of the other boys at a campout, he was hit in the head with a rock. When he regained consciousness after a few moments, someone jokingly called him Rock, and the name just stuck.

He was an energetic little boy with a fiery temper and a mother who had too many kids to keep track of: six children born in six years. Rock was a handful, as were a lot of the other kids from our new neighborhood.

Though the new club was barely two miles east of where I lived, this neighborhood was considered the east side. There were subtle differences between the east side and the west side of South Central Los Angeles. Though technically the west side starts at Broadway, many really considered Vermont Avenue the dividing line between east and west. Once you went east of Vermont and hit Hoover and Figueroa, the neighborhoods began to get a little dicier, the houses a little shabbier, and there were more apartment buildings and motels. If you lived on the west side of Vermont in those days, you were considered a little better off.

Vermont Avenue is a busy commercial street that runs north-south, starting in the artsy community of Silver Lake near Griffith Park; going down through Koreatown north of the Santa Monica Freeway and through the historic West Adams district just south of the freeway; continuing past the University of Southern California, which is just a mile or two north of our club; and finally going to Watts, a few miles south of us. Much of the Vermont area was originally settled in the first half of the twentieth century, as evidenced by the remnants of art deco–era brick buildings, which are now barely discernible, sandwiched between newer cinderblock structures covered haphazardly with stucco or painted with garish colors. The store signs are crude and often hand-painted, with proclamations such as "We accept food stamps."

A couple of blocks east of Vermont is Hoover. From Martin Luther King Jr. Boulevard at the north to Slauson in the south, Hoover, and all the tidily numbered streets that bisect it, has long been a focal point for some of the most ferocious gang activity in Los Angeles. One of the worst areas was around 50th Street, which was where Rock, Carl Reed, and Jerome Taylor lived.

In the 1950s, a gang called the Gladiators called this area their turf. They controlled everything along Hoover from 45th down to Slauson—about ten blocks, according to a couple of OGs, or "original gangster" members, I know. Back then, gang activity usually ran along the lines of burglaries, extortion, prostitution, and such. The weapons of choice were knives, baseball bats, intimidation, and muscle. Gangster life thrived in this area due mostly to the goings-on on Figueroa Street, a couple of blocks east of Hoover, where all the motels, bars, and prostitutes were.

The rivals of the Gladiators were the Rabble Rousers, the Businessmen, and the Blood Alleys. Much of the mayhem of the Watts Riot was attributed to these gangs. Continued police presence in the area served to cool them down, while a purported gang truce helped stop gangbanging until at least 1968, when a fledgling organization of teenagers got together, called themselves the Crips, and proceeded to get busy.

The next year, 1969, is supposedly when the Brims gang, a.k.a. the Hatboys—a precursor of the notorious Bloods—started. Oh, these gangs, they had some big fun then! They hid behind cars when there were dances going on at Freemont High School or Manual Arts High School. When the dance let out, they leaped from behind the bushes, jumped on people, and took their leather coats, money, and watches. They used the proceeds to buy beer and weed, then they kicked back and laughed the night away. Soon, police and people at the dances got wise, and the gangs started targeting ladies walking to the store or church. Then they moved on to robbing the homes and cars of the remaining white folks, many of whom soon fled. Before long, they were jumping kids walking to school and taking their lunch money. Big fun.

Along with the Brims were the Pirus, named after a street in Compton. The Pirus were affiliated with the Crips in the beginning, so the story goes, until there was a falling out between the two groups over a woman, who was dating a member of each gang. From then on, the Pirus were Bloods.

The Crips began in 1968 or 1969 (depending on which OG you believe) when two Freemont High School students, Jimel Barnes and Raymond

Washington, took a walk up Avalon Boulevard and wrote the word *Crips* on a wall. "Check this out, Cuz," Raymond said to Jimel. "Crips will never die, they'll multiply." There are several stories explaining where the name "Crips" came from. According to Jimel, "It's from the cradle to the grave. C-RIP, may you rest in peace." Raymond was patterning his gang after an older, established gang, the Avenues. Since they were younger, they were the Baby Avenues, which became Avenue Cribs, then Cribs, and somewhere along the way, just Crips. Others say the reason the name eventually morphed into Crips was because part of their look included using walking canes, which made them look like cripples—crips. The canes were also used to cripple people. Then there was the word *crippin'*,—which meant robbing and stealing—which may also have had a part in the evolution of the name.

However their gang name was coined, Jimel and Raymond soon hooked up with their friend Stanley "Tookie" Williams, who shared their passion for extreme bodybuilding and biceps the size of telephone poles, and the three of them became the godfathers of one of the most notorious and bloody gang movements in history.

As is well known today, gang members used a code of dress to identify themselves. In addition to the canes the Crips carried, for instance, the members were also identifiable by an earring worn in the left ear. For other gangs, it was the hats they wore: acey-deucies, derbies, brim hats, etc. Still others dressed in starched, pressed khaki pants, called Dickies, and blinding white T-shirts. Later, gang members were identified by colors: red for Bloods, blue for Crips. There was also a code language, the most common example being the use of "Cuz" and "Blood." The Crips used "Cuz" because apparently the rules on the street back then dictated that you didn't engage in a fight to help another person unless they were related to you. The verbal okay to get involved became "That's my cousin." On the flip side, "Blood" is supposed to mean "brother." Both describe exactly what many young kids are seeking when they join a gang: a family.

The calling cards for all gang activity were intimidation and fear. Defending your turf required soldiers to support you in battle, and those who didn't voluntarily decide to join a gang were jumped in front of their homes or at school until they made up their minds to enlist—a gangster's version of the draft. Out of fear, there was a need to "identify," or become part of a gang for protection. The strong preyed upon the weak, who then cultivated bad-boy personas that only perpetuated the violence.

Some joined out of fear, while others needed a sense of belonging. Whether it was society telling them that they were unfit to live in their neighborhoods or their parents neglecting them for whatever reason—divorce, drugs, jail time—many of these kids were searching for the love they didn't find at home. They needed someone to respect them and listen to them, to show them how to live life. The older gangsters, with their attitudes and nice clothes and free time, became the people youngsters turned to when they had problems—not the police, whom they were wary of; not their teachers, who were overburdened; not their ministers, because many of the families didn't go to church regularly; and not their fathers, the people from whom they desperately needed love and guidance but who, for one reason or another, were absent. Into the void stepped the gangbanger.

The very year the modern gangs were being formed was the same year I decided to form a "gang" of my own. What I was looking to provide were some of the same things the gangs were giving the kids: leadership, respect, and a sense of belonging. While gangs had their code words, hand signs, and style of dress, we had our T-shirts, behavior standards, and plenty of sorely needed affection. Many joined gangs to get respect; we provided and fostered our own kind of respect.

While the gangs' hook was protection, ours was sports—and with sports, you had to get physical. I was there at the club every day, with my tracksuit and my sneakers on, mixing it up with the kids. I never ran this program sitting down. After our games, when we sat on the grass, or later on the linoleum floor in our new building, I got right down on the floor with them and let them touch me, sit on me—they just needed that contact. Kids were constantly jumping on my back, hanging on me, and I loved it. I showed them it wasn't unmanly to hug. I didn't know any other way; that's how I was with my own kids, and I looked upon most of these kids as an extension of my family.

And it was a growing family. Once we moved into our new location, we saw a surge in new members, with Carl, Jerome, and Rock among them.

Carl was a tough little guy from a tough little street. The Crips and Bloods were just beginning to gain a toehold in our area, especially on Carl's street, where there were a lot of teenage boys with nothing to do and ripe for recruitment. These boys were into sports—football, baseball, basketball, you name it. A vacant lot on their street was their own private football field. Our Coliseum, they called it, after the professional sports complex a mile or so north where the Rams and the USC Trojans played. Their favorite place to go, however, was a tiny grassy park up on 48th Street and Hoover. It was only about two acres, but big enough for them to get a good scrimmage going. One day, though, a bunch of the regulars met up there only to find some city dump trucks unloading giant boulders the size of washing machines right in the middle of the field, making it impossible for them to run and play. "Playing football here tears up the grass," they were told. Some believed the city was actively discouraging black teens from congregating at the park. Whatever the reason, they no longer had a place to play within walking distance.

We didn't have grass, just an asphalt parking lot, but we made the most of it, let me tell you. We played touch football every day. When a bunch of the parents donated some of their Blue Chip stamps, we were able to buy a couple of basketball hoops and some balls. We utilized every inch of that space.

I got right in there, showing them how to do a layup or guard someone. If any of the kids didn't play by the rules or were bad sports, they had to do laps. If that didn't shape them up, they were suspended from the club.

I didn't get involved with just the kids, though. Every time we had a new member who wanted to sign up, I went to the parents' house and talked to them. I wanted everyone, including the parents, to be clear about our standards. Sure, this was a club meant for kids to have fun, but I felt in order for it to be positive for everyone, we had to have standards. Disrespect of anyone in the club was not allowed. Members' clothes had to be neat and clean. No fighting or bullying. Just basic things.

The reason I got the parents involved was because I knew that I needed their help to really make a difference for their children. If I had to suspend a kid because he was stealing or getting into fights, I wanted his mother to stand behind me and support the punishment we gave out. I didn't want any misunderstandings. Getting parents on board in the beginning meant that we often didn't even have to suspend the kids; just saying, "I'm going to call your mother and see what she says" was enough to get that kid to straighten up.

That was how I found myself standing in front of a large, two-story Craftsman home on 50th Street one evening in early 1972. I was going to speak to Carl's mother.

Carl was one of eight children. His mother, Laura, a wonderful, soft-spoken lady with an iron will, had left her children's abusive father in the Midwest and moved to Los Angeles to start over. After going through a rocky spell, she met and married her current husband, who owned this well-maintained house.

Carl was a smart kid, a smart kid with a smart mouth and a temper to match. He had opinions and views on everything and was quick to let you know what they were. He loved to talk back. He was also devoted to basketball, and I knew the only reason he wanted to join the club was so he could use our courts, the only ones in the neighborhood. I didn't mind; whatever it took to get these kids to come.

I really liked Carl's mother, a God-fearing woman who insisted that all of her children attend church weekly. She was also a firm disciplinarian who demanded respect. Unfortunately, the family lived in an increasingly troubled neighborhood. Angry, fatherless boys from around the area were preying on the angry, fatherless boys of this block. Carl, who was barely a teenager when they moved there in 1968, got jumped several times soon after they arrived and adopted more of a tough-guy attitude to defend himself. One of the first kids to gang up on Carl was Jerome Taylor, who lived across the street. He and two other young teens didn't like Carl's mouth and decided to teach him a lesson, his mother told me. When she heard what happened, she went to talk to the boys' mothers, who pretty much adopted a "boys will be boys" attitude. So instead she talked to the boys.

"You know," she told them in her sweet, quiet voice, "you boys are cowards. It took three of you to beat him up; the next time you disagree, at least do it one on one." They hung their heads.

"And you know that Jerome he's now friends with? I'm not so sure about his family and his parents. His uncle is trouble, that's all I can say. I think he's in jail. It's a bad house. Bad. And he and Carl are now so tight. So I said to Jerome, 'I'm not gonna let my son go to your house. If you don't want to stay away from him, you can come over here, but just know that whatever I'm gonna do to him, I'm gonna do to you, so if you don't like that, then you can stay away.' And he said, 'Momma'—he calls me Momma—'you can do that.' So I said okay. I've practically raised him ever since. He just needs a positive influence, like Carl does. Maybe you could take Jerome in your club, too?"

I told her it was no problem.

Carl had a lot of pride and was an intelligent, natural-born leader. In any other circumstance, he probably would have been the school's class president, captain of the basketball team, or both, and headed for a nice college back East. In our neighborhood, though, success was measured differently according to the amount of respect you garnered. In order to get respect, you had to be tough, and you had to back up your words. Carl was tough.

By the early 1970s, around the time I was talking to Carl's mother, the Crips and Bloods were already sniffing around our neighborhood, looking to claim more territory. "Sometimes there'd be twelve or thirteen gang people at my gate," Carl's mother told me. "I'd see them walking down the street with guns and everything. It's nerve-racking."

Tired of being jumped, Carl got some of the kids on the block together and organized things. "Enough of that," he said, "We gotta get our street together. We're gonna be 5-0," he christened his gang. "We're gonna watch each other's backs." Before he knew it, everyone was down. Soon, no one could come on the block unless Carl or one of the other dozen or so members of his gang said so. In these streets, the name of the game was survival, and Carl wanted to make sure he won that game, with points to spare.

Like a lot of kids I met in this community, Carl had a lot of anger. He always seemed to be beating someone up "because I won't take nothin' from nobody," he liked to say. The problem was, there was bound to be someone tougher. But Carl never showed any fear. One morning, he came out of his house to get the newspaper for his stepfather and found himself staring down the barrel of a rifle held by a Crip, who said, "You better join the Crips or you're gonna die on this block." Fifteen years old at the time, Carl had nerves of steel. He simply stared the guy down, took the paper, and walked back inside. "Inside, I was scared as hell," he told me years later. "But part of the survival trait is to never show fear." He was one serious kid. And now he was a member of Challengers.

I'd dealt with some tough kids over the previous two years, but some of the kids in this new neighborhood, like Carl, were something else. They weren't as trusting, and it took a lot to win them over. I couldn't get any message across to them unless they trusted me and believed I knew what was best for them.

Part of gaining someone's trust is simply spending time with them and being consistent. The first step was showing kids that the rules I set were for everyone, every day, no exceptions—in fact, my brother-in-law Michael was suspended on several occasions. The next step was just listening to the kids and to the parents. As I said, I needed them to back me up when their kids were at home or if I had to discipline them at the club.

That's how I got to Carl, through his mother. Carl loved, respected, and feared his mother, and I used that to every advantage.

"Lou, if you have any problem with Carl," she told me that first night while Carl was listening, "you just call me, and I'll be right there."

One day, about a month or two later, Carl and his friends were playing basketball outside. Rock, who was two years younger than Carl, was horsing around, being silly and teasing him. I had to separate them several times that afternoon. "Stop laughing, man! I'm trying to make a shot!" Carl would yell as Rock cut up during one of Carl's free throws. But Rock wouldn't stop. Finally, it got too much for Carl. He popped him one and busted his eye right open; there was blood everywhere.

"Get out! You're out of here!" I screamed at Carl as I ran over and held back little Rock, who was holding his head yet still trying to charge Carl. "You're out of here for a week!"

"Oh, man!" he yelled back, stomping and throwing the ball against the fence. "It's not my fault; I told him to stop clowning. He's always clowning and bothering me."

"I don't care what he does. Hitting him is not going to solve it. If you tell someone to stop bothering you, and they keep on doing it, you have to tell me or another adult, you understand?" I could tell I wasn't getting through. Carl was used to handling things his own way, with his fists. It's how he protected himself and his family. He got into fights all the time protecting his sisters, like the time a bully hit one of them in the back with a two-by-four because he thought she was cute but she wouldn't talk to him. Raised in this environment, Carl knew the way to survive was to be the toughest, the baddest. And here I was, trying to make him follow a whole new set of rules. He wasn't ready. He wasn't going to take any orders from me.

"You're suspended for a week," I told him.

"I don't give a shit," he shot back, standing straight up, fists clenched, in his tough-guy posture.

"Okay, a month then," I countered, trying to hold my temper as best I could.

Carl took a step closer to me. "You can make it a year, partner, but you can't make me get out of here! Just try!"

The thing I always had going for me was my size. I was six-two and 250 pounds, so there weren't many people willing to take me on, as my sergeant in the Air Force had correctly surmised. That's how I was able to hold my own with so many of these tough kids. The only thing they respected was someone tougher and stronger than they were.

However, Carl was different. Even though he was a good head shorter than I am, with the wiry frame of a fifteen-year-old, he had stared down the barrel of a rifle and lived to tell about it. He had spent years honing his tough-guy persona, and he wasn't about to back down in front of all his friends; his pride wouldn't let him. I could tell what was going on in his mind: I can take this guy, no problem! I can work him!

I wasn't about to get into a fistfight, however. Being tough is one thing, but I was trying to set an example that fighting wasn't the answer. So I used the ace up my sleeve. I called Carl's mother.

In an instant, she came barreling up the street in her station wagon. Carl was still mouthing off about how he wasn't going anywhere and no one was going to make him. Then he saw his mother.

"Carl," she said in a strong voice that meant business, "What's going on here? You don't want to do what Mr. Lou say?"

Carl emerged from his pack of cronies and sauntered over to where his mother and I were standing near her car.

"It wasn't my fault," he complained. "Rock was bugging me all day and he wouldn't stop..."

"Get in the car."

"But Momma..."

"Get in the car!" she commanded.

Carl didn't move. He puffed up his chest like a peacock, preening for his buddies who were watching from over at the wall.

"Mr. Lou says you are suspended for a month, Carl, but you won't listen to him. You won't leave. Excuse me? Is that the way I raised you?"

"Now, Momma, I—," he protested.

"I said, is that the way I raised you?"

"No, ma'am," he said quietly so his friends couldn't hear.

"That's right. Now get in the car," she ordered. But Carl's pride again got the best of him, and he wanted to show his bad-boy friends that he was still in charge, so he made a face, rolled his eyes, sighed theatrically as if none of this bothered him, and stood his ground.

Carl's mother reached her limit. *Bam!* She smacked him across the head. Stunned tears sprang to his eyes.

"You get in that car right now, or you'll have more of that when you get home, you hear?" she shouted for all to hear.

Carl had no choice but to get in the car. He kept his head down so his friends couldn't see the tears, but they could see his mother smack him one more time before she started the car and left the parking lot. The rest of that day, I didn't hear a peep out of anyone.

A few days later, I noticed Carl over at the far corner of the property on the street side of the fence, talking to Jerome and a few others. I could tell by his expression that he was trying to talk them into something, but for some reason, his close friends weren't listening.

The following week, Carl was back at the fence again. It looked like he was motioning to his friends to come out to where he was, and they were shaking their heads. Finally, I saw him stomp off, slamming his basketball in angry dribbles back up the street. All his friends were in the club, and he had no one to hang with.

Later, I found out that I was right; Carl was lobbying his friends to drop out of the club to teach me a lesson and show me who was boss. Carl's mother told me she overheard him on her front porch one evening trying to rally some of the guys to do some sort of retaliation. But nothing ever came of it. His friends liked it here; they chose the club over Carl.

When Carl's suspension was up, I wasn't sure if I'd see him again, or whether I wanted to. But he came into my office the day his suspension expired and, much to my surprise, apologized.

"Uh, I'm sorry for fighting," he said in a monotone, refusing to look me in the eye. Even with all the trouble he caused me, there was something I liked about Carl. He had real leadership qualities, and I admired that; he just needed to be pointed in the right direction. So I decided to cut him some slack.

"It's okay, man," I said. "I know you're a good kid; you've just got a temper, that's all. Just don't fight here anymore, that understood?"

"Yeah, Mr. Lou," he replied.

"All right then. Why don't we go out and play some ball, show these kids what's what!" I said, putting my arm around his shoulders as we walked outside.

From that point on, I had little trouble from Carl. If he started acting up, I threatened to call his mother, and he backed right down. Eventually, he got the message, and instead of fighting me, he started to listen to what I had to say. It took a while, but once Carl came on board, all his friends followed along, and they all behaved themselves while they were with me.

☙

After the article about us appeared in the paper, one of the many calls I received was from someone at the Dodger organization, offering us free tickets to a home game. About 100 kids went, including Carl, in a caravan of station wagons, sedans, and pickup trucks.

We all had so much fun that day. I think I can count on one hand the number of us who had been to a professional baseball game before. We took up almost one whole section. I didn't have any qualms about controlling such a large group; I knew most of the kids well enough now—and they knew me—to be able to anticipate trouble, which, of course, never happened. People commented to me that day about how well-behaved our group was, something I heard again and again throughout the years on countless other field trips. In my mind, it was simple. The kids had earned the right to go based on their behavior at the club. They knew it was a privilege to be invited to something like this, and I made sure they treated it as such. It goes back to what I've always known: If you set certain standards of behavior and follow through on making sure they're adhered to, children will work to achieve those standards.

I let Carl and his friends know right from the start what we were about and that I was not going to tolerate any antics. Carl being Carl, he challenged me every step of the way until he realized I wasn't going to budge. When he had nowhere to play ball and no one to play with, he realized he needed to get with the program, and he did. I'm not saying those first few months were easy for either of us. Carl could see through B.S. in a minute and use it to his advantage. What I had on my side was that I didn't have any B.S. I just wanted to help.

One Sunday afternoon in 1972, I was driving a few of the boys around in the station wagon as we came back from church. I often encouraged members to come with me to church. "It doesn't matter which church you want to go to," I told them. "I'll go with you to whatever church you want, as long as you go."

My upbringing had revolved around church and spirituality, and I credit that with helping me grow to be the person I became, so I was saddened by the fact that many families in this community were turning away from the church, leaving their children without that firm foundation of morals that did so much to shape my character. So once a month or so, I spent part of my Sundays in different churches with a group of Challengers kids.

On this particular day, we took our time coming back from the church we had visited on Normandie and 42nd Street. In the car were seven or eight guys, including Michael and Kenny. The thread of our conversation had nothing to do with God or the sermon we had just heard. Instead, the topic was girls, as usual—in particular a date I had chaperoned for some of the boys in the car the previous night.

By now, it had become a tradition that as a reward to some of my best junior leaders, I drove them if they wanted to take a girl out for a date. For those guys, most of them now fifteen or sixteen, this was far better than a dance. None of them had access to a car to take a girl out properly—something I could definitely relate to, remembering my youth in the South when I walked those dirt roads—so this gave them a opportunity to impress their girls.

"I know you guys want to take girls out on dates, so here's what I'm gonna do," I told the five or six I had chosen for that particular occasion. "I'll pick you up in the station wagon and take you over to pick up your dates. Then I'll take you all downtown. There's a theater on Broadway, and next door is Clifton's Cafeteria. You can take them to dinner and then to a movie.

"Now," I continued as I let that sink in, "I respect you guys; I trust you guys. I chose you because you are my most responsible leaders. I'm not gonna baby-sit you, you understand? We've talked enough now about how to act in public, how to eat in a restaurant, and how to treat a girl, so I'm leaving it to you. I'll drop you off at 8:00 and pick you up at 12:00. How's that sound?"

They were ecstatic, of course. Right away they started planning what they were going to wear and who they were going to invite and strategizing about how much money they would need to buy dinner as well as popcorn at the movies to treat the ladies right. Everyone had a plan, it seemed, except a kid named Chris.

"Oh, yeah, bighead Chris," Kenny laughed that day in the car on the way back from church. "Lou, check this out. We're at Clifton's last night, you know, and we all buy our girls what they want, but not too much because we gotta save some for the movies. But not Chris! Oh, no! He's being Mr. Big Shot, buying his girl everything. I mean cream pie, you name it." Everyone was laughing at Chris, who was in the backseat with his head down, looking sheepish.

"So we go into the movies," Kenny continues, shouting above the laughter, "and we look around and say, 'Hey, man, where's Chris?' and then we look back outside, and he pulls his pockets up and whines, 'I got no more money!'" Kenny and the others busted up laughing at Kenny's imitation of Chris. "Man," he said when he could catch his breath, "we just died!"

"So what did ya'll do?" I asked after they had calmed down.

"Well, we pooled our money, left the ladies inside in the lobby, went back out, and got him and his girl in."

I didn't say anything at the time, but I was so proud I thought I would burst. This was exactly what I had been aiming for when I started taking all those boys to the park. The camaraderie, trust, unity, and respect they demonstrated was a direct result of the years I had spent laying the groundwork with the standards I set out for them, and here it was being played out: They didn't leave their friend hanging. But that didn't mean they were going to let him off the hook.

"Chris, next time, don't try to act so big like a millionaire and blow all your money," Michael said.

"Yeah?" retorted Chris, who, tired of taking it and deciding to dish out some of his own, shot something back about how next time, he wouldn't have to worry because his girl was going to pay for him, or something like that. If he thought that would quiet down the teasing, he was sadly mistaken.

"Ooohh! Whoowee! Listen to Mr. Ladies' Man! Ha, ha, ha...."

Oh, to hear those boys talk! The way they told it, they would give Romeo a run for his money. They liked to act as if they knew all about women and sex, bragging and bagging on each other, but the truth was that they knew about as much as I had at their age, which wasn't much until my cousin Willie took me under his wing.

"...and did you see her boobs, man? I tell you...."

"Oh, please, that's nothin' compared to her butt, brother...."

"What you talkin' about? You ain't never got as close as that! How would you know?"

This could go on for hours. They never tired of this subject.

"Hey, you guys," I busted in after a while. "Tell me. What's the most wonderful thing about a girl?"

"Whooaaa! You mean only one thing? Gotta be her boobs, man! Ha, ha, ha...."

"No way," another interrupted, tracing his palms over an imaginary Coke bottle. "She gotta have a nice body all over, you know...." More laughter.

"Not even close," I said once they quieted down. "You want a woman who respects herself, because that way she'll respect you and you will respect her. The most important thing is respect."

There was nothing but dumbfounded silence for the briefest of moments before they all erupted in surprised guffaws. Considering the audience, I wasn't surprised. I was telling these kids—some of whom had been saying the nastiest of curse words since they were babies and thought showing disrespect to their parents was a way of demonstrating how to be a man—that sex with a woman wasn't the most important thing. I knew it was a stretch to expect a group of hormonal teenage boys to understand this concept, but I believed it had to be said. I demanded and expected better from them; I was going to do everything I could to make them respect themselves and others around them, including women. "You gotta rethink that whole attitude," I said over and over during rap sessions. "I'm not gonna let you talk or act like that here. If you want to act like a punk, then you can go home."

Even though they probably didn't want to hear what I had to say, I said it anyway. And, being realistic, I knew it wouldn't sink in right away. So I talked a lot about sex and how not to get a girl pregnant, which was something not a lot of people talked about with kids in those days. Nowadays, they hand out condoms at school like Halloween candy, but back then, the subject was still more or less taboo. But because I talked about it openly, without any shame or embarrassment, many of the boys felt they could trust me and occasionally asked me to buy them condoms. So I did. At least that was two less teenage parents, I reasoned as I made another trip to the drugstore, where the cashier probably thought I was some sort of sex maniac.

In addition to being the subject of sex talks, however, girls were becoming more of a hot topic in those days for another reason: Girls wanted to be Challengers, too.

Ever since Milton's sister Valerie had begged to go with us to the park that first day, I had been besieged by members' sisters and cousins and neighbors who wanted to join the club. Girls tried to climb into the truck whenever I stopped for the boys, or girls playing at the park tried to mix in with one of our games. Parents were bugging me, too. "Can't you do something for my daughter? You've done wonders for my boys; now I need help for my girl, too." Valerie was one of the most vocal lobbyists. Every day, she and two other girls on my street waited in front of my house until I got home from the club. They blocked my path to the front door as soon as I got out of my car. "Now listen, Mr. Lou," Valerie would say, "you always have the boys, but you got to have something for the girls, too. What are we supposed to do? We wanna come to the club, too!"

Frankly, I didn't want girls in the club. I felt I didn't know what girls needed or how to relate to them, and I was especially afraid of what would happen if we let girls mix in with hundreds of hormonal boys. How could I have open discussions with the boys if girls were around?

After we got our new building, things only got worse. Girls from the new neighborhood yelled at me through the chain-link fence, asking when they could come. Eventually, I realized I was going to have to incorporate them in some way.

So I made Sunday afternoons girls' day. No boys. Girls could come and play just like the boys did on the other days. Some of the mothers volunteered to come and organize things for them, and Barbara Walker, Toby's wife, also helped. The Sunday experiment didn't work out very well, though. The girls still felt isolated—they wanted to be part of it all. So one day, I brought it up at a rap session.

"We need to let girls into the club," I said. I was immediately showered with no's and boos.

"All right, calm down, calm down!" I said. "It's not going to be so bad. We need to let girls in here because they deserve to have the same kinds of advantages you're getting."

"But they're gonna change things, Papa Lou," someone piped up, followed by a loud chorus of agreement.

"I know you think that, but it's worth a try. Look, I've decided we're only going to have girls come on a limited basis, just a few hours on Saturday mornings. So don't worry."

Barbara set up a little area at the corner of the gym, near the Ping-Pong table, for the girls to do arts and crafts. After a while, we started taking girls on field trips with us, to places like the Science Museum or Disneyland. Before long, we all realized that the club wasn't going to come tumbling down because we let females in the door, and at that point, girls were made welcome whenever they wanted to come—they became official, full-time members.

Much to my surprise, I found that there wasn't much difference in mentoring girls and boys. Both need structure, discipline, attention, affection, and leadership. Just like boys, girls needed to be shown how to respect themselves and others and resist the lure of juvenile delinquency, drugs, and teen pregnancy. And, just like boys, girls needed help with school so they could set reasonable goals and attain them. Girls make up half of this community, and I realized I couldn't possibly have much impact here unless I addressed the needs of both girls and boys.

Looking back now, I can't imagine the club without girls. Allowing them to come was one of the best decisions I made, even though it wasn't common practice then. Most of the clubs in the national Boys Clubs movement were for boys only at the time.

It worked for us, though. At first, of course, there was some resentment. The younger boys had to give up one of their bathrooms, but the older boys loved having the girls around, especially once they saw that the girls weren't going to disrupt their sports; they had different interests, such as Double Dutch and drill team.

What did surprise me was that girls could fall prey to gang behavior. Like boys, they found it necessary to identify with the gang or faction on their block. In fact, one of my biggest problems at first was the intense rivalry between the girls on 50th Street—Carl's street—and the girls on 51st Street. I found out right quick that girls demonstrate their toughness differently than boys. While it was easy to spot two rival gang members getting into it—a fistfight was hard to miss—catching girls in the act required nothing short of covert operations training. Girls, I noticed, didn't get physical very often. Instead, they used classic undercover tactics: rumors, innuendo, and manipulation—divide-and-conquer kind of stuff. At first, I didn't know what to do.

After a few months, though, things began to settle down. The standards I set for the boys went for the girls as well. Once they realized that we expected them to respect each other—and that we would enforce it—they started to get the message. We gave them responsibility, encouraged them to develop leadership skills, and emphasized the need to have a positive attitude, just as we did with the boys. In addition, having girls in the club brought things into a whole different light for the boys. Their hygiene improved; they learned how to interact in a positive, respectful way with the opposite sex; and, most important to them, they got dates.

In addition to the infrequent dances and parties and station wagon dates we had, once a year I organized a trip to Knotts Berry Farm, Magic Mountain, or Disneyland for the older teens. They raised money all summer for the trip, holding bake sales and whatnot; I rented a couple of buses, and we went with a few parent volunteers on one of the last Fridays of the summer.

The kids looked forward to the trip all summer because the teens were allowed to ask dates. More often than not, the boy members would ask the girl members of the club. It was a nice, fun way for a boy to ask a girl out without having to worry about driving or coming up with the cash to pay for it. And more often than not, it was a first-time experience for both.

As the time for the trip drew nearer, I found myself acting more like the host of *The Dating Game* than leader of the club. Some of the boys were very shy about asking a girl they liked, and I could tell they needed a little bit of help, so I'd bring it up at a rap session.

"Who are you taking?" I would ask one or two of the more confident boys who I knew had a date already. Then I would ask one of the boys who I knew didn't have a date but had his eye on a particular girl.

"Hey, son, come on up here," I'd beckon. Reluctantly, he would come up to the front of the room. "Who are you taking to Knott's Berry Farm?"

"I dunno."

"Oh, that's too bad," I would sympathize. Then I would look over to where the girl he liked was sitting. "Hey, there, baby dolly. Who are you going with?"

"No one," she would giggle.

"No one!" I would say in mock horror. "A good-looking, nice girl like you? Well, since neither of you is going with anyone, why don't you two go together?" And then smiles of relief would creep across those two faces as the whole gym erupted in applause. A lot of couples started that way, several of whom ended up getting married. Some of their children are members of the club today.

We used the trips in other ways, too—as the carrot to encourage good behavior all summer. "Only my best leaders will be allowed to go with us," I said at the daily rap sessions. "And being a leader means being respectful, having a positive attitude, and doing what staff and parents tell you." Needless to say, as the summer weeks wound down and the trip came closer and closer, we rarely had behavior problems, which was remarkable considering the 600 or 700 kids who came every day. Many were seeing for the first time how having a positive attitude affected how people perceived them and opened up many more avenues for them.

Just as I did with the boys, I gave the older girls leadership positions in the summers, supervising the younger members. In the early 1970s, I started a summer program called the Tiny Tot Development Program for four- to six-year-olds—the kids who soon would become full-fledged club members. In the program, some of the girls who were thirteen and up taught fundamentals to the youngsters, such as how to tie shoes, the ABCs, or how to play games. It really taught the girls a lot about responsibility and nurturing and gave them little time to get into trouble. Before I knew it, most of the unpleasant behavior that had occurred when we first admitted girls disappeared.

The rival girls from 50th and 51st streets, for instance, ended up forming drill teams together, which they took very seriously. They had a team for older members and one for younger girls, and it was really wonderful to see how the older girls came together and worked hard to achieve such precision in addition to mentoring and teaching the girls on the younger team. They marched in front of us on our annual Sports Day, performed at our talent shows, and even marched in the annual parade in Watts. I was really proud of them.

More girls, however, meant more equipment to buy. At first, all we had for the girls were jump ropes made from old telephone cords. They made do until I could get enough money together to buy real ones. I also got another Ping-Pong table when I found that the girls could be as competitive at that as the boys.

Once the word got out that this was the place to be, we were inundated with girls from all over the area. Back then, it wasn't unusual for a family to have six or seven kids (it seemed Ruby and I were the only people content with having only two boys), and the influx of girl siblings was like a tidal wave. The friendships that were formed at that time endure to this day, and some of those girls now have their kids in the club.

Just as it had been for the boys before I started Challengers, there was nothing positive in the community for girls to do after school or in the summers. Increasingly, with the breakdown of families that began in the 1960s and scores of teens being left to fend for themselves, that void led to a wave of teenage pregnancies and girls dropping out of school. It's hard enough to raise a child properly in the best of circumstances, but the trend of babies having babies served only to rob younger generations of any chance at a positive future.

I'm happy to say that none of the girls we brought into the club became teenage mothers. Most, if not all, graduated from high school and some from college. We count among our female alumni from that era a sheriff's deputy, an accountant, and a political aide—but above all, caring, positive individuals who took what they learned at Challengers and became responsible adults.

11

Leading the Charge for Change

Not everyone can be a leader, but everyone can possess leadership qualities, such as commitment, accountability, and consistency. Young people need caring, positive leaders in their lives to motivate and better prepare them for a productive future.

—Lou Dantzler

By the summer of 1973, Carl Reed was sixteen and old enough to become a junior counselor. Mayor Tom Bradley, who that year made history as the city's first black mayor, had been a supporter of ours since we got the building in 1970, when he was city councilman. He and our councilman, Gilbert Lindsay, had arranged for us to participate in the Neighborhood Youth Community (NYC) program, which the City of Los Angeles organized to address the issue of summer employment for poverty-level youth.

The way the NYC worked was that the city gave money to participating corporations and businesses in the area to hire employment-age teens for the summer, giving thousands of kids their first real work experience and first real money. In 1971 and 1972, Bradley saw to it that we qualified for this program, and thus we were able to pay some of our older members, including Michael, Milton, and Kenny and Keith Rodgers, to be junior staff members for the summer. They helped with the hundreds of kids now enrolled in our summer program. For all of them, and later for girl members who participated in the program, it was their first job and first real responsibility. In 1973, Carl became one of them.

⮝

I'd met Bradley when he was our district councilman in 1971. While the members and staff were fixing up the club, Toby Walker was busy on another front: forming a board of directors for Challengers to help with fund-raising. He and Carl Moser asked some of their prominent friends to come aboard and help us out, and one of them was an architect named Kaz Yamimoto, who was very connected downtown and was friendly with Bradley.

What I didn't know was that Toby and Carl had been constantly working behind the scenes on my behalf, trying to get funding for the club. I was busy renovating the place and had my hands full looking after all our new members, so I had no time for anything else. You can imagine what a shock it was when Toby announced at our first official board meeting, in the summer of 1971, that we had our first grant.

"The Boys Clubs have given us $5,000," he told us, and a collective whoop went up around the room.

$5,000! I thought. Wow, now we can afford to fix the floor, buy a pool table, maybe some more baseball gloves....

"...and I think we should use it to hire a full-time director," Toby finished.

A director? I thought, my spirits sinking. Someone who's gonna come in here and tell me how to run things, make all sorts of changes?

My spirits sank even further as one by one, the board members approved the idea of using the funds to hire a director. Toby could be very convincing.

Then Toby said, "There is only one person I know of who could run this place as it needs to be run." He paused and then looked at me. "Lou, would you consider taking the job?"

Everyone turned in my direction. Of course, I thought, Toby would never try to take this away from me! He had told Ruby in that first phone call that he wanted me to do this as a full-time job.

"The Boys Clubs gave us this money with the condition that we find matching funds to hire a director, which would make your yearly salary about $10,000. Can you live on that?"

At the time, I was making almost twice that from my custodian job and various side businesses. It would be a huge cut in pay; I didn't know how Ruby was going to feel about that. But I really didn't have to give it any thought. Money or no money, this was what I'd always wanted to do.

"I'll do it," I said.

I spoke to Ruby about it that night, and she agreed—this was the right thing for me to do, and the club was where I needed to be.

A few weeks later, I went downtown to Councilman Bradley's office with Toby, Carl Moser, Kaz Yamimoto, and Al Secrist of the Boys Clubs. The organization wanted to make an official presentation of the $5,000 check to me, and Yamimoto had arranged for us to do it in Bradley's office to generate some publicity. We all got there and shook hands and made small talk, and then it was time for the presentation and photo. Suddenly, Toby and Carl realized that no one had brought a camera!

"I'll be right back!" Toby announced, and then he disappeared. We made more small talk for a while until he came back, breathing a little harder but holding a camera.

"I borrowed it from a lady downstairs," he said, and we all laughed, even Bradley. We took the pictures, and it was done. Ironically, the mix-up with the camera worked to our advantage. While Toby was running around the building—he was prepared to buy a new camera if he had to, he told me later—I had a little time to chat with Councilman Bradley, who was a very personable man. Carl had told him a little of my story, about taking the boys to the park in the truck, and Bradley, a former officer with the LAPD, knew all about our neighborhood.

"I know exactly where that is," he said when I told him about our new building. "There are lots of alleys in that neighborhood, aren't there?"

"Yes, there's one directly behind our building," I told him.

"There's a Public Works program that hires cleaning crews to maintain alleys. Did you know that?" he asked me.

"No, sir."

"Yes, and I might be able to direct some of those funds your way, if your kids want to earn some extra money. Think they'd be interested?"

I told him about how we were renovating the club ourselves and that the kids didn't mind doing the work. "I think it's a great idea," I said. "It would be a great way to raise money for the club and for them to get work experience."

"Exactly," he said. "You know, I think your club is one of the most effective grassroots recreational and educational efforts I've ever seen. Let me know if there's anything else I can do to help out."

Thus began a fruitful relationship with a man who would soon become one of the most influential men in Los Angeles. Tom Bradley became mayor of Los Angeles in 1973, and for the twenty years he was in office, he was one of our biggest supporters. He always made time for us and visited frequently, and I will never forget it.

In addition to the Public Works jobs, Bradley turned us on to those NYC jobs through the city. If ever there was a government-sponsored program that was the right fit for us, this was it. It allowed us to accept as many new members as we could fit in our space, without increasing our payroll. The older kids could mentor the younger ones—something that benefited both—and get paid for it.

Now Carl Reed could use his leadership skills to do some good. Because he was obsessed with basketball, I made him coach of our basketball team, and he learned a real lesson that summer in consensus building, teamwork, and motivation. You don't motivate a winning team by beating them up, so he had to find other ways to get the job done. And he did, organizing and nurturing them along. He thrived along with the team. It was so heartwarming to see some of these guys, who were getting to the end of their teens, being so patient and caring with the guys just coming up under them. Sure, there were some scuffles here and there—I mean, there were hundreds of members by that time—but it was really something to watch all these kids from different neighborhoods and, yes, different gangs, coming together and more than just getting along. They were helping each other grow up.

By 1974, the grocery store that had become our club was really beginning to take shape. Where the produce section once was, we now had a boxing ring. The old dairy section was a woodshop. The parking lot was home to our basketball court, baseball diamond, and football field. We finally had enough money to buy real doors to replace the plywood-and-padlock affair we'd used to replace the store's glass doors. It may not have been pretty, but it worked for us.

Still, even with the help of the junior staff, our club was full to bursting. There were so many kids who wanted to come that we had to start a waiting list. Another, more pressing problem, however, had to do with different kinds of growing pains.

When Carl and his group joined the club, some of our original members felt threatened. Here were these new, badass guys, they thought, coming into *their* club and throwing their weight around. Kids who had been with me since the beginning resented the attention I gave the newcomers. They saw me treating these troublemakers the same way I treated them, and they didn't like it.

It's a funny thing, being a surrogate father to so many teenage boys. They all want a piece of you; they all want your undivided attention, that special one-on-one relationship. The fact that many of them called me Papa Lou illustrated that.

As I said, I was never one to run my program sitting in an office. I was always on the floor, mixing it up, playing with the kids, encouraging them to do better. That's how I got them to trust me and listen to me. They needed to know that I cared, and the way I showed it was by spending time with them. But with the hundreds of members now on our rolls—600 to 700 coming for our summer program alone—I was stretched pretty thin. There were times I could barely walk through the club, I had so many boys hanging on my back. I loved it, and they did, too. It was just hard for these emotional, hormonal, competitive boys to share.

The one who seemed to have the hardest time was Michael. He took particular pride in being my brother-in-law, the one who was closest to me. For him, seeing the attention and support I was giving to Carl was too much. And Carl, who at the beginning felt we were invading his turf, had his own axe to grind.

"You guys gonna sing today, Michael?" Carl taunted one day. "Singing is for sissies, you know. Real men don't sing and dance."

"Shut up, man! You don't know what you're talking about!"

"What's that?" Carl's voice instantly dropped from teasing to threatening. "You talkin' to me, partner?" Both of them had their backs up.

From across the room, I recognized from their postures what was going on. I strode over, for about the fiftieth time, to break them up.

"There a problem here again, fellas?" Silence. "I said, *Is there a problem?*"

"No, Lou," they said in unison.

"Fine, then put your fists down. If you want to fight, take it into the ring."

A local business had donated the boxing ring to us soon after we moved into the building, and we used some Blue Chip stamps donated by parents to buy gloves, a heavy bag, and padding. In addition to allowing us to give boxing lessons, the ring was a great way to settle problems. If I noticed trouble cropping up that might turn into a fistfight, I reminded everyone that the gloves and ring were nearby. More often than not, after a few rounds, two former adversaries would end up as friends and sparring partners.

But Michael and Carl never took it to the ring and were never going to become friends, at least not then. Between them there was a deep-seated animosity: They were two strong-willed, smart, opinionated loudmouths who had met their match in each other—except that even Michael knew Carl could take him down if he wanted to. And Carl, for some reason, just couldn't leave Michael alone; he teased him mercilessly, especially about his singing.

Michael, Kenny, Keith, and Milton had formed an a capella singing group and modestly called themselves Sheer Ecstasy. They practiced all the time at the club and sang in all our talent shows. I took them under my wing and showed them some tricks about performing that I had learned as a member of the Sheiks when I was in Saudi. They were so good that I took them with me when I went to fund-raise at places such as the United Way.

In addition to giving the group exposure for their singing, these performances also gave the boys a chance to mingle with successful people in the corporate world, thus further broadening their horizons. They took their singing seriously and were quite the little stars around the club. That aroused envy in some of the other members, particularly Carl. He teased the four members of Sheer Ecstasy no end. Keith, Kenny, and Milton were just as angry about it as Michael but realized there wasn't much that would stop him. They just tried to avoid him and his friends as much as they could, which wasn't easy considering the limits of our space. When it got too much for them, they came to me, and unfortunately, it was becoming a regular thing.

"Okay, so you're not going to take it into the ring," I said to Carl and Michael as they stood there in front of me, silently glaring at one another.

A teenage Lou looks after one of his nephews
on the farm in Cameron, South Carolina, in the 1940s.

Lou in Saudi Arabia

Before Challengers had a building to call their own, the clubhouse was a shady tree in the park.

Playing tug-of-war in the park often helped our members forget the real war in the streets.

We began every trip to the park with a healthy round of calisthenics,
as we did here at Griffith Park in 1969.

When tempers flared, Lou encouraged members to take out their frustrations
in the ring—and sparring partners often became lifelong friends.

Football great Fred Williamson (left) *at the first celebrity basketball game,
in 1976, in the Challengers Gym—a former grocery store*

Sidney Poitier, on one of many visits, talks with members in the club library.

*Actor Richard Roundtree helps Challengers members with
their homework on one of his weekly visits in the 1980s.*

*Denzel Washington plays ball in 1993 with club members,
observing, "What Lou has built is an oasis."*

*Mayor Tom Bradley brings basketball superstar Magic Johnson
to Challengers. Magic has been a frequent supporter
and source of inspiration for the club since his first visit in 1980.*

Lou and wife, Ruby, on their 40th wedding anniversary, 2001

Lou with sons Corey (left) and Mark (right)—the next generation of Challengers leaders—1989

Lou introduces President George H. W. Bush before a speech
carried live on national television, delivered
from the Challengers Gymnasium in the wake of the 1992 riots.

"But you two are going to have to learn how to get along. You are two of my top leaders; you are here to set the example for the younger kids. How can you expect to teach them anything about respect and leadership if you two guys are always going at it?"

They hung their heads a bit and shook hands when I forced them to, but I could tell nothing was resolved. Within a few days, I overheard Michael referring to Carl as "the gangster" and Carl later teasing Michael about his diminutive height.

The discontent wasn't evident just in Carl and Michael's fighting, either. I heard it from everyone. "You pay so much more attention to the new guys, Papa Lou," a teen from the days in the park complained, while at the same time, newer members insisted that I favored the old timers— "the originals"—with the best summer jobs. I couldn't win.

By mid-1974, with the summer school break just a few weeks away and the possible influx of hundreds of boys—and now girls—looming, I knew I needed to take action.

Mayor Bradley came through once again with City of Los Angeles money to hire summer workers. We received enough funds to hire many of our oldest members to be junior counselors once again. Challengers still had only two year-round, paid staff members: me and my friend Howard Banks, who had quit his custodian job at the school district a year earlier to help me at the club. So we needed as many junior counselors as we could afford. I gave the question of who I should offer counselor jobs to some thought and decided that maybe one way to ease the tension and friction was to appoint a couple of head junior staff members from each faction to supervise all the other junior staff members and keep the peace. Maybe giving each side an equal piece of the action, an equal piece of ownership in the program, would calm the storm.

From the "original" side, I had Terry Smith and Michael head things up. To represent the "new" members, I chose Carl and Jerome. Jerome Taylor had been Challengers' first Boy of the Year, an award we had started giving out the previous year to the member who had demonstrated the most growth in attaining strong character and leadership skills. Jerome had definitely grown in this club, that's for sure. Once a tough little kid who would beat up newcomers on his block as soon as look at them, Jerome was now one of my best junior leaders, setting the example of what a young male role model should be.

Another budding role model was Kenny Rodgers. When Honda Motor Corporation donated ten mini-bikes to our club, I set up a program to teach kids between the ages of twelve and sixteen riding skills, teamwork, laws of the road, and safety, and I put Kenny in charge.

Only the most responsible and hardworking members were chosen to be in the mini-bike club; kids who were ditching school or having behavior problems had to work those things out before they were allowed to participate. As a result, parents reported an increase in school attendance and completed homework assignments by a number of boys who had previously shown little interest in school.

Once those boys started learning how to do their figure-eights and wheelies, demonstrating them in the alley behind the club, neighborhood boys who weren't sure about joining a club with so many rules soon put their doubts behind them. They agreed to abide by our standards. They wanted to ride mini-bikes, and where else would they get a chance to do that?

I was so impressed when I saw Kenny with these boys. Sometimes, people at the club called him Baby Lou because he did so much to emulate me, and it was true. He took the standards of leadership, responsibility, and hard work to a whole new level with that mini-bike club. "Lou, you always told me to lead by example, and that's what I'm doing," he said.

Kenny followed my lead by picking members of the group and elevating them to leadership positions, and one person he chose was Kelvin Smith. Kelvin was one of the first boys from the neighborhood to join our club when we got the building on Vermont. Nine years old when he joined, he came from a family with seven kids who lived right behind our club. Now fourteen, Kelvin was the captain of the mini-bike squad. When Kenny said, "Okay, guys, we need to tear down and drain the engines," Kelvin made sure the guys did it. "C'mon, guys, you heard him. Let's tear these engines down and drain them." He could dismantle the engines and put them back together quicker than anything you ever saw. And he wasn't only good with engines. Like Kenny, he had real leadership capabilities as well. He could motivate the squad and get them to practice riding drills even though all anyone ever wanted to do was go full throttle down 51st Street from one end to the other. Kelvin had them practicing their figure-eights, made sure they wore their helmets, and above all, had them working as a team.

As for Carl, he was still crazy about basketball, so I let him head up our basketball program. He too had really come a long way from the tough gangster who had challenged me a few years earlier. When he first started playing on our basketball team, he did more punishment laps than I could count and sometimes sat out more than he played—he didn't want to hear anything about rules. Now, he was enforcing them.

When I drove through the neighborhood in the days after Carl first joined, I often saw him and his friends sitting on a stoop or standing on a street corner in the middle of the day, during school hours. It was obvious they had no intention of going to class. Now, three years later, Carl had gone to night school and taken extra classes at lunch so he was able to graduate from Manual Arts High School on time, with his class—one of the few kids on his block to do so. He had plans to attend college in the fall. Before that, however, he had his summer job at Challengers.

Carl had a particular talent for coaching. His passion for sports and his naturally competitive nature made him an exceptional mentor —he was really beginning to shine. Years later, even Michael would admit to having learned a few things from him. At the time, however, he saw nothing but red when it came to Carl.

When I gave Carl the full responsibility for coaching our basketball team, we were playing in the Vermont Square basketball league. Up until this point, my attention had often been diverted to more pressing matters, such as building and maintaining the club, and a winning team wasn't my top priority. In other words, we got beaten a lot. Carl would have none of that.

"Time out, Lou," Carl said to me at the beginning of the summer of 1974. "Let me take over the team, really build a program. There are some guys in the neighborhood who don't belong to the club who might join and want to play for us. Let me recruit them."

Though Carl still had a fiery temper, he'd learned to control and redirect it. He completely bought into the standards of the club, and I had seen him enforce a lot of the rules myself, breaking up fights; enforcing the dress code, which prohibited gang attire (which he was really helpful at spotting for me); and punishing kids for cursing or bullying. So I let him run things as he needed to.

The real turning point with Carl had come several months after serving his month-long suspension for hitting Rock. Once we fixed up our new building and started using it on a regular basis, the teens began clamoring for a dance. One Saturday night in the fall of 1972, I told them they could have one and invite whoever they wanted.

Looking back, I still can't believe how naïve I was. When I said they could invite whoever they wanted, I had no idea they were going to ask the whole of South Central! More than 300 teenagers showed up for that dance, with me the only chaperone. I wasn't nervous because I knew most of these kids by now—even some of the nonmembers —and they knew me. If they got out of hand, they knew there would be no more dances. I entrusted some of our older members with the responsibility of taking care of the younger ones, especially the girls. "I want you to be generous, courteous, and respectful, and, above all, set a good example," I told them. "I need you to help me regulate things."

The first few hours went fine, with everyone dancing to the music on our portable record player and enjoying the punch and cookies some of the mothers brought by earlier. Everyone was happy and relaxed; the lights were low, the music loud—no problem.

About 11:00 p.m., just when the kids settled in to a favorite Smokey Robinson slow dance, I noticed a group of unfamiliar faces enter the gym. Right away, I spotted the gang attire, as did most of the kids at the party, who backed up and gave the toughs a wide berth. I moved as quickly as I could across the gym floor, but it was crowded and I couldn't move very fast. By the time I reached the gang members, knives were drawn.

I flicked on the lights and saw two of the guys make a play for Carl, who was slow dancing with his girl. I found out later that these gangsters had heard the noise at the club and had come to check it out when one of the attendees—not a club member—shouted something threatening at them and then disappeared into the crowd. As the gangsters entered the packed gym looking for the instigator, they laid eyes on Carl, who at that time led a rival gang.

Gangsters or not, I wasn't going to let these guys do their business here. I stepped between Carl and the lead gangbanger, one of the ones who had a knife.

"Hey, man, be cool!" I firmly said in as calm a voice as I could muster, looking the leader right in the eye. "I'm not going to have any of that here. You need to take that outside."

The gang leader, who couldn't have been more than seventeen or eighteen, had the demeanor of a criminal who had done hard time. He shifted his gaze from Carl to me, sizing me up. Remember, in those days, I was still pretty athletic, carrying about 250 pounds on my six-foot-two frame, which, thanks to mixing it up with the kids every day, was mostly muscle. I held his stare.

The gang leader must have sensed that I wouldn't back down, because he slowly lowered his knife. The others followed suit. Carl, unarmed but with fists ready for action, let his hands drop to his sides.

I didn't take my gaze off the gang leader. Our eyes locked for a few more moments, and I could tell he was weighing his options. Finally, he seemed to come to a decision, because he nodded to his cohorts and they left. The gym, which had been dead silent during the exchange, suddenly sounded like a wind tunnel as 300 terrified teenagers let out their breath in unison.

"This dance is over," I announced, and I started to call parents to arrange rides home.

Though I could tell everyone was disappointed, I didn't hear any arguments. Too many of these kids, including Carl, had been to neighborhood parties that had ended in bloody melees when a rival gang showed up. They knew I had ended the party to keep everyone safe.

Though I wasn't surprised that everyone obeyed my order—including the gang members—some of the teens were. They couldn't believe that the gang members walked away without taking anyone's leather jacket or money and that there was no bloodshed.

From then on, our dances were for members only, and I made sure to alert the police in advance and have plenty of adult chaperones on hand, just in case. I learned my lesson, thankfully, without anyone being hurt.

One unexpected benefit of that incident was that from that point on, I began to notice a change in Carl. It was subtle at first, but he was paying more heed to my advice and adhering to my rules with fewer arguments. I don't know if it had anything to do with my standing up to those gang members, but I sensed Carl was truly starting to embrace my program. I had no idea at the time how much of an impact it would have on his life and the lives of countless youths coming up under him.

~~~

Now, two years later, Carl was our basketball coach and was doing an amazing job. He was open to learning things from me, and he had some innovative suggestions of his own.

I gave him my blessing to go recruiting for the team in the neighborhood. As I've said, sports were our hook to get kids to come to the club. Once we got them inside, they began to buy into our standards, and the results were often nothing short of amazing.

As Carl walked to work every day, he saw a young boy of about eleven or twelve who played basketball as if the sport had been invented for him. Lanky and tall for his age, he played with a grace and confidence that guys twice his age didn't possess. Carl knew the kid from his days of playing football around the 49th Street park and knew he lived nearby.

"Hey, Chris," Carl called over one day. Chris Esteves, who was practicing free throws, passed the ball to a friend and ran over.

"What's up, Carl?"

"Hey, man, I'm putting a team together at Challengers, and I'd like you to play."

"But I'm already on another team." Chris played on a team with some of the best players in the community that was part of a league run by Eli Sherman of the Westside Jewish Center. According to Carl, the team's coach was a guy who had been there for close to twenty years and had long since lost his enthusiasm for the sport. He spent most of his time getting high.

"We won't have any of that on our team," Carl told Chris.

But Chris wasn't sure. The team he played for, which frequently drew high school and college recruiters, was considered something of an all-star team. "Man, that has nothing to do with the coach," Carl said. "It's because none of the brothers have the means to get out to Sherman Oaks or wherever to play on any other team. It's just the luck of the location. We're going to build a program at Challengers, and I'm gonna talk to Sherman about getting into that league."

Carl had some work to do to get Eli Sherman to allow the Challengers team into his league. "Are you a member of the Westside Jewish Center?" Sherman wanted to know.

"No," Carl admitted. "But I'm putting this team together, and we want to play in your league. It's a great league."

"Son, we've got some of the best teams around; you don't want to do that," Sherman said.

"You don't have to put us in the best division," Carl countered.

According to Carl, Sherman thought for a moment, then said, "Okay, bring the money by Monday, and you've got a deal. Fee is $100."

Unfortunately, I was plowing all of our meager budget into the summer program, so I told Carl he would have to fund-raise for this money on his own. "No problem," he said.

He told me later he got some of the cash from his mother, but most of it came from the drug dealers and gang members in the hood. At the time, these were the only people Carl knew who had that kind of money. Even gang members could do some good sometimes.

Once he secured a spot in the league, Carl went back to Chris and some of his friends and talked them into joining the club. That season, the team finished third out of forty teams in the league.

Carl's success, however, didn't come without friction: friction from the other players in the league, who laughed at the Challengers' raggedy uniforms, and friction from Michael.

Every morning, I had a meeting with the four junior counselors in charge: Michael and Terry, Jerome and Carl. We talked about what we were going to do that day, how we were going to group the kids, what age group was going where—all the logistics. By this time, we had things down to a pretty tight system.

Back when the park was our playground, I'd learned that I lost kids quickly if things were too tame (milk and cookies didn't sit well with some of the older members) or too challenging (younger kids wandered off when they couldn't play at the level of the teens). It was better to group the members by age. I'm sure this is written down somewhere in some handbook for taking care of large groups of children, but I never read it. I was going by intuition, and it worked; we had less trouble and more interesting things for everyone to do. The six- to nine-year-olds were grouped with one set of counselors, the ten to thirteens were with another, and the fourteens and up made up the oldest group.

One day during a morning meeting toward the end of the summer of 1975, I noticed things were a little more tense than usual. When I asked Michael why he had such a scowl on his face, he erupted.

"It's ridiculous, Lou!" he burst out. "Carl is letting some of those kids get away with murder...."

Before the next few words came out of Michael's mouth, Carl was on his feet.

"What are you talking about, man?" he shouted, moving toward Michael. Jerome and Terry were quick to step between the two of them.

"All right, settle down! Cool it!" I boomed over all of them. "Sit down! Now, Michael," I said, glaring at him, and he sat down. "What are you talking about?"

"It's Chris. That ballplayer, Chris Esteves, that Carl recruited to the club last year. I thought he was all right, but I think he's starting to change, and he needs a firmer hand. Yesterday I could swear he came in to the club high—I'm pretty sure he had been smoking weed, and all Carl did was tell him to sit down and get himself together. He's babying him, Lou; he's letting him slide just because he's his star player."

"Now hold on..." Carl burst in.

"Just a minute, Carl," I interrupted. "Is this true? Did Chris come here high?"

"Yeah, Lou," he admitted. "I'm working with him though, I'm on him every day, and I'm seeing progress...."

"Oh, bullshit!" Michael spat. There went his mouth again.

"That does it, partner! I'm not taking this shit anymore!" Carl yelled back. "I'm sick and tired of always being the bad guy around here!"

From there the language got even more colorful as the two of them jumped to their feet and screamed at each other, face to face, fists clenched, chests swelled—like two angry roosters fighting over the pecking order. As I jumped in the middle and tried to calm things down, I realized that all the anger, resentment, and hostility from the past three or four years hadn't dissipated; in fact, it was worse than ever.

I don't recall which one offered to take the other outside to "finish things," but I do recall my reaction: "Both of you—get out! You're both suspended! *Get out of this club!* You are supposed to be the leaders—I can't have you behaving this way."

So they left. Michael left for good. He was nineteen and had other interests, which didn't include taking care of kids. He had a part-time job at a local TV station, which eventually led to working for legendary producer Norman Lear, whose hit shows included *All in the Family* and *The Jeffersons*.

Carl, on the other hand, displayed real talent and commitment to the kids of this neighborhood. It was clear he could have a bright future if he could just harness his temper. To his credit, he tried awfully hard. In addition, he hadn't laid a finger on Michael, though I'm sure he could have made short work of him. A couple of days after I suspended him, Carl came in and apologized, and I gave him his job back.

As for Chris, Michael was wrong. What seemed like babying was actually Carl riding Chris, trying to keep him on the straight and narrow. When Carl drove through the neighborhood and saw Chris hanging out on a stoop with some of the other neighborhood guys, Carl would stop, go over, and encourage him to come to the club instead. When Chris was considering forming his own "group" at 52nd Street Elementary School, he had Carl to talk to about his sense of isolation and need for a place to belong. Carl could identify. For some kids, gangs really are more about caring and friendship than about the other stuff. Chris, who came from a single-parent family, craved the acceptance and camaraderie that forming a group in elementary school could offer. The only problem, and Carl knew this from experience, was that these groups often evolved into gangs.

Like Carl, Chris was very bright in addition to having tremendous athletic ability. He was named one of the best middle school players in the state—but he was also in danger of throwing it all away. But Carl wouldn't give up; he shadowed Chris. That day at the club, the day that proved to be the straw that broke Michael's back, Chris had indeed been smoking pot.

"I was walkin' through the alley behind the club," Carl told me the day he came back. "And there was Chris, smoking some weed. I took it away from him, and he was pissed. And I told him, 'Listen, life is like a circle. There's always going to be someone to take the dope dealer's place or the lawyer's place; you just have to choose where you want to go. Do you want to be in a vicious circle or do you want to be in a successful circle? You make the choice.'"

I sat back and listened to this man—and he was a man now—and had to pinch myself. This was *Carl*. Had any kid given me a tougher time? And now he was reading chapter and verse of the club's philosophy to another kid.

Chris, who was wildly recruited by every high school in South Central, disappointed a lot of people when he chose to go to Grant High School, miles away in the San Fernando Valley. Grant was one of the two top academic schools in Los Angeles; Chris wanted to get an education.

Today, he has a PhD. Dr. Chris Esteves is a minister, and he and his wife, who have been married for more than twenty years, have three beautiful daughters. In his sermons, he often talks about his juvenile delinquency and how Carl helped him turn things around. Yes, the branches on the Challengers tree were definitely growing and flourishing, I am happy and proud to say.

12

Aiming Higher

Often people ask me, "What school did you go to?" and I tell them, "The school of Life." I learn by doing.

—Lou Dantzler

In the fall of 1974, I got a phone call from Toby Walker.

"Lou," he said, "I just wanted to tell you how happy I am with what you've done with the club. What you've been able to do in such a short period of time is remarkable; I mean that."

I was very touched. "But Toby," I protested, "I wouldn't have been anywhere without all you've done for us."

"Oh, now, you know that's not true," he laughed. "If it wasn't me, it would have been someone else you dragged down there, believe me!"

We both laughed for a moment.

"Which brings me to why I'm calling," Toby paused. "Barb and I are moving to Newport Beach in a few weeks. I won't be able to be involved with the club anymore. I'm out."

I was thunderstruck. More than that, though, I was anxious. For the past four years, Toby had been my rock, my sounding board, my chief fund-raiser, and the person I turned to for advice the most. And Toby, I found, never gave me bad advice. I had come to rely on him so much and learned so much from him that I didn't know if I could run the club without him.

I credited him with taking our fledgling club to its current level; I talked to him every other day and depended on his support and input, and now he was leaving. I was devastated.

"Now listen, Lou," Toby said. "I don't want to come back and see you in the same circumstances in twenty years, with this same old raggedy building, always scrambling to meet payroll. You've gotta keep moving upward! Don't go back—go forward! You understand me?"

I understood. I was used to Toby pushing me. Looking back, I can see it was because he had confidence in me, but at the time, I wasn't so sure.

"But Newport is only about an hour away; you could still be involved," I said, giving it one last shot.

"Lou, you're fine now, ready to be on your own. I've been watching you lately, and I think you really have a handle on all this. People give money to people they like, and they like you. The great heartwarming thing about introducing you to people is that you always bond with them in some way. It's not a question of getting dough, and it's not just 'Let me tell you how great it's gonna be.' It's because they like you. They believe in you. When I met you, I liked you and wanted to help. I know other people want to help for the same reason. You've built these relationships, and now they're your own. I know you'll be fine."

There was finality in his voice; I knew there was no changing his mind. He, of course, had all the confidence in the world in me, but that was nothing new. I remembered that it was Toby who said at that first board meeting, after I agreed to become the club's director, "Now we have this $5,000 grant from the Boys Clubs, and we've got Lou who's agreed to lead this." He turned to me. "Remember, Lou? Remember that one day we were sitting around with the kids, and you said, 'See that little girl over in the corner, the one about eight or nine? Well, she just watched her dad get shot last week.'? That's what this place is about—I don't care if they're wholesome or not. I'm just glad they're here."

Then he said to everyone, "And Lou is the one who needs to be here working with these kids. So what are we gonna do for him?"

He challenged the board, and I remember thinking to myself, Damn! This is great; this man has so much faith in me. But a lot of my confidence came from the fact that I had Toby backing me up. I knew I could run the program, no problem, but could I find the money to keep it running?

I always joked with people that we would be happy to operate on a shoestring budget if we could just afford the shoestring. Responding to the needs of almost 1,000 boys and girls—our membership around 1974— required constant fund-raising, and Toby was the master. One of his big scores early on, in addition to finagling his way onto the board of the United Way, was the California Community Fund, which ended up giving us money regularly. In addition, Toby did all of the grant writing in the early days, which was great because I knew nothing about that. I mean, we didn't even have a typewriter. He sat through endless United Way board meetings to make sure we got our share—about $8,000 a year at the time—which ended up covering a good chunk of our operating expenses.

I recalled a conversation Toby and I had had the previous summer during a camping trip for the kids that Carl Moser had arranged to Camp Hess Kramer, a popular destination for white kids from the west side, in the Santa Monica mountains.

"Lou," Toby said when the kids had settled into their cabins after a full day of swimming and hiking, and I was expressing amazement that Carl would arrange such a nice thing for us, "people will want to help you if you do something yourself. That's why I got involved with you. You weren't just sitting around saying, 'Oh, I wish I could help these kids, but no one will give me any money!' No, you went out and did it, and that made people want to help you. You didn't just sit back and wait for me to set everything up before you said, 'Okay, I want to be a part of that.' No, that's not you."

I hadn't really thought of it that way, but he was right. I was never one to sit around and wait for things to happen. I knew that even though I had people like Toby behind me, things weren't going to come easily, that it was always going to be work. And Toby had confidence that I could fly on my own.

It wasn't long before I found out he was right, as usual—I had established enough relationships with people that I was able to carry on without too much of a ripple. However, I still missed him, missed talking to him and bouncing things off him. I took his parting words to me, about moving forward, as a challenge. I vowed that the next time Toby saw the club, he wouldn't recognize it.

⤙

A few weeks after Toby's announcement, I got another important call, this time from Al Secrist, regional service director for the Boys Clubs. He was the one who had come down to Tom Bradley's office when the Boys Clubs of America presented us with that first check for $5,000. Since then, Al and his staff at the regional office had been wonderful, helping me get acquainted with the ins and outs of operating a Boys Club—everything from running programs to staff management to fund-raising. Al also introduced me to other Boys Club directors in my area. I met guys from Hollywood, Santa Monica, East L.A., and Watts, who shared their experiences with me. The learning curve was steep, but everyone made me feel welcome.

That's why I was so excited to hear from Al that I would soon receive an official letter of acceptance as an affiliate of the Boys Clubs of America. I don't know if our process of acceptance was swift or lengthy, but, as I came to understand once I got more involved with the Boys Clubs movement, most clubs are started and supported by organized entities, such as school boards, housing authorities, or service organizations such as the Kiwanis Club or Lions Club, which had contacts and financial backing to get something like a Boys Club off the ground. When I started with those original twelve boys, I had none of that. Challengers was an exception. Apparently, there weren't many guys driving around poor communities in pickup trucks looking for people to help.

Accreditation meant, to me anyway, that I was on the right track and that our club was being recognized for its efforts. It also gave us more credibility when we approached potential donors; everyone knew of the Boys Clubs.

Originally founded in 1860 in Hartford, Connecticut, by a group of well-meaning ladies who invited some street urchins into their homes for tea and cake to get them off the street, the Boys Clubs of America had by 1974 swelled to include more than 1,000 affiliated clubs. Their chief aim, like ours, was to provide safe, positive places for children to go when they weren't at home or school.

For many children, a Boys Club in the neighborhood meant the difference between a life of crime and a life that was productive. Though most early clubs operated fairly independently of one another, they each hit upon almost identical formulas of organization and operation, which came to be recognized as the Boys Club approach. For instance, clubs are centrally located so members can easily walk to them; every child is welcome to join, regardless of race, religion, or background; dues are low and are never considered an important source of operating revenue, nor are there any additional fees for services; a child can come any time the club is open and find something to do (what has come to be known as the "open door" policy); there is a wide variety of activities available; the clubs themselves are privately supported, representing the tradition of volunteerism in America; and finally, the primary mission of each club is guidance and individual service.

Club leaders soon realized that their function was more than taking the children off the streets and providing "fun and games"; they were there to have a positive impact on the children's lives and help them become productive adults.

As the national organization grew during the twentieth century, so did club membership and the organization's dedication to supporting club leaders. As the movement spread westward, regional offices were established with support personnel. Training seminars for program directors and executive directors were organized, providing a wealth of information about how to get the most out of a club's board, how to organize a summer or after-school program, how to design and market a good fund-raiser, and more. Regional service directors like Al Secrist were there to provide leadership, advice, and support, and directors like me turned to them often.

⤬

Thus, the timing of our official affiliation couldn't have been better. I know I could have handled things on my own, and we could have stayed our course in a consistent line, but I wanted to grow, to reach even more at-risk children. Having the Boys Clubs behind us gave us the support we needed to aim higher.

That doesn't mean it was easy, not by any stretch of the imagination. Just hanging out a Boys Club sign didn't mean the money started flowing like a river; for us, it still was more like a trickle. But we were getting better every year, and to me, that's what counts.

Once we became officially affiliated, all sorts of things started to change. For one, I was invited to more meetings and training sessions. The first training session I attended was held in a hotel in San Diego, which the Boys Clubs paid for. I did a lot of listening and observing during those two weeks, and I learned a lot. Most tellingly, I revised the Challengers budget dramatically. Before I left for the training, our budget was about $35,000 a year. When I returned, I tripled it. Part of this had to do with the confidence I gained at the session. When people heard how I had started my club on my own and devised these successful programs myself, they all looked at me in amazement. Most had been hired by club boards and worked at existing clubs. That made me feel good.

By far, though, the biggest eye-opener for me came several months later, in 1975, when I attended my first Boys Clubs National Conference in Chicago. I went with one of our board members and Howard Banks. Other clubs had whole teams of people, but Challengers had just the three of us. Again, thankfully, the national organization paid for our travel expenses; they knew we were still struggling.

Almost as soon as we reached the conference, held in a huge downtown hotel and convention center, with official-looking people in suits all over the place, wearing badges and greeting each other like old friends, I was ready to come home. I'd never felt so out of place in my whole life; I didn't know anyone. After every meeting or seminar I attended, I just went back to my room. Everyone else seemed so busy and important that I didn't want to bother them. I did a lot of listening and observing, though. As much as I learned at the seminars, I learned more from watching other people.

One person I kept a close eye on was Dan Swope, director of the Boys Club in Chicago. He was one of the few other blacks at the conference, and he was impressive. I toured his shining, orderly, well-run facility, with its in-house radio station that broadcast simultaneously at the conference, and I was blown away. So this is what potential looks like, I thought. Man, I'm gonna have this one day, too.

I watched how Swope and another black man, Dick Jordan, a national staff member from Boys Clubs headquarters, moved through this confer-ence with all the confidence in the world, and it really impressed me. Someone introduced me to the two of them, a "Hello, how are you doing?" sort of thing, but that was it. I was also impressed by Jesse Jackson's key-note address, and I went home determined to take Challengers to the next level.

And just in time. That July, gang violence escalated to some of the bloodiest levels yet seen in our neighborhood, an area already reeling from recent increases in gang battles. According to Rock, who lived smack in the middle of it, a turf war started between two rival gangs, and the neighborhood from 48th to 54th streets and Figueroa to Vermont became a virtual war zone. The territorial dispute erupted into a full-scale, daily barrage of tit-for-tat shootings. These retaliatory shootouts occurred in the front yards and on the doorsteps of homes just steps from our club and eventually culminated in the death of one boy who was shot and killed on his own front porch, around the corner from Challengers.

The police stepped in at that point and were able to calm the situation down. Unfortunately, it felt to us like the calm before the storm.

13

Reaching Out with Hoops and Hope

Sometimes I say to people who want to help, "We're walking in this direction. Want to go for a walk?"

—Lou Dantzler

In the fall of 1975, we did our best to put the summer's violence behind us. It was time for our annual awards banquet fund-raiser, something we'd been doing since 1971. This time, however, I wanted a bigger, better event than we'd ever had before, something that would not only generate a lot of money and publicity but would also encourage people to come down to the club to see for themselves what we were doing.

Up until this point, our fund-raising activities revolved around my presentations to the United Way and different events the parents put on, such as our annual pancake breakfasts, held each summer around Sports Day. The breakfasts didn't generate big dollars, but they were still one of my favorite events because they brought together the community; people from all over the neighborhood lined up around the block once they smelled the bacon and sausage frying. The first year we did it, it was an ad hoc sort of affair where we spooned pancake batter into frying pans heated on camp stoves—it took forever. In the second or third year, the International House of Pancakes began donating the batter, along with a professional-grade batter dropper and cooktop just like they used in the restaurant. We could feed more people, and it helped a lot.

We tried other ways to bring in money, too. For a few years, I sold Christmas trees on our lot, flocked them and everything, and I think one year we cleared about $2,500. That was our monthly payroll at the time. Another year, we held a carnival with rides and other attractions. It was a hit with the kids but also attracted the wrong element. I worried so much about everyone's safety that we didn't do it again.

Sears was very helpful at that time, too. In addition to giving us toys for Santa to hand out to the kids at Christmas, they let us set up a wrapping station in their store on Pico. We bought wrapping paper, ribbon, and tape, and Sears let us have the gift-wrapping concession for the whole store for the entire season. Parent volunteers, staff, and even some of the older club members worked there every day during store hours. After the expense of the wrapping paper and other supplies, we cleared $5,000 or $6,000, a nice sum.

All these fund-raisers were great, and I especially liked how they got the members and the parents involved in helping me build up the club, but it soon became apparent that in order for us to expand and improve our building and programs, we had to start attracting dollars from people outside the community, people who could afford an ongoing financial commitment. So we decided that instead of the usual dinner, we would do something special.

We booked the grand banquet room at the Hilton Hotel near the University of Southern California, about a mile away from us. That alone let people know we were taking the event up a level. I knew that just to pay for the room, we had to reach out to more people—not just the parents and loyal supporters who came year after year. I talked to everyone—board members, parents, friends—about whom to invite and how to get them there, and I eventually struck pay dirt. Someone gave me the name of a public relations man named Warren Lanier, who represented some of the popular black entertainers of the time. I thought it was a long shot, but what did I have to lose? "The worst they can do is say no," Toby Walker always said—so I gave Warren a call.

The man on the other end of the line was so friendly and enthusiastic that I invited him to come down and meet me at the club so I could show him around. To my surprise, he accepted.

That day, as I gave him the tour and told him what we had been doing and would be doing for the kids, I was bowled over by his enthusiasm for Challengers.

"You know," he said, "I'm from the streets of Philadelphia, and I know that what you're providing is exactly what these kids need. I'm very aware of what it means for kids to have a neighborhood club to belong to because, as a kid, I participated in programs after church and after school just like what you're doing, and it was great. As poor as we were, our community was rich with people who wanted to make sure every kid had a chance to be somebody." He particularly related to my struggle to help these children since he knew as well as I did that South Central, unlike his neighborhood in Philly, was not rich with people willing to help kids. And he was in the position to help us.

"We're having a dinner in a few weeks," I said as we stood in the gym that day, "to give awards to the kids who are doing outstanding in our program. I want to get a couple of celebrities to come to the dinner to encourage the kids and make them feel special; they'll help us attract other people, and we'll raise more money."

Warren bought into the idea right away. Within days of his visit, he called me and said baseball legend Maury Wills and football great Fred Williamson would come to the dinner and act as emcees.

I was thrilled. This would be the first time anyone famous had anything to do with the club. Wills, who was the hero of the Los Angeles Dodgers, and Williamson, a football legend turned movie star, were more than I could have hoped for.

⤳

We had a packed house for the dinner. Sheer Ecstasy kicked things off, as they had every year, and then I let Wills and Williamson take over.

Warren had talked to them beforehand about our organization, and both said they'd be happy to get up and say something to encourage the kids. When I saw the looks on those kids' faces while Wills was speaking, how impressed they were that a celebrity was talking to them and encouraging them, I said to Warren, "Look at them. Isn't it amazing? Those kids are just awestruck. I wish there were some way I could get these guys to get involved on a more regular basis, to do something that would really uplift the kids and the community."

Warren, who agreed with me, said, "Lou, all athletes and celebrities travel on an ego trip. What we need to do is take advantage of this situation, challenge them in public so they can't back down." Apparently, that gave him an idea, because the next thing he did was turn to Williamson and say, "You know, Fred, Maury just said that he wished there were some way he could help more. You know that celebrity basketball team I helped you organize? When you get up to speak, why don't you challenge Maury to bring some baseball players to play your team in a celebrity basketball game to help the kids?"

Williamson must have thought this was a good idea, because the next thing I knew, he got up and challenged Wills to get some of his baseball associates to play him and his celebrity team in a charity game, with all the proceeds going to Challengers.

"You're on," Wills said as cheers and applause thundered through the banquet room. It was unbelievable—these guys actually were going to come down and help us out!

Well, it didn't take long for this to get around; word spread like wildfire through the community. Williamson and Wills made good on their promise and brought their teams down a month after the banquet, on January 17, 1976, to participate in our first Celebrity Basketball Game, which was held in our little gym with its linoleum floor and was a complete sellout. We had to borrow bleachers from a nearby school to seat the more than 600 people who started lining up early in the morning to get in. To my knowledge, this was the first time anything like this had ever happened in South Central. Celebrities and sports stars tended to avoid this area, though it was only a few miles from where they lived.

For some reason, Wills, who was a CBS commentator at the time, wasn't able to come to the game. But instead of backing out entirely, he called on his friend Frank Robinson, former baseball MVP who also had the distinction of being Major League Baseball's first black manager, to coach in his place. His team of athletes was stacked with names I had read about and seen on television for years: the Los Angeles Rams' all-pro Tom Mack, the Dodgers' Willie Crawford, the Baltimore Orioles' Tommy Davis, the San Francisco Giants' Von Joshua, and former UCLA All-American basketball player and actor Mike Warren.

Fred Williamson's team wasn't lacking in the celebrity department, either. Far from it. His team included a young actor named Lawrence Hilton-Jacobs, who was currently starring in one of our members' favorite shows, *Welcome Back, Kotter*, and Johnny Brown, who was appearing in *Good Times*. Other actors rounded out the team, including none other than comedian Richard Pryor.

Seeing Pryor, who was on his way to becoming one of the hottest and most popular entertainers of the time, walk into our gym, josh with folks, and ad lib the physical comedy that made him famous, was surreal to me, not to mention hilarious. He couldn't play basketball worth a damn, but that made it all the more fun.

Early on, it was apparent that Williamson's team of celebrities was no match for Robinson's team of professional athletes. No matter. At the end of the first quarter, when Williamson's team was trailing 20–8, Pryor, whose jersey number was 000, was asked what he was going to do to turn things around.

"This is part of our strategy," Pryor cracked. "We're letting them *think* they're good. We're gonna kill 'em. They haven't got a chance. The score will be something like 90–23!" Everyone in earshot was dying with laughter. The truth was, the only time Pryor's team managed to put some points on the board in the second half was when Pryor staged a game-stopping stunt, like pulling down the pants of the guy trying to make a shot. That broke the concentration of the opposing team all right—unfortunately, it broke the concentration of his own team, too! In the fourth quarter, he was the top point maker for his team, but it wasn't enough to save them. They lost 72–46.

"I usually score 50 to 60 points a game," he deadpanned to sports reporter Brad Pye of the *Los Angeles Sentinel*, who covered the game and doubled as the announcer. "But I had to give the guys a break. I didn't want to hurt their feelings; I didn't want it to get in the papers that Robinson's team lost. He might lose his job!" Everyone was busting up, including Robinson.

There was so much good feeling at the club that day. I mean, this was long before TV shows like *Battle of the Network Stars* and celebrity golf tournaments became common. People in the community were beside themselves that celebrities such as Pryor, Robinson, Williamson, and even Richard Roundtree from *Shaft* took the time to come down to South Central. No one ever came to South Central, but here they were, parking their beautiful Cadillacs and Lincolns and Mercedeses in our dusty parking lot. Roundtree couldn't play because of an injured knee, but he came anyway and agreed to act as referee, along with news anchorman Larry McCormick.

They all came, and they were gracious and friendly and willing to mix with the awestruck kids. Pryor even chatted with a few of the neighborhood folks while he was changing in the bathroom, making jokes and signing autographs.

I know everyone had a great time, from the celebrities and athletes right on down to the youngest members, who, for the first time, got a chance to meet and see and touch real black celebrities and heroes—people who looked like them, came from similar backgrounds, and went on to achieve success. I know it fired the ambitions and imaginations of many of our members at the time, including Carl, of course, who had such a passion for basketball. Kenny and the other members of Sheer Ecstasy mingled with actors and singers whose acknowledgment meant the world to them.

We charged only $3 a ticket for adults and $2 for children, though we could have asked much more. We wanted the game to be affordable to average people from the community, so we kept the price low. The local Anheuser Busch distributorship, Westside Distributors, underwrote the whole game in addition to providing refreshments and equipment. That was the beginning of a fruitful relationship with Westside's Ed Lara, which lasted more than two decades. That help meant that what we earned at the door, we kept.

For us, though, it wasn't just about the money. It was also about the recognition this event gave to our club and the sense of pride it instilled in our neighborhood. For months, even years, people talked about that day. Again and again, I heard, "Lou, you must have some amazing connections!" and while it was actually Warren Lanier who got things started, I soon found that the game had ongoing benefits.

Part of my plan from the time I formed this organization was to get successful adults—they didn't have to be rich and famous, just hardworking, law-abiding, caring people—to get involved with the kids and share their life experiences in hopes it would expand the kids' horizons and give them the confidence to achieve their dreams. For a long time, we had people from places such as the telephone company and McDonald's and other local businesses volunteering to mentor teens, and it really had an impact. We even had police officers from our precinct, which at that time was the Southwest Division, run by Capt. Steve Downing, stop by and take an interest. One early field trip in the late 1960s was a tour of Capt. Downing's stationhouse, and I introduced the kids to some of the police officers. I wanted the groups to have positive impressions of each other. I also wanted to let the police know what I was doing so that if someone saw a black man riding around in a truck with a group of teens, it wasn't cause for alarm. After we got our building, we had regular friendly visits from local LAPD officers, who stopped by to shoot pool with the kids.

At the game, as I was talking to and thanking the celebrities for coming down to help us out, I made my pitch about coming back on an ordinary day to get to know our program and some of the kids. I didn't really expect any of them to make any sort of commitment, so you can imagine how surprised I was when a few weeks after the game, I got a call from Richard Roundtree, who said he was coming down to see us. He told me how impressed he was with what our club was doing and how well behaved our members were.

Thus began what soon became Richard's weekly trips to the club. He came for a few hours every Wednesday when he wasn't shooting a movie. At first, of course, the kids were a bit starstruck and would stand off to the side and stare at the man they knew as Shaft, but after a while, everyone began calling him by his first name, and he really mixed it up with the kids.

We became used to the sight of him pulling up and getting out of his car in his tracksuit, ready to play a game of basketball or participate in one of our daily afternoon rap sessions. He was always very low key and unassuming, and I think that's why the kids warmed up to him so much and trusted him. He didn't do this with television cameras watching, mind you; he truly wanted to participate in the lives of these kids.

∽

After a couple of months or so, Richard and I had a conversation about my desire to get some of the older teens prepared for real-life situations, such as job interviews or applying to college, and he agreed to help. The next time he came, he brought a whole mess of electronic equipment with him.

"It's videotape recording equipment," he explained. "It's just been sitting around collecting cobwebs."

He taught us how to use it, and we set it up in a room to use for mock job interviews. Oh, this was something! Kids could see right away how they looked and sounded on tape. I had shot many club events, such as our Sports Day, with a 16mm movie camera—no sound—but then I had to have the film developed and set up a projector so we could watch it. The new videotaping equipment was something else entirely! We could shoot the kids doing their interviews and show them the result immediately—it was just like being on TV. Once word of this got around, everyone wanted to do mock interviews, some of which Richard himself conducted.

I was really impressed by how down-to-earth he was. We talked about everything and soon became friends. He even came to our house for dinner a couple of times, and he brought his girlfriend at the time, actress and professional tennis player Cathy Lee Crosby. Soon she started coming with Richard to the club, teaching the kids how to play tennis on the court we rigged up with a net in the gym.

In addition to admiring how down-to-earth and easygoing Richard was, I was really impressed with how well he related to the kids. When he said something, they listened. He shared my philosophy that the best way to reach kids was to just spend time with them and listen to them instead of telling them what to do. "I like just being here and showing them that someone is interested in them," he said to me one day, and I couldn't have agreed more.

Richard's involvement didn't end with just coming to the club. On one of his regular visits, he noticed the mini-bike squad performing their precision drills. You could tell he was impressed by how seriously the boys took their membership in this squad. After talking with Kenny and some of the other boys, it soon became apparent to him that what they wanted more than anything was the chance to take the bikes out into the open somewhere.

Richard offered to take them all to the desert. Those boys came back so dusty and tired and happy that they all decided to do it again. Getting out in the wilderness, away from honking horns, police sirens, and brick walls, and having the chance to breathe fresh air and travel as far as the road would take them was an invaluable experience that kids like Kelvin remember to this day. Not to mention having a celebrity escort, who by this time had appeared in the landmark television miniseries *Roots.* Having an icon like that take an interest in them did wonders for their self-esteem.

One day, Richard brought a friend along. When I saw the familiar car pull up, I went out to the parking lot to say hello as I always did. When I saw the person getting out of the passenger side of the car, I stopped dead in my tracks.

"Lou," Richard said, "I'd like you to meet a friend of mine."

And there stood the most elegant, well-mannered, handsome man in the middle of our hot, dusty playground, a man whom I had admired and respected for so many years. It was Sidney Poitier, who was to Hollywood what Jackie Robinson was to Major League Baseball: simply put, the man who broke the color barrier. Right up there with Martin Luther King Jr., this was a hero I never thought I'd have the chance to meet, let alone see at work!

Richard and I took him on a tour of the building, and in that unmistakable voice of his, he kept telling me how impressed he was with my work. *Impressed with me?* I kept thinking. I must be dreaming. I mean, I had just seen him in his latest movie, *A Piece of the Action,* in which he costarred with Bill Cosby. It was about two conmen who become involved with helping inner-city children, and it had a great impact on me, especially since Poitier directed it. It was one of my favorite films. And here he was, in our club!

Like Richard, he didn't bring any movie-star attitude to the club. He was there for the kids. He took the time to stop and talk to many of the members that day, some of whom were too young to know who he was, and then I took him upstairs to our library, where he sat with the kids, answered their questions, read them a few books, and even played a game or two of chess.

He came for another visit months later—"I just dropped by to see you," he said—and again, he was very pleasant, down-to-earth, and inspirational (not to mention generous, giving us a sizeable donation), and the children really responded to him. To me, if ever there was a person who exemplified a positive black male role model, it was Sidney Poitier. His willingness to come down and give something back—like Richard Roundtree, Maury Wills, Fred Williamson, and all the rest—was something that the children and other people of this community really appreciated and were proud of. Not only that, but these icons of our time demonstrated to our members that people who looked like them could make it out and live successful, productive lives—a lesson I hoped they wouldn't soon forget.

14

Having Choices, Making Choices

I am going to do everything I can so these kids have all the tools they need to succeed, and it will be their choice whether they want to use them or not.

—CARL REED

Ten years later, in 1986, when the euphoria of that first Celebrity Basketball Game was a fading memory, I stood in that very same gym and, for the first time in many years, began to despair.

About a year or so earlier—I can't recall exactly when—I starting hearing about something called crack. More and more often, it was cited as the reason for local violence, and I finally asked some people in the neighborhood what it was.

"It's the latest drug," I was told. "People are taking to this more than marijuana and PCP. It's starting to cause all sorts of trouble." While this sounded alarming, I didn't pay too much attention once I learned that crack was a form of cocaine. I mean, where would folks in this neighborhood find the money to support a coke habit? Wasn't cocaine for movie stars? I figured folks would try it a couple of times to act cool and then go back to their sherm sticks (marijuana dipped in PCP) or bottles of Night Train.

Well, I figured wrong. Like almost everyone else, I underestimated crack. What most of us found out too late was that sometime in the early

1980s, some enterprising genius had come up with a way to convert expensive cocaine into a cost-effective, potent, highly addictive drug for the masses. It was the drug equivalent of Chinese takeout: It was fast and cheap, and soon after you finished using it, you were hungry for more. It caught on and spread through South Central like wildfire.

Crack can be made in any kitchen by mixing cocaine with water and either ammonia or baking soda. The mixture is heated on a stove to remove the hydrochloride (crack got its name from the cracking sound it makes when it's being cooked), resulting in a crystalline substance that can be smoked. Smoking it, rather than injecting or snorting it, gives crack its awesome power, since gases travel more quickly to the brain, creating a greater rush.

As I stood in the gym that day, I wondered how much lower our community could sink. Lately, with alarming frequency, I'd seen one home after another, one family after the next, succumb to the scourge. Lives were lost, but so was a way of life—simple civility.

Families were torn apart as parents of young children became hooked, as did singles in their twenties who had the income to support their habits, then it was just a matter of time before it reached the schools. Kids began supporting their habits through petty crime and then selling the drug themselves.

And it wasn't just families; whole neighborhoods were torn apart. Throughout South Central, rental properties were quickly transformed from family homes into crack houses. Newly prosperous dealers were willing to spend a few hundred dollars a month for inconspicuous single-family houses to use as their bases of operation, so upstanding, hardworking people saw a sudden increase in traffic on their normally quiet streets. For several months, I'd been seeing an ice cream truck endlessly circle the streets of our neighborhood, but it never seemed to stop for any kids. I only saw it in the evenings as I was locking up, and when it did stop, customers didn't come away eating Popsicles or snow cones.

Yes, I had definitely underestimated crack. I still can't believe the speed at which its devastation spread. When I was in school, I learned in science class that something as small as a pebble rolling down an unstable hill could trigger a landslide that could take out the whole side of a mountain. Well, crack was that pebble. What looked insignificant at first destroyed nearly everything in its path.

As if that weren't enough, crack brought an even more dire consequence: increasing violence. It didn't take long for the Crips and Bloods to realize the economic potential of crack. Battles intensified as each set vied for part of the financial action; gangs were becoming moneymaking enterprises. With their increased cash flow, they took ever more deadly steps to protect their territories. Unfortunately, knives, fists, and the occasional revolver—the weapons of choice for gangsters of the recent past—were no longer enough. When crack dropped into the community, so did automatic weapons.

Like many in our area, the first time I heard the *rat-tat-tat* of automatic weapons fire, I thought I was hearing firecrackers left over from the Fourth of July. Then came the police helicopter banking in tight circles overhead and the squad cars zooming down the street, sirens blaring. This was no childish prank. Ambulances came and went away empty. The coroner followed.

It was also around this time that I began to see a gradual decline in our enrollment. For the first time in the history of our club, our waiting list no longer numbered in the hundreds. Attendance in our after-school program had dipped from a daily high of 400 to just over a couple hundred a day. When I went to schools to talk up our programs, only a handful of kids showed up. When I went to parents' homes to try to get them involved at the club, I was met with dazed expressions. Slowly, it dawned on me: Crack was winning.

More and more, people saw selling drugs as a viable way to make a living—better than having a part-time job and working toward a high school diploma. I don't think anyone realized the toll that this feel-good drug would eventually take on our community. No one yet understood that the damage alcohol can do over ten or twenty years, crack can do in a year or less. Everything about crack was quicker, costlier, and worst of all, more violent.

Teeming with little squadrons of middlemen armed to the teeth, our community had truly become a battle zone. The storm of violence had arrived.

It was depressing. It was dangerous. All the hope we in the community had had at the celebrity game a decade ago, when our club received a much-needed shot in the arm, had all but evaporated in the face of this deadly epidemic.

In the intervening years, our club had received terrific support from people such as basketball superstar Magic Johnson, who came down with Mayor Bradley to mix it up with the kids, play a little ball, and show them that success can happen for kids from a Boys Club like them. We had other high-profile donors, too, including the Los Angeles Olympic Committee.

In 1984, the Olympics brought hundreds of millions of dollars into Los Angeles, and a tiny bit managed to trickle down our way. The Olympic Committee donated and built a $35,000, state-of-the-art, professional-grade hardwood basketball court to replace the linoleum floor in our gym. Peter Uberroth, the committee head, who drove by our club every day on his way to events at Exposition Park and the Coliseum north of us, came to the dedication ceremony. I have Bob Gay, field deputy to Councilman Gilbert Lindsay, who sat on our board, to thank for getting the committee's help. There's nothing like hearing a basketball being bounced on a real hardwood floor, then having it spring back up to meet your hand in an instant, just like in the NBA. The kids went crazy for that floor, proud to have something as nice as they would have in any suburban high school gym.

The new floor was great, but it was no match for a crack epidemic. For the first time, I didn't feel optimistic about the future of the hundreds of children who spent their afternoons running, skipping, dancing, striding, and fast breaking across that floor. It was hard to be optimistic when our community was being compared by some to Beirut or Vietnam. There was a difference, but not one that worked to our advantage: A soldier wounded three times in Vietnam was sent home. In South Central, there was no escape: Home was the battleground.

Once-beautiful Craftsman homes were fortified with bars on their windows and doors. Rusting fences surrounded the perimeters of post-age-stamp yards. Streets were marked as "territories" by jumbles of words and symbols spray painted on every available wall and sign, and enemies who dared to enter forbidden territory did so at their own risk. Ever-increasing numbers of young "soldiers" patrolled blocks of decaying concrete. None of the property was truly theirs, but what they did own was the respect and fear of the people they held hostage to their ever-increasing brutality. Countless lives, innocent and otherwise, were sacrificed in the name of "putting in work" for their neighborhood and strengthening their gangs.

On quiet afternoons just before three o'clock, when school let out and hundreds of children came streaming and screaming through our doors, I sometimes liked to walk through the gym, hearing the faint echoes of my footsteps as I thought about how I could reach out to these kids who, at ever younger ages, were being lost to the streets.

<hr />

When Carl Reed joined in the early seventies, he was not yet fifteen. Back then, I still had time before he moved into manhood to shape his character and show him a more positive path. The harsh realities of that time consisted of petty crime, alcohol and marijuana abuse, and fistfights. A decade and a half later, I was dealing with a neighborhood overtaken by car-jackings and armed robberies, PCP and crack abuse, drive-by shootings, and third-grade kids getting jumped on. Now, if a kid like Carl came into the club for the first time at fifteen, it would be too late.

So far, I had been simply responding to the crisis as things popped up—comforting a seven-year-old whose mother hadn't been home in days because she was off smoking; trying to get help for another boy whose older brother was pressuring him to join his gang by beating him up whenever he came home; trying to get a mother to take more interest in her son, who was a child of rape—those kinds of things. Parent involvement was also at an all-time low. When I had our regular monthly parent meetings, the same eight or ten parents showed up.

After all these years of building relationships with the parents and kids, I figured that eventually people would understand that in order to belong to this club, they had to agree to the terms: Parents had to be involved on a daily basis in the growth and development of their children. Most, unfortunately, had to be convinced. Once they were, however, and they saw the positive changes in their children, even some of the most recalcitrant parents (or uncles or grandparents or aunts or older brothers) bought into the program, and some even helped recruit more kids. But it didn't happen overnight.

I remember sitting in Catherine Williams's house a few blocks away from our club and being almost in tears—I had had a parent meeting, and only a half dozen people showed despite the fact that we had more than 500 active club members.

"How can they possibly expect their kids to do anything positive with their lives if they don't take the time to support what I'm trying to do for them?" I asked Catherine, one of my strongest supporters and a neighborhood activist whose mission was to improve the community through better policing and better cooperation among families. We were of like minds.

"You just keep doing what you're doing," she said in her calm, soothing voice. "What you do needs to be done."

I had relied on Catherine's support a lot in those first few years. She and her husband were plugged into the community in ways that were extremely helpful to me. They were in some ways like parents to me, and I always left their immaculate house feeling better than when I arrived. While I was always confident about what the children of this community needed, it was just nice to have someone like Catherine to back me up those few times when it got too much for me.

Lately, I had been feeling that way more and more often as the Crips and Bloods went on a recruiting binge and neighborhood after neighborhood fell. Children, boys and girls alike, desperate for a sense of belonging, protection, and respect, felt compelled to join. For kids in this neighborhood, joining a gang was as natural a rite of passage as hanging out at the mall was to suburban kids. In order to really improve things and make a dent in the madness, I knew I needed to take a more proactive approach.

⤙

"Oh, Lord, give me strength," I whispered as I bent down to rub a scuff mark off the gym floor.

"Talkin' to yourself again?" came a voice suddenly from over by the open door. The voice sounded familiar, and I looked up to see who it was. Unfortunately, because of the bright afternoon light behind the speaker and the relative darkness of the gym, I couldn't see who it was.

"What, you don't recognize me after all this time, Lou?" the man said in a teasing tone, coming closer.

I was used to this. Scarcely a week went by that a young man in his twenties or early thirties didn't wander in to see me. Former members, they would drop in to reminisce and see what I was doing. It was great to see those guys, many of whom I didn't recognize because when they had left, they were little more than skinny messes of elbows and knees with peach fuzz sprouting on their upper lips. They came back all filled out and dressed up, ready to show me the men they had become. They all remembered me—there was only one of me!—but it was impossible for me to remember all of them. There'd been literally thousands.

Nevertheless, I was happy and proud to see all of them—happy that they had made it out of adolescence alive and well and were prospering, and proud that they came back to show me.

"Hmm," I said, launching into my routine as the visitor came closer, "I don't recognize you yet. Wait, turn around!" And we both broke up laughing. This was the joke shared by all former members of the club from the 1970s. In those early years, I needed to give some of the kids a good slap on the backside when they crossed the line. For those who made crossing that line a habit, the joke was that I knew their backsides better than any other part of them.

I remember one kid in particular from those early days. Tracy Taylor grew up on 48th Street in the midst of all the gangs, but he came to the club religiously and generally was a good kid. One day, I got a phone call from the lady who worked in the liquor store across the street from us on 51st. It seems she'd just caught Tracy stuffing candy in his pockets and making a dash for the door. He had his club shirt on, so when she caught him, she called me instead of the police. I went over there and brought him back to the club, gave him a few swats, and then had a talk with him. Years later, he came to the club for a visit.

"You know, Lou, that was the last time I ever stole anything," Tracy said gratefully, proud to be able to show his own clean-cut fourteen-year-old son the place where he grew up and pleased to tell me about his corporate job and his happy, sixteen-year marriage. "You saved me," he said.

Tracy was lucky. South Central kids who got caught shoplifting usually spent time in the criminal justice system, which for juveniles meant being booked and fingerprinted, being sent to juvenile hall, and facing a hearing. The judge could order the teen to be sent to juvenile lockup or one of the several youth detention camps operated throughout Los Angeles County, which often did more to turn troubled kids into hardened criminals than the streets did. Tracy's membership in the club meant his boyish mistake didn't lead to becoming another crime statistic. All he had to face was a few quick swats; he didn't have to learn the hard way.

"C'mon now, Lou—you must recognize me by now!" the young man in front of me said as he laughed and turned around.

"Man, look at you!" I said to Carl Reed as we hugged each other. "The last time I saw you, you were a skinny little thing with a huge natural, and now look," I said proudly as I took in the close-cropped, neatly dressed Carl who stood ramrod straight before me.

"Where you been, man?" I asked. I hadn't seen Carl since he quit in the late 1970s. The argument he had with Michael over Chris Esteves was the beginning of the end of Carl working at the club. He had put everything he had into coaching our basketball team. He'd had some terrific success and really seemed to learn a lot by following my example of visiting members' homes and trying to make sure they went to school and made good grades. But he was also attending junior college at the time and was soon burning the candle at both ends. Something had to give, and he decided for his future that he needed to go to college full time. It was the decision I would have made for him, though he made it all on his own. He planned to marry a girl he knew from the club and go to Cal State Chico, in northern California, which he did. The last I had heard about him was that he dropped out of college a few months shy of getting his degree because his wife became pregnant, and he wanted to support his family.

"So I joined the Air Force, Lou," he told me as we stood there in the gym. "I've been stationed at Travis near San Francisco for the past few years. But then they wanted to transfer me to Germany. I didn't want my kid growing up as a military brat, so I took a discharge instead and got a civilian job there in the aerospace industry."

"That's great, man. I'm proud of you," I said. "So what are you doing here?"

Carl sighed. "Well, something happened last December that really woke me up. The doctor found something in my colon and said they were going to have to do surgery to find out if it was cancer or not." He paused, then spoke in a low voice. "You know, with all the crazy situations I was in when I was younger, this was the first time I ever felt really scared that I was going to die. Here I'm only twenty-eight years old and facing cancer. I mean—a gangster looking to jump me? That I knew how to fight, but cancer? No way. It freaked me, Lou, it really did. And so I did what my momma always taught me to do, and that's look to the Lord. I said, 'Lord, if you bring me through this, I want to go home. I want to go home and do what I was meant to do, which is help kids in the community, give them direction on what I went through and try to spare them.' So I went through the operation and they cut the polyp out, and it was benign. The next week, I left there, and here I am."

His words echoed off the walls of the gym. The Lord truly works in mysterious ways, I thought. Here I was, beginning to despair, and for some reason, by divine intervention or whatever, Carl appears to give something back.

"Oh, your coming back home is a godsend," I said as we walked back to my office. "Things have really changed since you've been away. When you were here, we had problems with the gangs out there and all and people getting into trouble, but it was nothing like it is now. Our membership is actually flat for the first time in our history. Kids are not joining here at eight, nine, ten anymore, and if you don't get them by that time, you might as well forget it. Kids aren't joining because they're making money in those streets, and they like it. How are we supposed to compete with that?"

"I know, Lou. I know what you mean," he answered, then began to tell me how hard it was when he was in his senior year of college and was getting all this pressure to support his wife and their baby on the way.

"Everyone was pissed at me for leaving college," he told me. "My mom, everyone. But I had to take responsibility, so I decided to go into the Air Force. I wanted to take care of my son. And people here said, 'Why are you gonna do this?' I mean, I could have gone back to selling drugs—I had a connection where I could have sold coke and made a great living—but I said, 'No, it isn't right.' In the Air Force, I listened and watched the other guys who had it all together—just like I used to watch you, Lou, and saw how you did things. And so I studied and passed my tests and kept getting promoted, and I followed orders and learned discipline and how to be on time. Can you believe it, Lou? And you always said I was a discipline problem," he laughed.

It was true. Carl had always had trouble following someone else's orders, but this was a different man, someone who had grown up and gotten a little life experience outside the confines of the straitjacket of South Central. He epitomized all that I was hoping for all the kids in the program.

"Listen," I said. "We really need someone like you now. I mean, you just said you understand that temptation of street life. You lived it. Most kids here see the ballers cruising around in their $100 tennis shoes and shiny cars and then go home on the bus to an empty fridge and wonder why they're staying in school when they could be making a couple hundred a day on the corner. It's becoming harder and harder to compete with that.

"I mean, I had a meeting the other day in west L.A., and as I drove down one nice little street, I saw these white kids with their backpacks and clean clothes running through a pile of leaves on their way to school. The smiles on their faces and the confidence they have—I mean, they just have no idea. Around here, kids walking to school keep their heads down; there's no running or horseplay. They're afraid, and the sad part is, they take this all as a natural part of life; they don't know any differently.

"Yesterday, I was driving to the bank down the block and saw a group of boys—they couldn't have been more than eight years old—playing handball over the chalk outline of a dead body. There were bloodstains and everything. Now, is this the life for an eight-year-old? Or a seven-year-old, or six? I'm telling you, unless we do something, we're gonna lose all these kids."

I paused for a minute and then looked at Carl. "We could really use you here, man. Will you think about it?"

Carl turned to me, and on his face I saw a look that I can only describe as a mixture of surprise, happiness, and pride. "When should I start?"

I started Carl as a recreation leader, in charge of organizing all the sports activities, and he took to it like a fish to water. Within weeks, he made changes that reenergized that whole program. Kids couldn't wait to play with Carl.

I took him with me when I went into the schools, and he was such a natural that he was soon doing it on his own. Carl could definitely speak the language of the kids coming up; he was one of the OGs—"original gangsters"—and he knew exactly what these children faced. He was living proof that they could make it out of these streets—that anyone could.

"I had a lot of anger," he would say. "I was always beating up somebody, 'cause I wouldn't take nothin' from nobody. And then I got to know some criminals; they saw I was tough, and they wanted me on their side. So I mixed with the wrong element because to be the nice guy my mother raised me to be wasn't possible. I joined Challengers because I realized I wanted to belong to something positive." Those kids listened.

Carl's old friends sent their kids to the club. "Reed is up there, he's my boy," they'd say to their children. "Go up there and see him; I don't want you to be like me." His old gang friends finally saw the value of what he had done, and they were proud, too, if a little perplexed at how he was able to accomplish all he had.

As I always said, Carl was a natural-born leader, and smart. If he had been from a different neighborhood, he probably would have ended up with a Harvard MBA and running a big company. But Carl and I both believe that God had a different plan for him, that he was put in this neighborhood and went through all he did so he could teach what he'd learned to those coming up after him. Carl was smart enough to take what both his mother and I had to offer and seize it.

"You can't let up on these kids," he told me one day that summer. "Just like you didn't let up one me, Lou. You gotta push them to take education seriously. There's so much competing for their time. Some of these kids are seventeen or eighteen when they finally realize the importance of education, and by then it's too late. And they should be mad. Mad at their parents. Mad at the schools that failed them. But they won't be mad at the club, because I am going to do everything I can for these kids so they have choices."

As he was talking, I remembered what his mother had told me when Carl was at the height of his gangbanging.

"I never give up," she said. "Never. Because every night at ten o'clock, if he isn't at home, I go and find him. I've done that for a year. And he thinks I will get tired and give him to the street, but I never will. I tell him, 'You're gonna get tired, not me. If you do something, I'm gonna know it.'

"And he complains, 'But everybody else lets their kids steal bikes and stuff.'

" 'Well, not you.' I tell him."

She was a strong lady, and Carl had the wisdom to finally listen to her. Now here he was, giving it all back. I couldn't have been prouder if he had been my own son.

It wasn't long before Carl moved up the ranks to program director, in charge of all the programs and staff. Then I sent him to executive management school, one of the most advanced training programs within the Boys Clubs. When he came back from that, there was no stopping him. After some discussion, we took what he learned at the seminars and decided to implement more of the national organization's strategies, such as the Five Core Programs.

The Five Core areas consist mainly of programs that help with character and leadership development, education and career development, health and life skills, the arts and sports, and fitness and recreation. We had been focusing on all these things for years, but what the national Boys Clubs programs offered were easy-to-use plans and resources to organize and implement them. Once we did that, we found we were able to really streamline our organization and use our resources to the fullest. Instead of having kids just come after school and play and maybe do homework, we now had a schedule and a plan for each age group, and the results were amazing.

By the late 1980s, I found I had more time to focus on development and fund-raising because our programs were being run so tightly. We saw a surge in membership—an upward trend that continues to this day. Once again, our waiting list swelled. Once again, I started thinking about expanding the club, and with Carl running things with the kids, I was free to go out and get the money we needed to grow. I wasn't going to let crack win this war without a fight.

15

Envisioning What Could Be

My powers of visualization help me stay on course. Everybody wants to put their ideas on you, everyone wants to change things and confuse things. What I've said before is that if you set your standards and want people to follow those standards, you have to set them and get them to follow it your way. I don't think it's going to be effective any other way. I had a vision about helping kids that started years ago and I never wavered. I had the confidence what I was doing was right.

—Lou Dantzler

One of my favorite memories as a kid was listening to baseball games on the radio at Willie's house. I loved the radio. Although it was only audio, I could picture in my mind everything the players were doing—every pitch, every popup, every steal.

When the broadcasts were over, we would go out and play our own game—"I'm Jackie Robinson, man! I'm Carl Furillo!" We used our imaginations, putting ourselves in our heroes' shoes. We pushed ourselves to become better at what we did. I pictured other things, too, like a better life for myself. Later, when I was the neighborhood gardener and kept running into kids with no direction, I could see ways to help those kids. I didn't have much else, but I had vision.

❧

You don't have to be professionally trained to achieve your goals, you just need imagination—and a willingness to learn and grow. You also have to have enthusiasm—you have to be very up and energetic. Leaders take an active role; they don't sit and wait for things to happen. This doesn't mean, though, that if you're enthusiastic, it's all going to work out. It just helps to stay positive and focused on your vision even when you hit bumps along the way. Sometimes, when I get knocked down or suffer a setback, I take a timeout to think about it. I go through it in my mind, and when I come back to the problem, I'm stronger.

When you're down, I think it's important to picture yourself getting up again, and you'll get there. Sometimes, once you're down, you start to find excuses that keep you from reaching your potential.

What I have tried to teach the kids at Challengers is that part of their plan should be striving for excellence at whatever they do. I tell them, "If you're going to be a janitor, be the best janitor, the best you have the power to be." I advise them to find successful people to pattern themselves after—as I did early on with Toby Walker—and that will help them get to where they need to go.

I wanted our club to be the biggest and the best. Although at the time, I didn't have a plan or know how I was going to get there, I did have a clear vision of how I wanted it to be, and I just kept taking steps in that direction, learning along the way. That's why I'm not totally surprised at how things worked out. It's what I had always envisioned.

I was also fortunate to find people who shared my vision, people who dropped into my life to offer help just when I needed it. It happened when my cousin Willie came back to South Carolina just in time to usher me through my adolescence. It happened when Toby Walker tracked me down and helped me get the club off the ground. It happened when Carl Reed decided to forgo a more lucrative career in the aerospace industry and help me build the club's program. It happened when Kenny Rodgers— who worked for me throughout most of the 1970s—left a burgeoning insurance career to come back in the late 1980s and help me start a new leadership program funded by the McCabe Foundation. Called Leaders in Training, it later became the model for a nationwide program.

And it happened once again in 1988, right around the time an innocent civilian in white, wealthy Westwood, near UCLA, was accidentally killed in a gang shooting; the rest of America discovered that gang violence didn't affect just blacks anymore.

⟿

We'd always had an excellent relationship with the Los Angeles Police Department, particularly in the Southwest Division, from Capt. Steve Downing on down through the ranks. Not a week went by without a squad car or two showing up at the club as officers came to kick it with the members. I can't emphasize enough how important that was for the children. What contact most of them had with the police revolved around loved ones or neighbors being led away in handcuffs, or worse. Seeing the officers at the club regularly on a friendly, informal basis really helped open the lines of trust and communication on both sides; the kids saw the people behind the uniforms, and the officers got to know the children and teens away from their usual circumstances. I'm pretty sure that's one of the reasons some of our former members, including Terry Baker, have gone on to become police officers.

When the LAPD reorganized their precincts and our block became part of the 77th Street Division, we developed relationships with a new group. That's why I wasn't surprised when a squad car pulled up one afternoon in early 1988, and I didn't recognize the uniformed officer who got out.

"Hello," he said as he smiled and stretched out his hand. "I'm Lt. Bruce Hagerty from the South Bureau CRASH Unit. Are you Lou Dantzler?" The CRASH Unit was the LAPD's gang task force, formed in the early 1980s to deal with the nearly 70,000 kids who were members of more than

600 street gangs. They had their work cut out for them. In 1987, CRASH investigated 387 gang shootings—about 1 a day.

"Yeah, I'm Lou," I said, hoping he wasn't there on official business. I never asked if anyone who joined our club was a gang member. As long as they didn't bring any of that business to the club, I didn't have a problem. Even gang members should have the chance to turn their lives around. I know we had members who belonged to gangs at one time or another, like Carl, but when they came to the club, they left other affiliations at the gate.

The house across the street with the bullet holes was one of the most notorious gang houses in the area, yet the two youngest members of that family attended the club. Everyone respected and adhered to our policy: no gang attire and no fighting. I welcomed them all and hoped we could encourage them to give up that life. I never judged any of them and treated everyone equally and with respect. I believe that's one of the reasons we've never had any gang fights or incidents at the club and no graffiti has ever marred our walls—quite a feat in a place where churches were sometimes tagged.

"What can I do for you?" I asked.

"I've heard a lot about you from some of the guys down at the 77th. I always loved playing with my own kids, coaching them and whatnot, and now they're growing up and don't need me anymore. But I like being with kids, and I want to get involved on a personal level with something positive for them. I am in public service, and since I derive my income from this city and community, and that income has allowed me to raise my family and provide a nice living, I believe it's time to give something back. Now I have the time. I heard about your club and the much-needed work you do for so many people in this community, and I thought I'd come by and see if you needed any help."

There was such sincerity in his manner, and I really liked what he said about giving back. It was exactly the way I always felt. Dealing with gangs as he did every day, he told me, he knew firsthand how much our program needed support. We talked for a while longer, and I really felt a connection. He was straightforward and friendly, and he really seemed to care about the future of the kids in this community. We were of like minds.

I told him of my vision for expanding the club and making it a haven for even more families.

"You see these houses back here?" I said as I pointed to the area directly west of us, to a row of homes in varying states of decay. "If we could somehow buy up some of those houses, we could build a bigger building, maybe have a grassy area for kids to run and play soccer. In the summers, it gets so hot here on the blacktop. We have a huge increase in membership, and we just need more space."

By the end of that first meeting, we agreed that instead of Bruce getting involved on a direct level with the kids, his personality and organizational skills might be better put to use as a member of our board.

Since we were first incorporated, our board always numbered between a dozen and a dozen and a half members. Some came and went, and others came to every meeting and stayed on year after year, making a real impact. I count Toby Walker, Carl Moser, Warren Lanier, and Bob Gay among the latter group. The president at the time was Brad Pye, the former sports columnist who was the announcer for our very first Celebrity Basketball Game. He liked what he saw that day so much that he kept coming back and became one of our strongest supporters. Once he retired from sports writing, he took a job as a chief deputy at County Supervisor Kenneth Hahn's office and really helped make a lot of things happen for us.

Another prominent member of our board around this time was a man named Michael Tennenbaum. I met him in 1980 when a mutual acquaintance—coincidentally, another police officer—introduced us. Well, *introduced* is probably the wrong word.

Michael is an investment banker, and at the time, he was a partner at a company called Bear Stearns. He was successful and influential in addition to being very generous. Like Bruce Hagerty, he wanted to do something for inner-city kids, but he didn't know how. When his friend at the LAPD told him about our club, Michael called and asked us to send him some information, which we did. He must have liked what he saw, because he called me and said he wanted to send us a check. I thanked him but said (as I always do), "Why not come down here with your check and see what we're doing?"

It's nice that people want to give us money, but I've always wanted them to see for themselves what the money is going toward. I want them to see the faces of the children when they receive new sports equipment, books for the library, or a van to take us on field trips. I also don't want them to write us a check once and go on their way; I want longer-term commitments—and I don't necessarily mean giving more money. I think it's important for kids to see people from outside the community come down here and give something back, to see that they care. I also believe that getting someone like Michael Tennenbaum or Toby Walker to come to South Central Los Angeles and see that there's more to it than the "black hole of urban decay" is beneficial to both sides. There is hope here, but how can anyone understand that unless they see it for themselves?

After some discussion—Michael didn't get where he was by letting others make decisions for him—he agreed to come down for a visit. As I took him on a tour and told him about my plans, I could tell he was receptive and really impressed with the club. He brought a check that day—a big check. It had a lot of zeros on it.

Not only did he give us money, he gave us his time and his wisdom. He was a shrewd and well-connected businessman who became one of our most valuable board members. Just as I had from Toby Walker, I learned a lot from Michael.

"You know, Michael," I said to him after a board meeting one day, "I'm starting to think bigger because of you." It was true. I had always talked about expanding, but with Michael behind me and pushing me, I felt more confident that I could achieve my dream.

At first, though, we expanded not our facility but our reach. Michael convinced me that instead of spending our resources on bricks and mortar, we should instead use what was already available in our community to reach more children.

"I've been talking to the board of education," he said to me one day, "and I've been telling them that we should take your after-school program right into the schools themselves, bring the mountain to Mohammed." So we went to the school board and made a presentation. They thought the idea was okay, but they wanted us to use an existing classroom or a corner of a gym—places that we would have to share and compete for space with others. I didn't like that idea much.

"These kids need to have a place of their own," I told them. "They need to feel ownership and that their place is special, just for them." Once the board members heard that, they cooled on the plan. I thought the issue was dead, but Michael was motivated and very passionate about reaching out this way. A few weeks later, he called and told me of a conversation he had with Mayor Tom Bradley.

"You know," Michael told Bradley, "I live in Malibu, outside the city limits. But I've supported you all these years, and I've never asked for anything, but I'm asking now, for this. I want you to tell the school board that we are an organization that can get things done, that having Challengers on their campuses will help them immensely."

Bradley had always been a champion of our club, and he went to bat for us again. After that, the tone of the meetings changed; it was a matter of when it was going to happen, not if. In 1988, we opened our first satellite club at Cienega Middle School. Hopes were high all around, but sadly, the program withered after a couple of years because kids didn't want to stay at school after dark, when the drug dealing and violence began—"nightmare time" was what one child called it.

So we closed the satellite and brought the kids to our main site, where their parents could pick them up safely. The gangs in our area knew us, respected our work, and gave us a wide berth. They never brought their trouble to our door. With the new influx of members straining our cramped space, though, I knew more than ever that we needed to expand.

This is why Bruce Hagerty was such a godsend. After serving on our board for barely more than a year, he became president; Brad Pye stepped down to devote more time to running for city council. Bruce and I discussed my vision of expanding the club in earnest.

We put our heads together and drew up a list of supporters we could get to help us. On the top of that list were Magic Johnson, who had been a board member since he first started getting involved in the early 1980s ("Every time I come down here, Lou, you don't let me leave before I write you a big check!" Magic would joke with me); Michael Tennenbaum; and Win Rhodes-Bea, whom I first met in 1987.

Win is the granddaughter of Max Whittier, a prominent turn-of-the-century Los Angeles oilman and developer of Beverly Hills. Whittier left a fortune when he died, which his children and grandchildren put into different philanthropic trusts that in turn begat numerous Whittier family foundations. Win was the trustee of one of those foundations, and she had a great interest in helping children. One Sunday evening, she was watching *60 Minutes* when the program aired a segment devoted to the "I Have a Dream" Foundation.

"I Have a Dream" was founded in 1981 by successful New York businessman Eugene Lang. Lang had been asked to give a speech that year to a class of graduating sixth graders from Harlem's P.S. 121—a school he had attended 50 years earlier. He intended to tell them something along the lines of "Work hard and you'll succeed," but on his way to the podium, the school's principal told Lang that three-quarters of the students he would be speaking to that day would probably never finish high school. Aghast, Lang then took the stage and made an extraordinary impromptu change to his speech: He promised college tuition to every one of those sixth graders who graduated from high school.

His commitment didn't end there. Once he got to know the beneficiaries of his largesse, Lang realized they would need more than just the promise of money years down the road. So he hired a full-time social worker and enlisted a local community-based organization to provide services and support for the children throughout the years that separated them from high school graduation. He also worked to maintain close personal relationships with each of the children.

In August 1985, all of the original 59 children were still in school. Word spread, and soon Lang incorporated the "I Have a Dream" Foundation, which ultimately led to the *60 Minutes* segment. It so inspired Win that she decided to start an "I Have a Dream" chapter in South Central Los Angeles, an area where high school dropout rates hovered around 40 percent, more than twice the dismal 18 percent of the Los Angeles School District as a whole.

Because Win had never been to South Central and didn't know how best to put her foundation's money to work, she hired a community activist named Myrtle Middleton to help her get the program started. It was she who called me one day and asked for help. She told me what they planned to do and explained that they needed a community-based office for their organization. One of the two schools to which they planned to offer scholarship opportunities was 52nd Street Elementary School, just a few blocks away from us. Did we have any extra room they could use?

"Of course," I said instantly. "Come on over and see." A few days later, she came with Win, an attractive, elegant woman who was equally gracious and compassionate—and generous. Her family's group of Whittier Foundations donated the entire $1.5 million needed to fund the whole "I Have a Dream" program for the two schools, which included counseling, tutoring, and field trips to help the children make it through high school in addition to individual scholarships to college or vocational school.

Win told me that day that she also hoped their program would expose the children to broader cultural and other areas, such as the business world. "I want these kids to have an opportunity to get out of the ghetto; I want them to have an opportunity for cross-socioeconomic caring."

When I told her that was what I'd been trying to do for almost twenty years for these same kids, many of whom would be beneficiaries of her new program, she became really interested, and we had a nice long talk, a conversation that continues to this day.

From that first meeting, Win and the president of her board of trustees, Arlo Sorensen, were among our biggest supporters. That's why, three years later, when Bruce and I were making a list of people who could help us mount a $5 million capital campaign, Win and Arlo were at the top. Their generosity and moral support over the previous few years had proven indispensable, and their commitment to this community was unshakeable. The first South Central class to be supported by Win's program—the class of 1987—was nearing the end of high school, with about 80 percent of them entering eleventh grade at one of fifty local schools. This rate was far better than the typical South Central graduation rate of 60 percent.

Our plan was to meet with Win and Arlo, discuss our plans, and ask for advice; maybe they'd even pledge some dollar amount for support. What we didn't figure on was walking away with a check for $1 million.

I think Bruce and I were speechless for about a week. This was by far the biggest donation I had ever seen, and Bruce was amazed at the amount of respect they had for me and how much trust they'd shown. They didn't ask us to write a proposal or a letter of intent or anything. They just gave us the money.

"You have an incredible relationship with her, Lou," Bruce said when he recovered his voice. "That really says something." So our capital campaign was off and running. With a million-dollar shot in the arm, we could approach business and civic leaders with real confidence—the Whittier Foundation was backing us up.

Bruce and I also decided that more publicity for Challengers would help our cause, which was why, in 1990, I agreed to two media requests. One in particular had far-reaching positive effects for the club.

The first was a request by the CBS news program *48 Hours*. The producers were devoting an entire episode to life in South Central— crime, gangs, urban decay, all that sort of thing. At first, I told them I wasn't interested; it was all about the forces in the community that I'd spent so many years trying to fight. My refusal must have intrigued them, because they called back and said they wanted to do a segment for the program on Challengers and how it was bringing hope to the area. I agreed. The segment, which I think lasted no more than seven or eight minutes, was a window into the club and all we were trying to do, and all in all, the result was positive. We fielded calls from all over the country after that program aired, and it really helped our fund-raising efforts.

Ironically, though, an appearance on a local cable-channel show had a more lasting influence on the club—it really changed our trajectory. The show was a public affairs program called *Good News,* which aired over the Christmas holidays in 1990. I was one of several panelists invited to discuss what each was doing to help the children of Los Angeles. Other panelists included a rabbi, a freelance artist, and a lawyer-turned-businessman named Richard Riordan, who started a foundation to put computers and a literacy program into area schools.

"None of these kids are born doomed to failure," Riordan said. "We've failed ourselves somewhere along the way." Not three years later, he became mayor of Los Angeles.

In the ten minutes I was allotted, I gave my standard United Way presentation about the club and the service I was trying to provide for kids in South Central. I'd said it so many times over the past twenty years that I didn't even have to think about it.

I left the studio and didn't give it another thought other than making a note to myself to call Riordan in a few days to see if he would come down and donate some computers. If I could manage that, I thought, the time I took to go on the show would have been worth it. I never did follow up with Riordan, though, because a few days after the program aired, someone who'd seen the show picked up the phone to call me.

Laura Peterson had devoted most of her life to kids. Growing up, she helped take care of her four younger brothers and sisters. In college, she spent her summers as a nanny. After graduating from the University of Southern California with a degree in education, she taught elementary school in Watts before eventually taking a job with Bright Horizons, a company that specialized in setting up, developing, and managing employer-sponsored childcare centers. As its representative in Southern California, Laura was responsible for building state-of-the-art centers for the children of employees of Sony, Mattel Toys, Universal Studios, and Warner Brothers, as well as Los Angeles' City Hall.

Sidelined by a knee injury, Laura found herself homebound instead of on her regular holiday ski trip. As she was lying in bed flipping through the television channels, she happened upon the cable-access program I had appeared on with Richard Riordan. She had known Riordan years earlier and was curious about what he had to say. She caught the tail end of his comments, and fortunately, I was up next.

The moderator introduced me as the founder of Challengers Boys Club, and Laura paused before changing the channel. She'd heard the name before but didn't know where, so she kept watching. Once she heard me talk about parent involvement and my approach to helping kids, she was interested. But it was bugging her—where had she heard about Challengers?

A day or two later, still laid up, she found herself flipping channels again. She stopped on a rerun of *MacGyver*. She had taken to watching the show from time to time ever since some kids at one of her centers had told her about it. Thinking it was one of those violent, shoot-'em-up cop shows, she was prepared to denounce the show until she saw an episode. Instead, she found that the title character was a cerebral action hero, a man who bested his foes with brains, not firepower. She was impressed.

The episode she absentmindedly tuned in to that day was a rerun of a Christmas episode from a few years earlier. When she heard MacGyver talk about going down to Challengers to help out the kids, Laura sat straight up.

≈

Years earlier, in the mid-1980s, my old friend Steve Downing came to pay me a visit. I hadn't seen him since he had retired from the police force a few years earlier.

"What have you been up to, Steve?" I asked. "Fishing?"

He laughed. "Now, Lou, you know I have no patience for that! I've actually been working as a television writer and producer. You know how I'd always written for cop shows on the side when I was on the job? Well, now it's turned into a full-time thing.

"When I retired, a friend of mine convinced me to be a story editor on *T.J. Hooker* and *Knight Rider*. Now I'm producing this new show, *MacGyver*, about a guy who gets all the bad guys but does it without guns. He uses his head."

I couldn't believe it. I never knew that Steve had done all this stuff in addition to being a busy police captain and helping out Challengers. In the early days, Steve was instrumental in helping Toby, Carl Moser, and me put together our board. Together, we'd recruited downtown business-people, convincing them to give something back to the community. "That's how you start fund-raising," Steve said at the time. "You extort rich businessmen—responsible people who want a healthy community to do business in—and give them the opportunity to do something." With

Steve's insight and Toby and Carl's contacts, we met with scores of the big shots, as Steve used to call them.

And now here he was, saying he was in a position to help us again. He had an idea for an episode of *MacGyver* that would feature the Challengers Club and be seen by millions—a great opportunity for publicity. It was a Christmas-themed episode in which MacGyver steps in to help the foundering boys' club. That show was so popular that throughout the series' seven-year run, Challengers was featured in several more episodes, one of which was actually filmed on our property.

During that time, I met the star, Richard Dean Anderson, a very down-to-earth guy who liked what we were doing and wanted to help. Soon after, we received a sizeable contribution from him, the first of many, and his support of the club hasn't been limited to breaking out his checkbook. In the years since our first meeting, Rick has attended countless pancake breakfasts, awards dinners, and other events in addition to being a prominent member of our board.

It was that first episode that Laura watched from her sickbed. And then it clicked: That was where she'd heard the club name before. She remembered that I'd said I was interested in expanding our facility and looking to reach even more kids but that I needed a lot of help. Laura knew she could help us—her job was building facilities for children. That Monday, she picked up the phone and called. From that day on, we've talked almost every day.

By the time I met Laura, we'd raised a considerable amount of money, but at the same time, it seemed as if we were barely out of the starting gate. We already had plans drawn up for a new building and had a projected budget of almost $5 million, a sum that sounded unattainable to me. Laura had extensive experience in facilities construction, so I invited her to sit in on our weekly construction meetings.

It was an exciting time. Months earlier, Bruce and I had talked to a large public relations firm about donating their services to us; we were going to need more help with our fund-raising campaign. At one meeting with them, we were kicking around fundraising ideas, and it was Bruce, I think, who mentioned the club's longstanding relationship with Magic Johnson. The mere mention of Magic's name caused a few heads to snap up.

"Why don't we plan a fund-raiser around him?" someone suggested, and the ideas started flowing. "How about we get people to donate money for every point he scores this season?"

"Magic's known more for his talent with assists than for high scoring," someone else said.

"Well, then, let's have people pledge a dollar amount for every assist: Help Assist Magic Assist Challengers." It was a great idea.

We spoke to Lon Rosen, Magic's agent, who, along with Magic, was 100 percent behind anything we wanted to do. He put us in touch with Bob Steiner of the Lakers organization, who proved instrumental in making things happen.

Not too long afterward, Laura came on board, and I told her about our Magic idea.

"It could bring us a lot of attention, but we need someone to run this thing from our end to make sure things are getting done," I explained. "I don't have the time, and Bruce is now head of detectives at the 77th, so he doesn't have much free time either."

Laura thought for a minute. "You know," she said, "I think I can help you. The company I work for has a program that allows its executives to volunteer at worthy organizations for a set number of hours per week. I could use those hours to help with this fund-raiser."

And she did. We moved beyond the idea of targeting individuals for contributions; we could raise a lot more money by enlisting the help of prominent corporations in the area, such as Arco and Bank of America.

The idea was to have them encourage employees to pledge a dollar amount for each assist. The Lakers used their contacts with sponsors to help us, Lon Rosen broke out his Rolodex, as did Michael Tennenbaum and others, and soon we had a hefty roster of companies willing to participate.

Here's how it worked: Each company adopted one home game, and to entice people to participate, the Lakers organization offered amazing sweeteners: floor seats, a promise to display generous pledges on the scoreboard, things like that. They also provided prizes—signed basketballs, jerseys—throughout the season and an end-of-season party for all participants, big and small, paid for by Lakers' owner Jerry Buss. The grand prize was a ride on the Lakers jet to an away game, tickets to the game, and a suite at the Lakers hotel. Soon we had more support than we knew what to do with.

That didn't mean it was easy, though. The public relations firm was helping us on a pro bono basis and couldn't provide much in the way of office support, just ideas and contacts. We had to follow up ourselves, and I was grateful and relieved that Laura shouldered most of that burden. By the time we held the press conference at the end of September 1991, we had sold each game for the season. Our hopes were really high. We expected to raise $1 million or more.

A few weeks later, Magic Johnson unexpectedly retired from professional basketball—he had contracted HIV. When I first heard the news, the assist-a-thon didn't even enter my mind. All I could think about was the pain that this kind, generous, talented man must be going through. In hindsight, Magic redefined what it meant to be HIV positive in much the same way he redefined basketball, playing things on his own terms, but we had no way of knowing that at the time, and like the rest of the country, I was in mourning.

In this gloomy state of mind, I did eventually have to think about the fund-raiser since the wheels were in motion and pledges had been made.

We called a meeting with everyone involved. The obvious choice would have been to cancel the whole thing, but many felt that we shouldn't let all this work go to waste; we were, after all, a worthy cause.

"A worthy cause?" Laura said. "What if we asked James Worthy to do it in place of Magic?" Lon Rosen graciously agreed to talk to Worthy about it, and he immediately signed on.

"We can call it Magic Gets an Assist for a Worthy Cause," Laura said. We all agreed that was a brilliant way to put it. By the end of the season, we raised nearly $100,000. and happily, Magic was there to support us every step of the way. He even came to the end-of-season party.

With the assist-a-thon behind us, we began to explore other ways to raise money for the new building, now projected to cost almost $6 million. Now a solid member of our team as well as our board, Laura joined Bruce and me at many of our fund-raising presentations to our expanding list of contacts.

One foundation we approached during this time was the McCabe Foundation, a strong supporter of many Boys & Girls Clubs (the national Boys Clubs organization had finally recognized that they were serving as many girls as boys and officially changed its name in the 1980s). I had met Jim Sheppard of McCabe in the late 1980s when Challengers and four other clubs in the southwest region were asked to start a pilot program focusing on leadership training for youth. The McCabe Foundation generously funded it. Jim must have liked what we were doing, because he and I struck up a nice friendship; I knew he'd be open to an appeal for more support.

Bruce and I talked beforehand and decided to ask for $400,000, with which we planned to hire staff to manage the capital campaign over the next four years. At the meeting, I explained that it was all about reaching more at-risk kids, and Laura followed me with her presentation of facts and figures. Then it was Bruce's turn to ask for the money.

"What we're looking for, Jim, is $1.4 million," he said casually.

"$400,000 would be used for campaign expenses, and..." he paused. "Jim, we would like you to donate the last million for the capital campaign."

Bruce and I hadn't discussed this, and all I could do was look at him and then Jim, who I was sure would say something along the lines of "Are you nuts?"

Instead, there was a pause, and then he said "Okay."

We were over the moon. On the heels of what we made from the assist-a-thon and the million Win Rhodes-Bea gave us, we were almost halfway to our goal! More than the money, though, it was incredibly gratifying to have all these people—Bruce, Laura, Win, and others—support our dreams and share our vision. For a sharecropper's son with little more than a high school education and a dream, this was amazing.

16

One Point of Light

Families can't thrive, children can't learn, jobs can't flourish in a climate of fear.

—PRESIDENT GEORGE H. W. BUSH, SPEAKING AT
CHALLENGERS BOYS & GIRLS CLUB

I always fall asleep on airplanes. I can't help it. Once the plane takes off, heading for the clouds, I'm out. It doesn't matter how uncomfortable the seats are or if I'm being crowded by the person next to me, I never manage to stay awake for long. But one particular flight was an exception.

On this trip, I think even if I had been in a coma, I would have kept my eyes open. I settled into the soft leather seat, as comfortable as my living room sofa. It tilted way back like a recliner, perfect for sleeping. Except there was no way I was going to drop off for a nap on Air Force One.

"We're getting ready to take off, Mr. Dantzler," a polite uniformed Air Force steward informed me. "Please make sure you're buckled in. And here's our itinerary for the trip," he said as he handed me a few pages printed on presidential stationery—with my name printed at the bottom. "Is there anything I can get you to drink?"

I looked over at Laura. She was as dumbfounded as I was.

The whirlwind of the two weeks preceding our cross-country flight on Air Force One still had me reeling. "I'm fine," I think I managed to say, and pretty soon the plane was taking off.

Across the plushly carpeted aisle was a distinguished gentleman who looked very familiar.

"How are you doing? Jack Kemp," he said as he stretched out his hand.

Of course, I thought, the Secretary of Housing and Urban Development. He was at Challengers when President Bush gave his speech. He was so outgoing and interested in our work that we chatted for quite a while. We told him the incredible story of how it came to be that the two of us were sitting on this plane. We hardly believed it ourselves.

For me, I told him, the whole thing began like a horror movie.

⌐

The verdict that acquitted four white police officers of beating Rodney King was read just after three o'clock in the afternoon, precisely when all the children and teens of Los Angeles were being let out of school. Bad timing, to say the least.

Our vans left our parking lot on that warm afternoon right around three o'clock, just as they did on any other weekday, to pick members up from school and bring them back to the club. We'd heard nothing about the verdict.

Soon, though, I realized something was up. I heard the wail of sirens to the south, and they didn't let up. Traffic on Vermont Avenue was backing up. We turned on our small TV to see what was going on, and the pictures were chilling. People throughout the community were spilling into the streets, angrily shouting into microphones and at TV cameras. The streets were gridlocked. I felt a pit in my stomach. I had seen this happen before; I knew what it meant.

I hurried outside to see if our vans were back yet. Only two so far. We ushered the kids inside the gym, and the noise of the police and television news helicopters became deafening. I was sure I smelled smoke.

About fifteen minutes later, the last van rolled in, and I slammed our gates behind it as a police cruiser raced down 51st Street, sirens screaming. The children who got out of the van were pretty subdued and watchful; there was none of the usual horseplay.

I paced back and forth in the yard, trying to ignore the angry shouting and what I thought was the sound of breaking glass in the distance. Meanwhile, calls from concerned and frightened parents were flooding our phone line. The smell of smoke became stronger and stronger. When the newscast showed violence erupting at the intersection of Florence and Normandie, I decided to close the club, load the kids back in the vans, and send everyone home. I think I held my breath the whole excruciating time it took for every last child to get home.

The next five days were a blur of panic and prayer, after which the armed soldiers departed and the cleanup began. Those days of deadly rioting were over, but they had laid waste to South Central Los Angeles, claiming fifty-four lives and costing the city close to a billion dollars in property damage. Residents and people everywhere began to take stock of what had happened and what it meant. The smoldering and shattered forty square miles of our community, ignored since the eerily similar convulsions of the mid-1960s, were once again the center of worldwide attention.

"I feel a deep sense of personal frustration and anguish," President Bush said about the verdicts that set off the rioting. We all did, but he was our leader, and he had to do something, which meant he had to come see the devastation firsthand and propose solutions. And Challengers was one of his stops.

To be honest, I didn't have high hopes that much would happen as a result of the president's visit, other than generating some publicity for us. Don't get me wrong; I was excited at the prospect of meeting the president, but I never expected much from the government. In all the years I had been running this club, I had taken very little public money, mainly in the form of funding for programs such as the one that paid for summer youth jobs for some of our older teens. Applying for government grants meant jumping through hoops, and the money came with so many provisions and restrictions that we might not have been able to finance what we set out to do in the first place.

I preferred to go after private money from people and foundations that shared my vision, and I was grateful to them all, including the Brotherhood Crusade; United Way; the Whittier, McCabe, and Firestone foundations; and corporate donors such as Anheuser Busch, Nike, Reebok, Citibank, McDonald's, Disney, and Taco Bell—as well as our local radio station, KKBT "The Beat," which has always done so much to spread the word about Challengers in the community. It might have been easier to depend on public funding because relying on private funds meant I had to hustle every day for money, but at least I was able to run the program as I knew it needed to be run.

So while I was honored to have the president as our guest, I really didn't see how we stood to benefit from it. All the same, Laura and Bruce convinced me to ask the Bush staff to grant us a private audience with the president as a condition of using the site, and they graciously agreed.

The fires had burned out, the smoke and ash had cleared, and people were busy sweeping the glass and debris away. For me, those first few days that followed the disturbance were a rollercoaster ride of frenetic activity and high emotion. I was still stunned and sickened by it all. The smell of smoke seemed to cling to everything, streets were next to impassable, and searching for an open grocery store was like trying to find a needle in a haystack. Still, one positive thing had emerged.

A couple of days after the disturbance was officially declared over, several of the area's gang leaders came to see me at Challengers. Knowing that some of those guys were the ones responsible for keeping our place intact, I received them as I did any visitor: with respect. I recognized some of them from the neighborhood; the others' faces were new to me. Though their clothing was familiar—it's hard to miss a true gangster—their demeanor was totally different. They looked haunted and chastened by what they and their soldiers had done. We talked for a while, individually and as a group, and all of them expressed a desire to see the violence stop.

I invited them to become involved at the club and told them our doors would always be open to them. The rest, though, was up to them. Something must have gotten through, because over the next few weeks and months, several of them came regularly to the club to talk to the kids and try to make a difference.

One of them was Rock, who had lost his way once he stopped coming to the club in his late teens. Carl had kept in sporadic touch with him. After the riots, when Rock came to see me, he showed me bullet scars from his years of running the streets. We had a serious talk about the direction his life was headed, and I sensed he was looking to make a change. Thankfully, he was. When Rock was a member of the club, he was the one I could always count on to keep things neat and orderly. He loved to organize things, so I offered him a job as custodian. Knowing how highly I value the club's appearance, Rock understood how important this job was, and he took to it with gusto. Soon he left his former life behind, and he's been with Challengers ever since.

I wish I'd had more time to follow up with the other boys, but all too soon, my attention was diverted. Barely twenty-four hours after Robbie Callaway told me of President Bush's plan to visit Challengers, a phalanx of vans, sedans, and Suburbans came careening into our parking lot. Laura, who was there with me, likened it to that scene in *Butch Cassidy and the Sundance Kid* when, right after Butch and Sundance blow up the safe on the train tracks, a train pulls up right behind them, one of the boxcars opens, and—*bam!*—a posse springs forth, ready for action. Only this posse was the Bush advance team that had come to set up for Friday's press conference.

Squads of people in suits scurried about, pointing, measuring, and speaking urgently into walkie-talkies. When we finally managed to flag someone down, she introduced herself as Judy Smith, assistant to Marlin Fitzwater, Bush's press secretary. She was very friendly and walked us through what would happen on Friday. It was amazing—within several hours, Pacific Bell was on site installing thirty-six phone lines. After that came the generators and portable bathrooms. They asked us to have the kids make signs welcoming the president, and soon we were hanging "Welcome, Mr. President" banners on the gym walls next to ones that proclaimed, "Never Stop Dreaming," "Be Part of a Solution," and "Preparation Is the Key to Success."

There was so much to do, so many details to keep track of, that I barely had time to think. We had to draw up a list of people we wanted to invite, which was a lot harder than you might think—our gym could hold only so many people, and the Bush team already had a list of 1,000, not including the press. From that Wednesday afternoon until Friday morning, Laura and I didn't sleep.

My overwhelming memories of meeting the president are of how proud I was that he'd decided to visit our club and how comfortable he made me feel. I mean, once I had the chance to sit down and talk with him, I felt very at ease. He was like a very real, attentive, and conversational father.

Before he gave his speech, we had a short meeting with him and some of his advisors in our cramped little library upstairs, just as his staff had promised. In the room with the Bush people were Laura, Bruce, and me as well as Richard Riordan, Michael Tennenbaum, Win Rhodes-Bea, California Governor Pete Wilson, Cardinal Roger Mahoney of the Los Angeles Diocese, and a few others.

We did little more than present our views on what happened in South Central and what was needed to improve things: more money for viable after-school enrichment programs; economic development that would provide stable, well-paying jobs, which would encourage more middle-class families to move back into the community; and more officers on the street who could focus on crime prevention rather than arrests after the fact.

"Studies show that the most likely hour of the day for a child to get in trouble is right after school—between 3:00 and 4:00 p.m.," I remember saying. "There needs to be a solid investment in this community—not just dollars but also people investing their time—in order to address our problems. Lately, it seems as if society is more interested in building prisons than in creating jobs to solve the problems of the inner city. What we need to do is make more of an investment in people, especially children, because they are our future."

President Bush listened to all of us and asked informed questions. I had the impression that he really understood what we were saying.

Our time was soon up. We went downstairs into the gym, which was packed to the rafters with dignitaries, club members, and parents as well as thirty or forty television cameras and photographers. Ruby and our sons, Mark and Corey, were there. After the governor and the other dignitaries finished their remarks, I went to the podium and introduced the president. I have never been one to script speeches; even if my words are going to be carried live around the world on CNN, I've always just spoken from the heart. I said that day what I still feel: that I found it incredible that I had started my life picking cotton in the fields and here I was, fifty years later, introducing the President of the United States. It was an honor.

President Bush embraced me warmly and thanked me before delivering a speech about his "Weed and Seed" initiatives, programs designed to use tough law enforcement to get dealers, drugs, and crime out of targeted neighborhoods such as ours (weed) and then provide educational and employment opportunities and related services to the people in those places (seed).

"I can hardly imagine," he said. "I try, but I can hardly imagine the fear and the anger that people must feel to terrorize one another and burn each other's property. But I saw remarkable signs of hope right next to tragic signs of hatred. This marvelous institution, this Boys & Girls Club, stands unscarred, facing a burned-out block. And its leader is this wonderful man next to me, Lou Dantzler. Its existence proves the power of our better selves, and let's never forget it."

I couldn't believe it: The President of the United States was praising me and the club on live television in front of the whole world!

"The people right here in this room know exactly what I'm talking about," he continued. "An officer in the LAPD who's the board chairman here...giving of his time, he knows what I'm talking about. You're the ones that have your sleeves rolled up, trying to help the other guy.

"This tragedy seemed to come suddenly, but I think we would all agree it's been many years in the making. I know it will take time to put things right. I could have said, 'put things right again,' but that would miss a point I want to make: Things weren't right a week ago Wednesday. Government has an absolute responsibility to solve this problem," he concluded. I couldn't have agreed more. He then announced that Challengers would be number 766 in his Thousand Points of Light program.

After his speech, there were the obligatory handshakes and photo ops—including one in which Bush received a hug from Korrah Murray, a ten-year-old member of the club—and then, almost before we knew it, the president and his team were off in a cloud of dust and sirens. The snipers on the roof vanished, the Secret Service and the press with them. An hour later, there was nothing left to do but clean up. It was over.

Or so I thought.

It's a funny thing about people. All my life, whether I've been talking to a hardened gang member, an international celebrity, or a high-ranking government official, I've thought of them all the same way—as people.

Everyone, no matter what their status in life, is deserving of respect and civility, and I believe that's one of the reasons Challengers has thrived: It's all about relationships. Gang members respect us because we show them respect as people; movie stars and sports figures help us because we give them space to be real people; and government officials, from the chief of police to the mayor and right on up to the president, applaud us because of our positive approach to helping our community.

When the Bush advance team descended upon us for those two hectic days, Laura and I spent a lot of time talking about our program with some of them. We really felt a connection with one person in particular, Deputy Press Secretary Judy Smith. She was down-to-earth and fit right in with us—she even mixed it up with some of the kids, jumping Double Dutch in her business suit. Laura worked with her closely and had a lot of time to talk to her about what we believed in—helping families take responsibility for their children and teach them how to live within and up to the standards of our society. Judy really seemed to like what we stood for.

As she and the rest of the team were packing up to leave, she gave us her card and told us that if we were ever in Washington, we should give her a call so we could meet again. While people in politics extend those kinds of invitations as easily as they draw a breath, Laura and I both got the sense that Judy really meant it.

"You know, Lou," Laura reminded me, "you have to be in D.C. on Wednesday for that Minority Male Initiative meeting." Community and civic leaders from around the country as well as the heads of all the major corporations, such as Nike and IBM, had been invited to come together and discuss the problems facing young black males in our society and what could be done in the public and private sector to address them. Dr. Louis Sullivan of the Department of Health and Human Services had asked me to attend.

Dr. Sullivan had gotten to know me as a result of our success with the Leaders in Training pilot program, funded by the McCabe Foundation.

LIT was designed to teach teen boys life and leadership skills. In the three years since Kenny Rodgers and I helped design and implement the program at our club, we'd seen spectacular results. Youths in the LIT program were more apt to stay in school and finish and stay out of gangs and off drugs; they were less likely to become teen fathers and more likely to attend college or get jobs after graduation. We had members being accepted to colleges like Yale, Cornell, and UCLA.

I liked and respected Dr. Sullivan and his staff, and that's why, when they asked me to attend the MMI meeting, I accepted, even though I knew I was needed at the club.

"We should give Judy a call," Laura continued. She was going with me to the meeting. We were pretty much inseparable around this time; I relied heavily on her advice and common sense, especially at busy times like this.

"You think so?" I said.

"Sure, why not? She was really great, and it would be nice to know someone in D.C., don't you think?"

So we called and asked if Judy was free for lunch on Wednesday after our meeting. Lunch was no good, she said; she was pretty backed up. I felt like an idiot for calling and was about to apologize for taking up her time when she said, "How about breakfast?"

"Sure. Would you like to meet us at our hotel?" I asked. "We're at the Marriott."

No, no, she laughed. She had a better idea. She asked us to meet her at the White House, where we could have breakfast in the commissary. I knew she worked for the president, but I was so naïve that I had no idea she actually worked in the White House. I tried to be casual as she explained which gate to enter and so forth, as if I were accustomed to popping in to the offices of the leader of the free world every day.

The next morning, Laura and I—a middle-aged black man and a young white woman—got into a cab in front of our hotel in D.C. and told the driver where we were going.

"No, that isn't where you want to go," the driver said when we told him which gate. "You want to go around the other side for the tour." He thought we were a couple of mixed-up tourists; the whole thing was surreal. Eventually, we convinced him we knew where we were going, and he took us there. As we approached the little gatehouse at the end of the driveway, I could see the driver casting us strange looks.

"Hello," I said to the guard. "I'm Lou Dantz–."

"Yes, Mr. Dantzler. Welcome. Can I see some identification, please? Are you Miss Peterson?" It was one of the few times I'd ever seen Laura speechless. She pulled out her driver's license. In a matter of moments, we were each issued a visitor's badge with a giant A on it and ushered into the White House, where Judy came to meet us.

She greeted us as if we were old friends, which, considering all that had gone on since we had met a week earlier, is what it felt like to me. As we stood there in the foyer, a photographer came and took some pictures. I looked around to see if there was someone famous behind us or something, but no, he was taking pictures of us. Judy handed me a large envelope that contained beautiful 8x10 photographs of me talking with the president during his visit just a few days earlier. Wow, things *must* have been crazy. I had no recollection of having a camera pointed at me at that point.

Judy then led us down a hall in the West Wing. This was years before there was a television show with the same name, so it meant nothing to us. All we knew was that we were in the White House! Laura had been on the official tour years earlier, which didn't include the West Wing, and she whispered to me that we were definitely behind the scenes. Judy pointed to a wall, and I was shocked to see pictures of myself and Challengers up there—the same as the pictures Judy had just given me—*in the White House!* Laura and I exchanged astonished looks.

Eventually, we made our way to the cafeteria and went through the motions of having something to eat. The whole time, Judy's beeper kept going off about every minute, and every so often she dashed off to return a phone call, then returned to pick up our conversation exactly where we had left off. She was amazing, let me tell you.

After a while, Laura said, "Where are we in the White House? Are we near the Oval Office or anything?" She was just making conversation, she told me later; she had no idea of what was to come next.

Judy looked at her watch and then said, "Well, why don't I take you on a quick tour?"

She walked us down a narrow hallway and told us she wanted to introduce us to her boss, so we met Marlin Fitzwater, and then she took us to the press room. From there she took us down a few more hallways, which became wider and more crowded with people. We came to a reception area, and Judy said, "And over there is the Oval Office."

"Is the president in there right now?" Laura asked. Judy looked at her for a second and said, "Just a minute, let me check."

Laura and I exchanged another look, like, *What is going on?* Suddenly Judy came back and said, "Come this way. The president will see you now."

Excuse me?

Laura said, "Oh, no! I wasn't asking for a meeting with the president. I just wanted to know if he was in the office today."

But Judy must have thought that the president had nothing better to do than spend his valuable time talking to us again, because suddenly the door of the Oval Office opened and there he was, waiting to shake our hands and say hello. "It's eight o'clock in the morning, Laura," he laughed. "Where did you expect me to be?" Now I was speechless.

Once we sat down in those wingback chairs—the same chairs you see in news footage when the president is talking to the Prime Minister of Israel or someone—he put us both at ease with his relaxed, genial manner, just as he had on Friday .

He started off by recounting how great the previous Friday was and how much he learned about South Central from us. He then asked me about my background and how it was that I was able to put something like Challengers together. He chuckled a bit about the pickup. I talked some more about my philosophy of parent involvement and trying to bring the community together. We talked about our funding sources, and he was clearly intrigued when I told him that less than 10 percent of our operating budget came from the government. He wondered why.

Then Laura spoke passionately and knowledgeably about how difficult it was to deal with government bureaucracy. "We have to be able to respond to the needs of these children as things happen, not when some governmental organization decides when and how we should respond. The reason Lou's program is so effective is because he's right there, every day, dealing with it. He's not in an office somewhere with statistics and reports. The work that needs to be done is on the front lines, and it is done primarily through nonprofits like us, which also don't have the resources to hire teams of grant writers and lobbyists who are experienced in getting government money. And then, once you get the money, you have to hire another team to evaluate how you're doing. Well, it's hard to evaluate a child's growth in character, his being on the verge of joining a gang but deciding to stay in school another year because of your program. How do you quantify that? What I mean is, it's important to let the people in their own community decide what needs to be done instead of one homogenized umbrella version of, 'If you give this, it should yield that.'"

Laura's tone was very pleasant and respectful, yet firm. I could tell the president was listening, especially when she talked about the frustration of dealing with red tape.

"What would it take?" he asked.

I said it would be wonderful if the government were willing to take a risk on a nonprofit organization and say, "Tell us what your needs are and how much money you need; tell us what your problems are and what your solutions are going to be, and we'll take a risk on you based on your reputation and your plan. If you haven't done what you've said you're going to accomplish after a period of time, then we're not going to fund you any-more." That way, we'd be held accountable, like a small business, yet also be able to run programs tailored to the needs of our own community. I think that clicked.

We chatted some more, as friendly as if we were on his front porch and he had all the time in the world. He talked about some of his own life experiences, and we shared some of ours. We laughed a bit and overall had a really nice time. Finally, as if in response to some signal, we all stood up at the same time, and the meeting was over.

"When are you headed back to L.A.?" he asked as Judy led us out the door that opened onto the Rose Garden. We told him about the MMI meeting that morning and said that we were leaving after that.

"Well, that was the most amazing twenty minutes of my life," Laura said as we took a taxi over to Health and Human Services.

We reached the meeting a bit late. The CEO of Xerox was speaking. Everyone had the chance to speak at the meeting, which was chaired by Dr. Sullivan, about what they were doing or planned to do to help the plight of urban black males.

As it turned out, though, I never had the chance to speak because shortly after we settled into the meeting, a woman came into the room and said, "Lou Dantzler?"

I wondered who knew I was here besides the people at the club. Sheepishly, I raised my hand. "I'm Lou Dantzler," I said.

"I have a call from the White House for you," she said, and you could have heard a pin drop. "Will you follow me, please?" I managed to steal a look at Laura before I left, and she looked just as astonished as I was.

When I got back to my seat at the meeting, I could feel many sets of eyes on me. "What was that about?" Laura whispered.

"Bush has to go to L.A. today, and he wants to know if we want to ride with him on Air Force One."

And that's how we found ourselves, barely two hours later, riding with the president on his private plane and talking to Jack Kemp. This was his first time on Air Force One, too, he confessed, and he was enjoying himself as much as we were.

Let me tell you, I have never had better service than we had on that plane. Everyone addressed us by name and offered us our choice of what to read, eat, and drink. It was like a five-hour vacation.

After a while, one of the stewards took us on a tour that ended up at Bush's office. "Come on in," he beckoned, dressed casually in a polo shirt and slacks. We chitchatted a while about things, such as his dog, Millie, and then he told us how much he appreciated our conversation in the Oval Office that morning. He's thanking *us*? I thought. As we talked some more with him, I got the impression that he really liked spending time with us because we were real people and had no agenda. It was fantastic.

Later that day, we touched down at LAX, and the president went on his way. I headed back to Challengers, back to reality. A few days later, Dr. Sullivan called. I apologized to him profusely for leaving the meeting early, but he understood. You don't say no to the president.

Dr. Sullivan then told me the reason for his call. It seemed Bush had decided to form a special commission to look into the reasons our inner cities were degenerating into war zones and the family structure was disintegrating. He asked Dr. Sullivan, as head of Health and Human Services, to spearhead the formation of the committee, which was to be called the National Commission on America's Urban Families. They wanted me to serve on it.

I told Dr. Sullivan that I was grateful but that I didn't know what I could possibly contribute to a committee that would be replete with nationally recognized politicians and community leaders. He wouldn't take no for an answer; he convinced me that mine was the type of voice that needed to be heard. I was in the trenches working with urban families every day, and I knew firsthand what solutions were needed.

I accepted. As I said, you don't say no to the president, however indirectly he asks.

17

Men in Charge

cA lot of the problems young men have out in the streets are really about trying to find their fathers and coming to some understanding of manhood. Without a good father, they'll find that understanding in the worst places.

— Denzel Washington

I sat in my office one afternoon in 1996 and looked at the handsome, well-groomed twelve-year-old boy sitting across from me. His innocent face belied all the trouble he was putting us through.

Barron had been a club member for a little more than seven years, starting when he was barely five years old. I had actually bent my rule—no kids younger than six—as a favor to his mother, whose older boy, then ten, was in the club. As a single mother, she had her hands full. Barron was as smart as they come, with enough energy to power a tractor-trailer, and she was pulling her hair out trying to keep him in line. He loved to question things, especially rules.

I took Barron into the club because I could see that a smart boy like that could all too easily get into trouble if left to his own devices on these streets. I took him on the condition that his older brother would look out for him.

Within weeks, staff members started complaining about him. My son Corey, who had worked for me off and on during school breaks and then full time since graduating from college, was as frustrated as any of them.

"You tell that kid something, and before the words leave your mouth, he's asking why," he fumed to me one day. "Why this, why that? He just won't shut up."

Yes, Barron loved to challenge authority. If you told him to line up, he'd ask why. If you asked him to tuck in his shirt, he'd do it halfway. He was always talking when he wasn't supposed to and trying to pass for older than his five tender years so he could be with the older kids.

Ever since the park days, I had separated kids into groups by age. What appeals to and is appropriate for a six-year-old is a far cry from what keeps a sixteen-year-old busy. We had separate areas and activities for different age groups, and it was effective. But it could also be a headache.

After our membership surged again in the late 1980s, I noticed how difficult it was becoming for the staff to determine who was supposed to be where. Keeping track of 500 to 600 kids is a big job. After talking it over with Carl, Kenny, Corey, and some of the other staff, I decided we should have the kids wear colored club shirts: light blue for ages six and seven, gold for eight to tens, green for eleven- to thirteen-year-olds, purple for those fourteen and fifteen, and dark blue for the oldest members. Not only did the colors help us keep better track of everyone, but I felt that wearing shirts that identified children as being part of a group gave them a stronger sense of ownership and belonging. It didn't hurt our image, either—the kids looked neater overall, especially since we mandated that shirts be tucked in at all times. I believe dressing neatly demonstrates respect.

The strict dress code limited problems with gang attire but also encouraged positive self-image, so parents backed us up with little if any fuss. I figured the kids would be a harder sell, given how into fashions and labels teenagers are, but they surprised me. Most of them, especially the younger ones, were proud of their shirts. When a young blue-shirt had his eighth birthday and received his gold shirt, you couldn't have wiped the look of pride and happiness off his face if you had tried.

The color-coding system, however, was the bane of Barron's existence; it identified him as younger than the kids he wanted to be with. Today, he had been sent to me—the last resort before being suspended, kind of like being sent to the principal's office—for once again talking back, challenging the staff, and sneaking off to where he wasn't supposed to be.

"What are you, Barron, almost twelve?" He nodded.

"It's seems like I'm always seeing you here in my office."

"But—"

"No buts! Let me do the talking here. I'm going to give you another chance because I can see you're a smart kid. Kenny's starting a new program for boys your age, and I want you to join. Understand?"

When people say government can't do anything positive for the folks in South Central, I have to disagree, even though I once believed it myself. Now, when people say, "Oh, politicians. They come and make promises, and then they leave, and nothing happens," I tell them about Men in Charge.

The MIC program is something Kenny and I came up with as an offshoot, of sorts, of the Leaders in Training program, which had proven to be so successful at teaching teen boys how to set reasonable goals for their future and attain them.

After President Bush recommended me for the National Commission on America's Urban Families taskforce, I got to know Dr. Louis Sullivan and the people at the Department of Health and Human Services at the monthly commission meetings, one of which was held at Challengers. Because Bush lost the election, the commission met for only eight months, but that was enough time for me to form what became lasting and fruitful relationships.

I had long been formulating an idea that would extend the mandate of the Leaders in Training program. Too many of the youth in our area were becoming parents before they even left childhood themselves. Statistics showed that fully one-third of teenage parents in Los Angeles were from South Central, which is striking when you consider that we comprised less than 10 percent of the entire city's population. And the problem was getting worse; teens were having babies at ever younger ages, some even before high school.

People writing about or trying to address this problem had long focused on the girls. I felt that if we could educate the young boys, show them what fathering children before they were prepared to care for those children did to their own lives and the lives of their offspring, we might make a greater impact.

I told Dr. Sullivan and his staff my idea, and they were cautiously upbeat about it. "Write up a proposal outlining your ideas, tell me how much you think you'll need, and we'll go from there," they said.

Now, four years later, we were about to implement a completely new program, funded by the federal government, just for our boys.

Kenny was my obvious choice to lead this ambitious project. Eternally upbeat and enthusiastic, he has a magnetic energy that makes young men want to be where he is. They get so caught up in what they're doing with him, it's just amazing. He is also full of energy—a definite plus when dealing with teenagers—and he knows the needs of the boys in this community almost as well as he knows himself.

It was interesting to see Carl and Kenny, once fierce rivals, work together. Even though Carl, as the club's program director, was Kenny's boss, there never was any sort of attitude problem on either side. They got along and respected each other, which was a great example for the kids. By the time Kenny started setting up the new MIC program, though, Carl was moving on.

The Boys & Girls Clubs had long been after me to replicate our success in other neighborhoods. After what happened with the club at Cienega Middle School, though, I was at first reluctant to try anything like that again. That was the main reason I was working so hard to raise funds to expand this club, so we could extend our reach in other ways. And we were almost there. Laura, passionate about this coming to fruition, had actually taken a two-year leave of absence from her job to devote herself full time to helping me raise the $4 million we needed.

Like me, at first she was leery of opening other sites when we were trying so hard to secure money for our own needs. With her business-professional hat on, though, she looked at the idea in another way. With more clubs, we could economize on staffing, supplies, and insurance: We could rotate staff where needed, extend our insurance as an umbrella for all the organizations, and buy all the supplies we needed in bulk.

By 1996, we were operating five other clubs. We took over an existing one in Echo Park, another gang-infested neighborhood just west of downtown, and an on-site after-school program at Lennox Middle School near the airport, as well as three smaller clubs located in housing projects. Lennox and the housing project clubs were somewhat small and were manageable with supervision by our staff. Echo Park, however, was another story.

Membership there had dwindled to barely thirty kids a day, and this was in one of the most densely populated Latino neighborhoods in Los Angeles. The staff was in low spirits, although for the most part, they were caring, competent individuals; they were simply overwhelmed. The gym was burned out, the air conditioning was broken, winos drank in the alley, and gangs ruled the streets. There was only one person I knew who could turn that place around: Carl Reed.

When I told Carl I was going to send him to Echo Park, I could tell he was disappointed. Here he was, running a big, successful club, and I was asking him to go to tiny, rundown Echo Park. He went, though, and gave it his all, and today, I'm proud to say, he has more than 300 active members. The club broke its affiliation with us in 1998 and became a full-fledged Boys & Girls Club. Carl took what he learned in all those years at

Challengers—both as a member and as a staff person—and applied that formula to his new situation. It worked.

"When I got there, Lou," he told me proudly, "people said I couldn't have parent involvement or color-coded shirts for members. The first parent meeting I had, I think seven parents showed. The staff said, 'Carl, why are you even bothering?' And I said, 'I've been places with Lou, and I've seen where he started. Let's be patient and consistent and see what develops.' Now we have over 250 parents at our monthly parent meetings. We have a brand-new gym, and downstairs is a library. I've been blessed."

Yes, Carl has been blessed—with a strong work ethic and the strength and wisdom to learn from all he went through at Challengers to become an even stronger branch on the tree, helping others.

When Carl left, I promoted Corey into his position. Carl had really taken Corey under his wing. He came in green, right out of college, while I was busy trying to raise funds for the new building. I didn't have the time to guide him, so Carl did it instead, and did it well. "Most of what I know about how to run a Boys & Girls Club is because of Carl," Corey says. "He took me aside one day and said, 'Corey, let's develop our own legacy. What can we do that Lou didn't do? What can you give to the club that Lou can't? Your own legacy is going to motivate you to reach the next level.'"

How right he was. He motivated Corey to find his own way to lead instead of letting him just stand in my shadow, and the result has been tremendous. Corey really grew into a leader under Carl. Yes, he has my physical presence and booming voice, but his style is all his own. When he ran his programs, the kids listened to him because of his leadership skills, not because he's my son. Today, I'm proud to say that Corey is my director of operations and often turns down job offers from other clubs as well as the private sector.

I can't tell you how gratifying it is to have your son want to come into business with you and share your life's passion. There's nothing like it. I had hoped Mark would be the first one to come to work at Challengers, but he had mixed feelings about the club. I think it was because he had to spend so much time there while growing up, and he wanted to try something different. He spent his first few years after high school in the military—coincidentally in the same capacity as I had thirty years earlier, top-secret communications—and then went to work for Southern California Edison, the power company. We didn't work together the way Corey and I did, but we were still close, and I was very proud of him.

Meanwhile, Kenny was having a ball starting Men in Charge. While in many ways MIC mirrored and duplicated some of the Leaders in Training program, it took things a step further and addressed the fundamental problem that boys always experience at adolescence.

Recent studies have demonstrated that between the ages of ten and thirteen, children go through as much growth and change in their bodies and brains as they do during the first three years of their lives. The difference is that infants generally receive plenty of attention and nurturing. Even government programs, such as Head Start, are specifically mandated to provide underprivileged families with assistance for their preschool children.

Rarely are these programs aimed at the needs of adolescents. It's a pity, really, because in many ways, the teen years are even more crucial to a child's growth and development. An adolescent's brain undergoes extensive changes during puberty, precisely the time when raging hormones—often fingered as a cause of negative teen behavior—begin to wreak havoc. It's also during those confusing years that children are trying to figure out who they are. Too often, especially in my neighborhood, they search for answers in all the wrong places.

Once kids reach junior high school, they seem so independent and able to think for themselves that parents often don't pay as much attention to them as they did when they were younger. Teens say they want to be left alone, and parents often comply. But I once heard of a study in which a social scientist interviewed more than 1,000 children and, to her surprise, found that teens were yearning for *more* time and *more* communication with their parents, even when they seemed to be pushing them away. "What the research shows is that it's the relationships, it's the connections, it's the people in children's lives who make the biggest difference," noted Ellen Galinsky, president of the Families and Work Institute and author of the study.

It's ironic that this crucial period of growth and change is the time when kids are most likely to experiment with drugs, alcohol, unprotected sex, and violence. Physically, they are starting to look and act like adults, but their brains are still immature and vulnerable. In particular, certain parts of their brains, such as the areas that control reasoning, aren't fully developed, so teenagers often can't think through what the consequences of their behaviors are, and they're impulsive. Because teens look and start to act more grown up, we raise our expectations, although when you think about it, that's hardly fair. How can we expect them to demonstrate adult organizational and decision-making skills before their brains have caught up to their bodies? If parents and other adults gave young adolescents as much attention as they give infants and toddlers, guiding them through this intensely emotional time, I believe we'd see a generation of well-adjusted young people.

This is what I was trying to do way before I had heard of this or any other study. Common sense told me that the kids I was dealing with were on the outermost margin of our society. There are far too few fathers present in our community, and mothers can be consumed by working to support the family, not to mention drug problems. These kids need even more attention and direction than even the average adolescent.

In short, my quarter-century of work with teenagers formed the basis of what I was trying to accomplish with Men in Charge: targeting young men between the ages of ten and seventeen and providing them with educational, recreational, and social activities that include plenty of one-on-

one interaction with positive adult male role models. I wanted the program to help give them more understanding of the responsibilities and consequences associated with early sexual activity. I also wanted it to help prepare young men for leadership roles in their families, schools, and communities as well as improve their knowledge and use of personal hygiene and health care. This program encapsulated all I had been trying to accomplish with Challengers for nearly three decades.

Kenny was able to go even beyond that by establishing a level of trust and respect with the MICs, as we called them, that allowed them to discuss intimate personal matters such as problems with girls and family members, and Kenny and Challengers were able to address them.

"I'm learning how to make good decisions now that will help keep me from making bad decisions later," is how one MIC described the program to me. It can't get much simpler than that.

≈

I looked across my desk at Barron, who I sensed needed someone to take him under their wing and help him channel all that energy and intelligence into something positive. He reminded me of plenty of other kids who'd come before him: intelligent and talented but with few places to channel his energies.

I thought about Eric, a young boy who was one of our earliest members from the days in the park. He and his older brother lived near 66th and Hoover; they were both talented in sports, good-looking, and bright. There was a certain intensity and purpose about Eric in particular, but I didn't realize at the time how much baseball and basketball meant to him. I remember being proud when he was named All-City in high school baseball and basketball. I remember congratulating his parents, Shirley and Jimmy Davis, when he was signed to play minor league baseball right out of high school. What I most remember, though, is almost dropping my dinner one evening when I turned on the television to watch a Monday night baseball game and saw Eric Davis starting for the Cincinnati Reds—the beginning of an almost twenty-year career in the majors. For kids in the club, Eric was a hero and an inspiration.

I also thought about John, a quiet, introspective, determined nine-year-old who came to the club for a couple of summers in the late 1970s. It was the first time he had ever been allowed to go that far on the bus by himself, he told me later, and he sees those bus rides—along with our regular field trips to the museums—as the beginning of his world opening up. There were so many kids who came to the club at the time John was a member, though, that I don't remember much about him.

I do, however, clearly remember the young, serious, clean-cut man in his early twenties who dropped by my office in 1991 to show me a video-tape of a movie he had just written and directed.

"It's called *Boyz 'N the Hood*," John Singleton said, and it was about growing up in South Central. He reminded me about his experiences at the club, and we had a nice talk. He invited me and some of our members to a screening of the film. Like everyone else who saw that powerful, groundbreaking movie, I was awestruck. It accurately depicted the struggles ordinary people faced growing up in our community and insightfully captured our experience in a realistic way without being exploitive or maudlin. I was so proud.

I thought about John and Eric, as well as all the other bright, talented kids like them who had come through here. Most of them used what we offered to grow in more positive directions. That's certainly what I hoped for Barron. But I also realized that kids like Barron walk a razor-thin edge: They can either choose to belong to something positive or let the elements of the street choose them. Michael and Carl fell on one side of that edge, but there were some kids who fell on the other. I knew that there were some I couldn't reach and thought of Jessie*.

Name has been changed.

I was first introduced to Jessie by Win Rhodes-Bea. Barely ten years old, Jessie was one of the children in Win's first "I Have a Dream" class at 52nd Street Elementary School, and his manner and personality demanded attention. Whether it was because of his intense energy and curiosity or his hard-to-control temper, he was difficult to ignore. By the time Win met him, he was already down with the local gang and causing a lot of trouble in class. Win asked us if we could help.

"He's by far the roughest of them all, Lou," she told me. "He can kick a ball farther than anyone else, but he will also steal other kids' lunch money. If we can get through to him, then I'll know what I'm doing is worth it."

Jessie lived in Carl's old neighborhood with an elderly grandmother who couldn't read but knew the Bible by heart. His father was in prison, and his mother had died of drug-related causes. It was a tough situation.

Carl took Jessie under his wing right away. He had grown up with Jessie's uncle, and he knew better than anyone else exactly the kind of life this kid faced.

For a while, it seemed as if things were really starting to turn around. Jessie began attending school regularly and tried to stay out of trouble. He made friends at the club and became really involved with the sports programs. He actually did his homework.

When he hit middle school, though, things changed. Adolescence, hormones, and the violence he witnessed on a daily basis—not to mention the absence of a stable home life—began to take a toll. Carl had to go looking for him in the streets when he missed coming to the club for days or weeks at a time. He'd drive over to Jessie's house, and there'd be guys drinking out of paper bags and leaning on the fence in front. With no one at home to continue what we were trying to do for him at Challengers, Jessie gradually sank back into gang life.

Eventually, he was expelled from junior high because he came to school with a knife in his pocket. After he got into trouble with the police, Win made arrangements for him to go to a boys' home about thirty miles away instead of juvenile hall. His first comment when he got there was, "Wow! I got my own bed and my own blanket!" It was a first for him.

After a brief stint at the home, however, Jessie was sent to a penal boot camp. Win went to see him there; it was a very painful visit for both of them. "He's too far gone," she told me with tears in her eyes. He managed to get himself discharged from there after a few months and returned to the neighborhood and Challengers, but a few weeks later, he was shot in the head.

He survived the shooting, but barely, emerging from a coma after two months. He'd been shot while wearing a hat that identified him as a member of the Hoover Crips. Carl visited him almost every day, and everyone at the club prayed for him. We didn't care how he had ended up in a coma; we just prayed.

Miraculously, Jessie regained consciousness with all of his faculties. As he went through a lengthy rehabilitation, he made a tremendous effort to turn his life around, and Win and Carl were right there with him.

Then I arrived at work one morning and was greeted by the sight of a squad of police cars in front of the bullet-hole house across the street from the club. I held my breath as I unlocked our gates and parked my car. I was used to seeing police in front of that house, but this time the situation felt more ominous. Yellow police tape was up around the perimeter of the front yard and part of the street. Crowds of neighbors milled around, trying to get a look at something. At the end of the driveway lay a pricey new white leather basketball shoe, resting in a pool of quickly congealing blood.

A police officer I knew was standing nearby, and I asked him what happened.

"Gang retaliation," he said matter-of-factly. "This guy," he said, pointing to the shoe, "robbed a dope house over on Hoover last night with Fat Boy*, who got shot 45 times and died at the scene. This guy, though, was

*Name has been changed.

lucky—at least at first. He was shot, but he got away. Then he came over here, and his luck ran out. I just heard he died at the hospital."

When the officer told me the victim's name, my body went cold. That was Jessie's prized sneaker. That was Jessie's blood pooling on the driveway underneath it.

My feet felt as if they were made of lead as I walked back to the club. Even with all the resources we had and all we had tried to do to help him, Jessie, barely into his teens, was lost forever.

❧

Every time a kid like Barron comes into my office, I can't help thinking about Jessie. I knew Barron would soon be at a crossroads —the same turning point that Jessie had faced—and I wanted to make sure we did everything we could for him. His neighborhood was the stomping grounds of the Rollin' 60s gang, and soon he'd be pressured to join. I felt the MIC program would provide him with the strong, adult male role models he needed to have in his life to make sure he made the right choice. I only wish we'd had the MIC program for Jessie.

It wasn't easy for Barron, especially at first. He still had his mouth and his attitude, much like Michael and Carl once had. However, he soon began to flourish under the care and guidance of Kenny, who knew well the types of pressures kids like Barron face. Kenny was tough but fair with his MICs, and he didn't let Barron get away with anything. All of Kenny's kids respected him. I kept a close eye on Barron as well and made sure that when he started to change for the better, he was rewarded. With good behavior and good grades, club members could earn things like an expense-paid trip to the Grand Canyon, underwritten by one of our supporters.

Thankfully, the attention and positive reinforcement really changed Barron's outlook. At seventeen, he was one of my most trusted leaders, going out of his way to mentor some of the younger kids. He was taking all advanced-placement classes at Dorsey High School and was making straight As, and he had his sights set on Caltech and Georgia Tech for college. We're lucky that we caught Barron at the right time; we were able to step in with our MIC program and show him a different path before the streets seemed like his only option.

Not long ago, Barron told me about a friend of his, a kid who had been his best friend in the neighborhood when he was younger. Barron's friend never came to the club, while Barron became more involved with each passing year. The tutoring programs, the computer and science lab, our partnership with NASA, our fully functioning radio and television stations, the field trips to places such as the Grand Canyon, the college tours all helped entice him to be there every day without fail, soaking it all in and eventually mentoring some of the younger ones coming up. He and his friend grew apart but occasionally ran into each another.

"What's he doing?" I asked.

"Running the streets," Barron answered. I didn't have to ask any more. I knew what that meant.

How many other Barrons are out there, waiting for someone to stick by them, take a chance on them? It would be great if I could say we could take in all the Barrons or Carls or Kennys or Kelvins or Jessies or John Singletons or Eric Davises the streets have to offer, but the truth is that the amount of money it takes to mount and run these types of programs is just staggering. Reaching out to a few more Barrons would mean an extra million or so tacked onto our budget every year. And it's just so hard to come by.

"If I could make the perfect family, it would have a father who was honest," wrote one of our young MICs, who lived in a foster home. "An honest father would be a good influence on me. He would be loving, so he could teach me how to love. The mom would be nurturing and caring. I would want the mom to be patient. My big brother would be truthful; I would have a sister that is very smart, and I would want to see her be respected."

Isn't that what we all want?

18

Never Give Up

Gangs are like war. In order to defeat them, you must cut their supply lines of fresh troops so there will be no one left to fight. In order to do that, you need to give those kids a positive alternative.

—Lou Dantzler

Five years later, in 2001, I stood on a large, dust-choked lot and signaled to Kelvin Smith. Spotting me, he broke off a conversation with several men wearing tool belts and came over.

"What's up, Lou?" he asked.

Kelvin was one of the first kids to sign up for the club after we moved into the old Vons building in 1970. He and his six brothers and sisters lived with his parents in a large house behind our lot. Kelvin loved the club. He camped out with me in the gym the night after we took the supermarket's glass doors out, and he was as happy as if I had taken him to Yosemite.

Kelvin was also the kid who showed such an interest in the mini-bike program, becoming Kenny's right-hand man and leading the others in maintenance and drills. He liked things with motors; the bigger, the better.

I wasn't surprised when I learned that he had started his own trucking and construction business a few years earlier, but I was grateful—grateful that he was back on track after succumbing to something so many young men in the 1980s did after graduating from high school: selling drugs.

Smart and blessed with good business sense, Kelvin did quite well in the drug trade. "But," he confessed to me after his son, Kelvin Jr., was born in early 1991, "something told me this wasn't right. This wasn't how I was brought up. It was leading me to a dead end, and I knew I had to do something."

Becoming a father was a turning point. "I flipped my whole life around. If my son's looking at me doing this, what is he going to think? The cycle is going to repeat itself. I've got to get away from this and do the right thing." He disassociated himself from everyone he was doing business with—a particularly hard thing to do in this neighborhood. Dealing drugs in South Central isn't like working in corporate America. You don't give two weeks' notice. His "business partners" were criminals and murderers. It took a lot of courage for Kelvin to take his life in a completely different direction.

He sold his house and moved in with his sister, then used some of the proceeds from the sale to buy a used Freightliner. Rock's brother, Pete, taught him how to drive a big rig, and he hired himself out as a driver to anyone who would pay him. Soon he bought another truck, then a tractor, and decided to get into construction.

Through all this, even during Kelvin's drug-dealing days, I kept in touch with him. I knew deep down that he was a good kid caught up in a bad situation. I told him that if he wanted to change things, he should come to me. And he did.

I'm also grateful that he's been such a big part of expanding Challengers. When I needed someone to demolish and remove the eight houses behind us to make way for the four brand-new, professional-grade tennis courts Win Rhodes-Bea had given us the money to build, I asked Kelvin if he wanted the job.

"I won't let you down, Lou," he said, and he didn't. In fact, the architects were amazed at how quickly his crew was able to raze and grade those lots—including the one where his parents' house had been. I was impressed, too, so much so that I had our general contractor hire Kelvin as a subcontractor to handle the concrete work for the tennis courts and the foundation for the clubhouse. He was one hard worker.

"Just like you, Lou," he said one day. "I'm the first one there and the last one to leave—I've modeled myself after you."

Some of the other subcontractors on the jobsite recommended him for other jobs. When Procter and Gamble, makers of Crest toothpaste, told us that they wanted to make Challengers the site of one of their first "Smile Centers"—a free full-service dental clinic for our members and families, completely underwritten by the company—I asked Kelvin to be the general contractor for the job. Recently completed, the Smile Center is as beautiful as any upscale dentist's office in Beverly Hills.

What's even more remarkable about Kelvin's business is his hiring practices. He recruits almost exclusively in the neighborhood, mostly current or former gang members, guys just out of jail or on probation who would have little chance of getting work anywhere else. He takes them on and trains them if they need it.

"I'll never give up on him," Kelvin told me one day, referring to his efforts to recruit a gang leader, a former member of the club. "I'm just like you, Lou. I never give up. That's what I've always respected about you: You never gave up on anybody. It's like when I was selling drugs, you weren't like, 'Ahh—you just a rockhead.' You still treated me like a human being and kept on me. And look what happened."

⤚

Kelvin's right. I never give up on people or ideas I believe in, such as raising millions of dollars to expand our club. It was an odyssey that took almost a decade and was fraught with setbacks and obstacles, manmade and otherwise.

It started with the Magic Johnson assist-a-thon, which derailed with news of Magic's condition and then got back on track with Plan B. Laura

Peterson was instrumental in salvaging that effort and went on to use her connections with executives at the major Hollywood studios—for which she has set up childcare sites—to launch another campaign. In early 1992, she received some terrific news: One studio liked what we were doing so much that they agreed to fund the whole expansion project! Before we could sign papers, though, the disturbances in April brought the whole plan to a stop. "We're so sorry," the studio people told us. "Now the money has to go to riot relief." That took the wind out of our sails, but we pressed on.

We found our momentum again, and we got some other major local companies to climb on board and say, "Okay, we're going to make this happen." Then the 1994 Northridge earthquake hit, devastating our whole city as well as the financial commitments to the new building. "Our money has to go to earthquake relief," we were told. Yet another setback.

When our capital campaign began in 1989, it was a time of economic prosperity that no one thought would ever end. "California is recession-proof," our civic leaders crowed. Who could have predicted the fall of the Berlin Wall, the end of the arms race, and the subsequent loss of tens of thousands of lucrative aerospace industry and defense department jobs, which were the underpinnings of our heretofore rock-solid economy? By the time of the 1994 earthquake, prosperity in Los Angeles was a distant memory for many families, including the ones in our community.

When the good jobs left, crime increased. In 1992, there were more than 1,000 homicides in Los Angeles—more than 3 a day. "White flight" swept through the city, and illegal immigrants, most from Mexico and other Central American countries, flooded into our neighborhoods, straining schools, housing, and social services. For Challengers, this meant adjusting our program to meet the needs of Spanish-speaking members and looking for ways to bridge the racial and language divide for both the children and the staff. We needed our new building more than ever.

The capital campaign took more than seven years, and I'm certain it would have taken much longer had it not been for the skillful and competent guidance of Laura Peterson and Bruce Hagerty. They brought the relationships I had built over the years to a whole new level and helped me form new ones.

After the 1994 quake, we decided to focus our fund-raising efforts in a whole new direction. We started with a series of "power breakfasts." Board members and other supporters invited friends who might be in a position to help us, and at my insistence, we hosted the events at the club instead of some fancy restaurant. The food was prepared by parent volunteers and served on paper plates. I wanted the people who came to really get a feel for what we were trying to do, something that I felt couldn't be accomplished with a slide show and a $10-a-head fruit plate.

I met a great many warm, caring individuals at those breakfasts—people who became true angels of Challengers. Long-time supporter Bernard Parks, now a city council member, reached out through his network, and those folks helped out considerably.

The Vons Corporation, our original angel, stepped in again, too. Bill Davila, head of Vons, who had been a generous and gracious presence in Challengers' life for some time, brought a whole group, including a friendly, energetic man named Dennis Holt. Dennis grew up in South Central Los Angeles not far from our club and attended Manual Arts High School. Even back then—the late 1950s and early 1960s—the school had its share of gang problems. Those were the days of the Gladiators and the Businessmen, as well as what Dennis called the Chicano gangs, from the east side. At thirteen, he became the only Anglo in a Chicano gang at Manual Arts, something he felt he needed to do as a matter of survival.

Dennis's luck changed dramatically when he befriended a police officer with a connection in Hollywood. After talking to Dennis and seeing that he was just a good kid in bad circumstances, the officer decided to take a chance. He hooked Dennis up with a job on *The Adventures of Ozzie and Harriet* TV show.

After hearing about Dennis's struggling family (his father had health problems that kept him from working), Ozzie Nelson gave him the job. That helped him support his family, and, he says, gave him hope and faith in his ability to survive. He worked there for seven years, finished school, and went on to found his own company, which became Western International Media, the largest media-buying agency in the world.

Dennis clearly understood what we were trying to do. He knew that there were many kids in South Central just like him—kids who had the potential and the desire to lead positive lives but had no one to show them how or give them the chance. He believed as much as I did in our need to expand, and from the first day I met him, he signed on to help make that vision a reality.

It is because of people like Dennis, Bill Davila, Magic Johnson, Win Rhodes-Bea, Jim Sheppard, Michael Tennenbaum, and Laura and Bruce, as well as countless others—including my wife, Ruby, who worked all those years for the telephone company, augmenting our household income so that even though my salary has remained the same since 1987, it hasn't pinched—that I am able to sit here today and survey what their dedication to my vision has made. They made it possible for me to realize my dream of improving and expanding the club to its current size of more than 50,000 square feet of indoor space to nurture the children of South Central. They enabled me to raise the necessary funds to make this club an oasis in South Central Los Angeles, which is how Denzel Washington, who became the spokesman for the national Boys & Girls Clubs organization in 1993, described us when he came for a visit with Barbara Walters that year.

Handsome, elegant, intelligent, and committed, Denzel, like Sidney Poitier, embodies what I see when I think of a positive black male role model. Perhaps most important, they both took the time to come down to our neighborhood to give something back. When Barbara Walters asked to interview Denzel for a special she was doing on Academy Award nominees—he had been nominated for *Malcolm X*—he arranged to have the interview take place at our club, spotlighting our efforts. Apart from that, he also spent a good part of that day simply mingling with the kids and playing basketball. Even Barbara Walters got on the court and took a shot or two!

I can't tell you how much it means to have someone like Denzel—or Will Smith or Shaquille O'Neal or Colin Powell, who all came to visit at different times—come to the club. We're a community that attracts media attention for crime statistics, but there's so much more here.

Shaq has come several times, once bringing two semi-trucks full of toys to distribute to our members at Christmas. When Colin Powell visited, he gave a stirring talk about what it means to never give up, using his own childhood as an example. He seemed really impressed with our club, remarking, "This is a great, dynamic place." To have this national hero take the time to notice our work was beyond anything I could imagine.

Even Henry Kissinger stopped by once and was interviewed by two of our members in our radio station. Having living historical figures such as Powell and Kissinger take the time to visit with our kids is invaluable to their self-esteem, not to mention a tremendous learning opportunity. Before occasions like these, I had the kids research the visitors in the library or our tech center so they could ask informed questions and really make the most of the visits.

In 1999, our new building was complete. What I had dreamed of since that day in 1970 when I first looked at the old, dilapidated Vons supermarket and imagined a spacious, clean club for the kids of this community was finally a reality. The Chicago Boys Club, which I visited during my first trip to a national Boys Club conference, had shown me what was possible, and we'd done it. We have a fully functioning, professional radio station as well as a state-of-the-art television studio where members can learn how to use the latest in cameras, sound, and editing. We have a science lab that rivals anything in an affluent suburban high school; a home economics room with a fully functioning kitchen to teach both boys and girls how to cook, clean, and do laundry properly; an arts and crafts center; an auditorium; a library; a tech center underwritten entirely by Citibank, featuring fifteen computers with high-speed Internet access and a full-time staff person to help kids research colleges and sort out their goals; a dental clinic; and a fully functional, restaurant-grade kitchen, built by McDonald's, which doubles as a training center for teens who need fast-food experience in order to get a job.

We have four brand-new, gorgeous tennis courts with professional-grade surfaces (donated by Nike), along with a clubhouse underwritten entirely by none other than Win's Whittier Foundation. It looks as nice as any country club.

It may be more than twenty years since I stood in awe of the Chicago Boys Club and its charismatic director and vowed that the children of South Central would have something as good as that to call their own, but now, here it is.

I often find it hard to believe all that I've been through since that first national meeting I attended in 1975. I felt shy and uncomfortable as one of the few African American attendees, and I decided then and there that one day, I would try to do something to change that.

There's no question that President Bush's visit and what followed did much to elevate my profile within the Boys & Girls Clubs organization. Afterward, whenever I attended conferences and meetings, scores of people of color sought me out for advice and fellowship. Just coming up in the organization, they were mostly looking for ways to improve their own clubs.

I mentioned this one day to a good friend of mine, Lincoln Ellis, executive director of a large Boys & Girls Club near Sacramento, who later established the Jackie Joyner-Kersee Boys & Girls Club of East St. Louis. He and I went back a long way. He was one of the few other African American executives at the time I was coming up, so we hit it off and often consulted each other on managing our respective clubs. Together we lamented the dearth of African Americans in leadership positions within the movement; I was probably the only one that President Tom Garth had ever singled out.

For some reason, Garth had a great affinity for me; he saw to it that I was appointed to several key committees and invited me to attend important meetings. I later learned from Robbie Callaway that Garth held our club up as an example for others to follow. He told Robbie that he wanted to raise the movement's profile—he wanted every Boys Club to be like Challengers.

Robbie heard other great things about us, too. When he was coordinating a Hollywood event with MGM, someone told him that if he wanted someone to deliver the goods, he should call Lou Dantzler. He did, and the event was a great success. Later, dozens of our members got to ride in the Hollywood Christmas Parade, and the Boys & Girls Clubs got huge amounts of free publicity. Robbie never forgot that and soon came through for us. When he became vice president of government relations, a newly established lobbying arm of the Boys & Girls Clubs that pursues federal grants, Challengers was always high on his list of clubs to receive funds.

"When I get in battles on Capitol Hill and I need inspiration," Robbie said once, "I think about what you did and what you continue to do. So dealing with the members of Congress or the White House doesn't bother me. I've used Challengers in major arguments with the Department of Education and folks on the Hill about the need for funding for after-school programs. Any dollars we give you, Lou, you always make sure they're spent appropriately, correctly—the biggest bang for the buck."

We were a mutual admiration society of two—he said he was inspired by my work; I was moved by his faith in me. When people like Robbie—or Toby Walker—put that kind of faith in me, it spurs me on to work even harder. I want to more than meet their expectations.

The access I enjoyed was not available to everyone. I was fortunate that Tom Garth recognized my efforts and took me under his wing; I wanted to make sure that others who were as committed and dedicated as I was would get the mentoring I'd sorely needed in the early years. So Lincoln and I and a few others put our heads together and decided to set up an organization within an organization: The Society for African American Professionals (SOAAP), which would provide resources and support to the ever-growing number of professionals of color within the Boys & Girls Clubs organization.

When we had our first meeting at one of the national conferences—it was the early 1990s, I think—we gathered in the coffee shop of the hotel. I recall looking up from time to time and seeing other Boys & Girls Clubs staff looking at us quizzically, wondering what a group of perhaps two dozen black folk could be doing together.

Our rolls now number almost 200, and we aren't meeting in coffee shops. Our group holds meetings in conference rooms at the national conferences, and we're included on the official Boys & Girls Clubs Conference program. Our mentoring organization has also been reinforced by the support of Judith Carter and Jim Cox of the national office, who, as the highest-ranking African Americans in the organization, offer inspiration and hope to all in the movement who want their voices heard at the national level.

If the 1960s were all about me finding my direction in life, the 1970s about building this program, and the 1980s about retrenching, then the 1990s— which had begun with so much struggle—ended with the fulfillment of my dream for the club. I had achieved what I set out to do, but that didn't mean I was ready to stop; I had more people to reach. I wanted to save this community, and I was going to accomplish that if I had to do it block by block.

Looking back now, I see that although much had changed, an awful lot had stayed the same. The burned-out block across the street had been partially rebuilt as a cinderblock mini-mall, flanked by a weed-choked vacant lot and a rundown used car lot. Our club, untouched and unscathed on a street that had seen the worst of the destruction from the riots, was still here and vastly improved—larger and newer, with more programs— but sadly, the social problems that led to the uprising in the first place remained the same.

There were some bright spots. The bullet-hole house—where four of the five children in that family had lost their lives to gang violence, and where Jessie had staggered to his death—had been sold to a nearby church, which converted it into a halfway/recovery house. At least now I no longer had to worry about gang activity unfolding in plain sight of our playground. You had to go down the street for that.

Yes, gangs, crime, and juvenile delinquency still infect our streets. Many kids still remain fatherless, schools are still overcrowded and overwhelmed, and well-paying jobs still elude far too many.

There are things about the club that have stayed the same, too—and that's all for the good. We're on the same site, with many of the same people and programs that have been there since the beginning. O'Melveny and Myers, the law firm Toby Walker convinced to help us, has remained our legal counsel and champion all these years, with partner Cheryl White-Mason being one of our longest-serving board members and someone I rely on for advice and support. Howard Banks, my friend from my days as a custodian and Challengers' first employee (after me), is still my transportation director, responsible for shuttling hundreds of kids daily to the club from area schools. Kenny still heads up our MIC program. Doris Hodge, one of our best parent volunteers from way back in the early

1970s, started working for Challengers in 1980 and still rarely misses a day. Toby Walker lives in Newport Beach but checks in with me from time to time and even came to the grand opening of our new building. Michael Tennenbaum and Magic Johnson continue to provide support and friendship as well.

There is one other person who became one of my strongest supporters and whose success epitomizes exactly what I'd hoped to do when I created the club. I always wanted people from the community to give something back and provide its youngest citizens with role models to look up to and emulate; people who looked like them and overcame similar obstacles to become successful in life.

Eric Davis was one of our first members, and the nearly ten years he spent in the club had a profound effect on him—so much so that even when he became rich and famous, he never forgot his roots. Over the years, he stopped in periodically to see us and encourage the kids, to say nothing of offering financial support. He was part of Challengers when our transportation services consisted of no more than the back of my lawn service truck. We shared so much over the years—including a surprise setback that neither of us could have dreamed of: cancer.

I remember riding in a limo from the airport in Washington, D.C., to Capitol Hill one day in 1997 with Eric, who was to be inducted into the Boys & Girls Clubs' Hall of Fame. It was great to see him again, but I was concerned because he had recently been diagnosed with colon cancer. It was a shock, especially for a healthy, thirty-six-year-old athlete in his prime. I wasn't downhearted, though, at least not after I saw Eric's attitude. It was the same as if he were facing a particularly nasty pitcher: He was going to do everything he could to beat it. Fear didn't seem to enter his consciousness.

When I went to the doctor about a year later complaining of cramps and bleeding and got the same diagnosis, I remembered Eric, and I knew that I had to deal with this the same way, with a positive attitude and a willingness to fight it aggressively.

Corey called Eric and told him what was going on, then Eric called and told me what I could expect. The student had become the teacher. I was no longer "Papa Lou" to him; we were now friends, and I'll never forget his kindness and support during that harrowing time—we beat the disease together.

A short while later, I was shocked when Eric came to our annual fundraising banquet and made a startling announcement: He was donating $1 million to the club.

"Lou, how far have we come from three cookies and a little milk?" he joked. "When I started, no one could envision what you put together today—well, maybe you did, but we didn't!

"I'm very proud to say I was part of the beginning. When you believe and have hope, anything can happen, and you believed in us. So I'm dedicating my life to paying you back. You taught me discipline, values, work ethics, things that have served me through my whole life, and I want this to continue."

And I know that it will. My son Mark, I'm pleased and proud to say, has now joined Challengers. When I had cancer and was in the hospital, he became very protective of me as well as the club. Although he had told me over and over through the years that he couldn't see himself working at the club, something happened when I became sick. He decided he wanted to be closer to me and share my life's work, the way Corey was. I was floored.

I thought that Mark would come into the club, see how much work it involved, and decide, after I got better, to abandon it, but he surprised me. He had a lot to learn, and his bosses—his younger brother and me—were tough taskmasters. But he persevered, bringing his enthusiasm and creativity to bear on the work, and he is now an integral member of the team. I'm incredibly proud and more confident than ever that Challengers will continue providing help to the kids of South Central for generations to come.

19

Native Sons

Everyone has the capacity to change, to do something positive with their lives, to make a contribution. Sometimes it just takes a while before they see it your way.

—Lou Dantzler

In the fall of 1997, I got a phone call that took me back more than forty years. It was from Freemon Thomas, my best friend from high school.

After I left the South, I kept in touch with Freemon sporadically, dropping in for visits on those few-and-far-between trips I made back home. But no matter how long it had been, when we finally did hook up again, it was like old times.

Freemon remained a high-spirited guy with a bit of the devil in him. With his charm and charisma, I had figured him for a career in sales, not the military demolitions expert he became. But now he was on to something completely different.

"Say hello to the newest county magistrate for Calhoun County," he announced to me on the phone that day. He was making history as the first African American appointed to the position, which made him the highest-ranking law-and-order man in the county. I just about dropped the phone, but he wasn't finished.

"I've talked it over with some folks here, Lou, and I'm calling to ask you to be the grand marshal of our annual Christmas Parade, coming up here in December."

I gave him the only answer I knew how to give to my oldest friend: "Of course I'll do it. This is home; what a great honor." I was extremely touched by Freemon's generosity and by how much things had changed in my birthplace.

In the summer of 1950, just after I turned thirteen and just before my cousin Willie went into the Army, I remember my mother telling me that we wouldn't be going into town for a while.

I was so disappointed. I had been hoarding nickels for weeks, and I finally had enough for a new comic book.

"But why...," I began, and she shut me down with that look of hers. There would be no explanations, and I knew not to ask again.

That night, though, I paid particular attention to the murmurings of my mother, aunt, and uncle out on the porch after dinner, and I caught some bits and pieces of why I was marooned on the farm. "...coming out in force...," I heard my uncle say.

"...much worse than the rally at Orangeburg last year, that's for sure...," my aunt agreed, almost whispering.

"...just keep your head down and doors shut, I guess, and don't let on to Lucious...," said my mother apprehensively.

I was still young and innocent enough to believe they were talking about the bogeymen in the woods being stirred up for some reason. Looking back fifty years later, I see that I was half right: There were bogeymen, all right, and they were stirred up, but they weren't the ghosts of my imaginings. These bogeymen were real, and they were out for the blood of the black folk.

A year earlier, there had been a spate of Ku Klux Klan rallies in Orangeburg, a large city twelve miles from us, and we didn't go to town for over a month. That was nothing compared to what came later.

After World War II, the thousands of black soldiers who had gone to fight for their country came home to find no room for them in the welcome wagon, particularly in the South. The ticker-tape parades and Veterans' Day honors were reserved for the white soldiers. These black men had fought long and hard for their country—in fact, the all-black Tuskegee Airmen made history not only for breaking the color barrier but also for sheer excellence. They completed hundreds of missions and lost not a single bomber to the enemy. Many African Americans weren't going to stand for being treated like second-class citizens any longer. Things were separate all right, but they sure weren't equal.

Sensing this shift in attitude, many Southern whites dug in their heels to preserve the Jim Crow society they had nurtured and cultivated for more than fifty years. Fearful that blacks might rise in standing enough to threaten their legally sanctioned superiority, Klan members were out in force. Incidents rose sharply in the years after the war, a reign of terror designed to put us back in our place.

When the Orangeburg rallies ended in the summer of 1949, we hoped that would be the end of it, but the Klan was just getting started.

First there was the fatal shooting of a black man near Columbia, followed shortly by the bullwhipping of Rufus Lee, a forty-year-old farmer taken from his home. Lee survived his ordeal and told the police, who were "working on apprehending the persons who were accused," according to the local paper.

The police investigation did nothing to quell the Klan's thirst for violence. Rumor had it that it made them even more determined to show the black folks a thing or two, and the numbers of confrontations and disturbances increased. Needless to say, tensions were high that summer. Willie heard that some Klansmen from Georgia were threatening to come up and assist their brothers to the north—that news chilled our blood.

We didn't venture any distance from the farm unless it was strictly necessary. Every far-off sound in the night had me tense and alert for hours. Then, one day in late August, we had a reprieve.

"Acts of violence cannot and will not be condoned in South Carolina," our governor, J. Strom Thurmond, declared. "If it reaches the point where local authorities can't handle a situation and the law enforcement division can't handle it, it may be necessary to call out the National Guard."

Folks on both sides of the color line were stunned. In 1948, Thurmond formed the segregationist Dixiecrat Party, which rabidly supported Southern white supremacy, and ran as its candidate for president. When he lost, he ran for governor instead, and as white South Carolina's favorite native son, he won. Two years later, to have Strom Thurmond openly declare that he would put a stop to Klan violence—with soldiers if necessary—was something of a miracle, at least to people in our neck of the woods.

"Strom Thurmond, I have lot of respect for him," Willie told me not long ago. He's a retired bus driver living in New York, married for more than forty years to Elizabeth, the girl I made him ask out all those years ago so I could double date with her sister, Rebecca.

"Here the KKK says, 'We gonna come to Columbia and get these niggers; we need to clean them out.' And Thurmond says, 'Call all the troops,' and it stopped them. They were going to protest and burn crosses on front yards and God knows what else. I mean, even if you're white, they make trouble for you, remember? If you're white and say, 'I have no trouble with black men,' they come and harass you, too. I never forgot what Strom did for us. I still respect that man for that. It was hard for a white man to take a stand for us back then."

I still talk with Willie every few weeks or so. One day, I called him to tell him something extremely ironic: I was going to present an award of sorts to Sen. Strom Thurmond, Republican of South Carolina, in a few weeks.

Thurmond hadn't become our country's oldest and longest-serving

senator by being rigid in his beliefs. While he liked to cloak his segregationist doctrines in the early half of the twentieth century in "states'
rights" rhetoric, he nonetheless moved with the times, albeit at his own
pace, even becoming one of the first Southerners to integrate his senato-
rial staff. And apart from being one of America's most famous Southern
firebrands, Thurmond had a genuine interest in the welfare of children,
especially disadvantaged children. In his capacity as one of the most influential and powerful senators in Congress, he helped secure government
grants aimed at the Boys & Girls Clubs.

As Thurmond neared 100 and announced his decision to retire from
Congress, Robbie Callahan wanted to express thanks from the Boys &
Girls Clubs for all he had made happen for us. And he wanted me, another
South Carolina native son, to be the one to formally thank Thurmond at
a Congressional Breakfast in September 2001.

"Lou," Robbie said when he asked me, "I know this is ironic, but that's
the beauty of it. It's a true American story, that a sharecropper's son who
went on to success took the time to say thank you to Strom Thurmond.
Though you may not agree on political or social issues, you're still able to
come together to try to help America's kids. We never would have been
able to get all the funding we did had Strom not supported us. He wanted
us to give the money to kids most in need of it.

" 'Which clubs are getting help to the kids that are hardest to reach?'
he would ask. And we used you as an example, Lou; we used Challengers
in our arguments with Strom Thurmond many times over."

I said yes mainly because Robbie asked me. In fact, when he finished
telling me all that Thurmond had made possible, I was honored to be the
one to thank him. I probably wouldn't have voted for him (even if, when I
lived in his district, voting had been an option for me), but I would certainly thank him. So I had the kids in the arts and crafts center make up a
large portrait of him, listing his life history and all his accomplishments,
which they researched on the Internet in our new tech center.

The morning of the breakfast, just a few days after September 11, 2001, I was seated at a table across from Sen. Thurmond. On my left was Sen. Orrin Hatch, and on my right was Sen. Patrick Leahy. At the table next to me was movie star Mark Wahlberg, who gave a moving speech about his desire to use his popularity with teens to help lead them to Boys & Girls Clubs and positive lives.

Then it was my turn. True to fashion, I had no prepared speech; I just spoke from the heart.

Even though I hadn't written anything down, I had thought a lot about what I should say. Should I recount my childhood as a dirt-poor share-cropper who often went to school without lunch because there was no food and no money? Should I make the point that all of us, whether a gang member, a sharecropper, or a United States senator, have the capacity for change and the wisdom to do so and therefore improve the lives of thou-sands of children of all races—just as Carl, Kelvin, or even Rock had done? I never give up on people because I know we all have it in us to do some-thing positive. More than anything else, I think that is the most impor-tant thing to remember.

As I sometimes did, I looked at my hands and realized that these hands, hands that had once borne the scars, cracks, and calluses of labor, hands that had swollen with bites from the chiggers in the cotton fields, had also had the opportunity to sweetly hold my wife as we slow danced to our favorite song, to proudly cradle my two sons when they were born, to rest gently on the head of a child who had no one else to show him affection, to pitch endless baseballs to kids who had no one to throw to them, and to shake the hands of all the people over the years—celebrities, business leaders, politicians, and everyday people—who helped me turn a dream that started in the back of my pickup truck into a reality that has touched the lives of more than 30,000 children.

Yes, these hands are smooth now; the scars have faded, the calluses worn away. They've changed through the years, just as the South that I knew growing up has changed, and some of its people, like Strom Thurmond, have smoothed and mellowed as well, accepting the fact that we are all people, deserving of the same respect and opportunities to thrive that other Americans enjoy. The South may rise again because of people such as Freemon Thomas; my dream is that South Central will someday rise again because of people like Carl, Kenny, Kelvin, Barron, and all the others who have dedicated so much to give its children a place to go and a place to grow.

Epilogue

Ever since that first summer, in 1968, people have asked me the secret of my success. Parents, politicians, police, you name it, they all want to know how I have been able to get the most at-risk and disaffected children to listen to me, respect me, and allow me to help them become productive members of our society. My answer is the same: What I do is simple, but it's not easy.

It's as simple as taking an interest in their lives and giving them a safe place to grow and learn. It's as simple as requiring a parent (or uncle, foster parent, or grandmother) to take an active role in shaping their child's growth and development. It's as simple as doing the same thing day after day, year after year.

Simple, yes. Easy? Definitely not!

You see, in order to gain the trust and respect of those I wanted to help, I had to be the tough guy, the one who enforced the rules—no matter what. I've been here every day, rain or shine, encouraging the same values and beliefs with every child and every parent who came through our doors. Everyone is expected to follow the rules—no exceptions. I don't worry about being popular; I worry about these kids. Schools have their three Rs, and so do I, but mine don't stand for reading, writing, and 'rithmetic. My three Rs are responsibility, respect, and reliability.

My belief is that too many of us don't take enough responsibility for our own lives and the lives of our children. We've become a society of victims—someone else is responsible for causing our problems: the schools, the media, and so on. And too many people wait around for someone else to solve them.

I have never taken any kind of public assistance, although there were times when I was eligible, such as when Mark was born and I lost my job. As I said, I was upset, but I didn't sit around counting grievances and bemoaning the fate of the black man. I felt it was *my* responsibility to feed my family. Later, when we wanted to buy a house and needed to come up with the down payment, I started my gardening business and took on other jobs to earn extra money. I did what was necessary to achieve my goals. It was hard, sure, but I believe the old saying that nothing worthwhile comes easy.

Respect is something that everyone wants but not everyone wants to give. I have found, however, that giving kids respect repays itself because they want to live up to it. I showed respect by letting them be part of the process. "This is your club," I told them in the early days. That's why they were so dedicated to fixing up the place; they wanted to impress me. I gave them a sense of ownership that made them feel that they belonged to something positive. I've long said that the reason so many kids join gangs is that they are looking for something to belong to, even if they know it's not in their best interest.

The club wasn't burned down during the 1992 riots for one simple reason: The people of the neighborhood—gangsters, working folk, welfare families—all felt that Challengers was their place, too, even if they weren't members. I showed them respect and they respected me, and the result was that the community pulled together to save something positive even while they were destroying just about everything else.

Respect also has to do with setting standards and making people live up to them. Most are more than willing to uphold the standards that we set. But there are a few who aren't, such as the lady who owed us $25 in late fees. We close at 7:00 p.m., and we charge parents $5 for every five minutes they're late picking up their children. This woman showed up at 7:30

one evening, and when I met her at her car and reminded her of the policy, she was hopping mad!

"No one ever told me about a late fee, and no one told me you closed at 7:00," she said angrily. "If I had known that, I woulda been here."

I told her that I was sorry, but we went over this at the parent orientation meeting all new families are required to attend. She hadn't come to orientation, she admitted; she sent her sister instead.

I asked her, "How do you expect to get any of this info if you don't come around?"

She didn't want to hear it. "I ain't giving you no more money!" she said, taking the club shirt off her daughter's back and throwing her club lunchbox out the car window. The girl, who was about eight or nine, jumped out of the car and picked them up, and as the mother drove off, the daughter had to run after her.

I feel sorry for that girl. I'd like to have her in the club. But I firmly believe that unless the parents are our partners, our chances for success with their children are slim. We have a waiting list with the names of hundreds of kids whose families do want the chance to make a positive difference in their children's lives, and I doubt that they would treat the club as a place to park their kids.

When parents are involved, they gain a different perspective on raising kids. One of the biggest fears some of these kids have is that I'm going to talk to their parents. That's why my relationship with the adults is so important. I can't do much if a child doesn't have respect for his or her parents and for me, so I'm strict with parent volunteer hours and late fees and dress codes. Sure, there are some who'd rather not enforce them— discipline and enforcing rules is a lot of work! But so is raising children to be responsible, productive members of our society.

If parents want to be part of this, if they want themselves and their children to be uplifted, they have to be willing to pay the price. Here, the price is their time. I tell all parents of prospective members up front, "If you don't want to be involved and volunteer, this is not the place for you."

Sometimes I have to ask myself what these parents think they're doing by buying kids whatever they want. Kids who don't have to work for things don't understand their value—but the parents think that giving their children things is love. Half a week's pay for a pair of basketball shoes for a ten-year-old? How is that teaching that child about life? I also think that many parents give children too much freedom and not enough structure. Kids need to know there are consequences for their behavior.

Often, parents chafe at our rules and pull their child out. Then later, when they realize what a difference our program makes (and at $75 a year, how affordable it is), they come back and become some of my most dedicated supporters. I hope that's what will happen with the girl who jumped from her mom's car to grab her club shirt and lunchbox—that she'll be back.

Being reliable—being the same place every day and doing the same thing—also sounds easy but is perhaps the most difficult thing of all. I've said before that the reason I'm still here after all this time is because I'm still here after all this time. I'm at the club every day. Children need stability and a sense of consistency in their lives, and I've worked to provide that. I'm down greeting the parents at 7:00 a.m. every day; I'm walking around. It's the only way to stay in touch and let people know you care.

You see, what I do isn't magic, it's just plain old common sense; the type of thing I learned at my momma's knee and what I credit with making me the man I am today. If we could get more kids into programs like ours, providing them with discipline and direction, I'm sure our society wouldn't have as many problems as it does. And if we could get more people to take an interest in communities like ours, I know there would be less violence and fewer disturbances like the one in 1992. It's not just one group that's to blame. Once they make it, people who grew up here often leave, never to be heard from again. Not everyone is like Kelvin or Carl, giving back to the community. Sometimes, we can be our own worst enemies.

Often, someone from a potential funding source will ask, "How do you know your program is working?"

I tell them, "I just look at their faces. The differences in their attitudes, how they talk with respect, dress better, how they look and practice hygiene. And parents tell me, 'I see such a change in my kid. I couldn't control him before, and now he treats me with more respect. I'm so grateful.'" That's how I know I'm reaching them.

The things I've learned over the past four decades working with children, such as setting standards and being consistent and fair with discipline, demanding parent involvement, listening to children and showing them respect, not being afraid to be tough, and giving kids positive alternatives to the streets, have helped provide more than 30,000 members with the foundation they need to stay out of trouble and become productive members of society.

It was interesting to me that the Boys & Girls Clubs of America recently opened a club in Malibu, one of the wealthiest communities in the United States, with an excellent public school system. Parents there were finding that a large bank account and good schools weren't enough to insulate their children from the lure of crime. Kids of all races and socioeconomic backgrounds can be tempted into trouble if there is no one around to expect more of them and give them positive alternatives. Just ask the parents at Columbine High School.

One afternoon recently, as the kids started arriving after school and the explosion of colored shirts burst onto our playground, I heard a shouting match erupt between two purple-shirts (fourteen-year-old girls) over by the snack counter. There was plenty of finger pointing, gesturing, and foul language to boot. Mark, whom I happened to be talking to at the time, strode over to the girls with me and pulled them apart. When they saw me, they froze.

"Hey, what are you doing?" I demanded. "You're supposed to be leaders [I knew both girls were in the Leaders in Training program]; you can't be acting like that here! Maybe I should put the two of you out for the summer."

That got their attention. It was only April, but already the staff and the kids were gearing up and looking forward to the summer field trips, special games, and activities. No one wanted to be suspended for the summer.

"What do you think I should do?" I asked them as dozens of members on the playground stood and watched. "How do you think I should handle this? Here you are, cursing and yelling in the club. You're leaders, maybe you should figure it out! Talk it over and let me know what I should do."

In full view of everyone on the playground, they went over to a picnic table and calmly talked it over. Then they came back over to me and told me they were wrong, and it would never happen again. Just to make sure it sank in, I had them go up to the tech center and write me a letter explaining themselves. While the grammar wasn't perfect, their letters were sincere; they really felt terrible about acting so badly, especially in front of the younger ones.

"Dear Mr. Lou," read one letter, "I apologize for the way I reacted. I will watch what I say in front of the little ones. We could have sat down and talked about it like two mature young ladies and not like children in the streets. This is a positive place for kids and I will like to keep it that way. Sincerely apologize, Janice*."

"Dear Lou," read the other, "...I don't mean to do all the things I do. I do them without thinking. Like yesterday, I lost my temper when Janice came up to set me tripping—acting ghetto and loud talking—with her hands in my face. When I asked her nicely, she...banged on me. I do realize that I could have taken this argument to a staff and they would have allowed us to settle our differences. I feel I made a bad choice, I acted very immature and not like a leader! But the next time I will be careful of confrontations and be sure to take them to staff! Signed, Whitney*."

*Names have been changed.

I've read countless letters such as this over the years, ones that apologized for "disrespecting my authority," "using violent words," and so forth. The year on the calendar doesn't seem to matter: 1972 or 2002, the kids have always wanted to test the limits and see what they can get away with. It hasn't changed, and neither have our standards since that first Saturday in Centinela Park.

You see, what I'm doing today is no different from what I set out to do in 1968 in the back of my pickup truck: give kids in this forgotten community the attention, caring, structure, and discipline that is often lacking in their lives and make sure it's provided on a daily basis. Our building may have changed over the years, and staff, members, and parents may have come and gone, but I'm still here, and my mission remains the same: to provide an oasis in a hostile territory, a place where kids can be kids, where they can learn how to treat each other and be treated with respect and can learn skills and behaviors designed to give them a better chance in life, all under the caring supervision of a staff of mentors offering positive alternatives designed to raise the awareness and self-esteem of at-risk kids.

The icing on the cake is the people whose aspirations to help others grew from coming into contact with mine. Bruce Hagerty, who remained our board president and a strong supporter for nearly a decade, retired from the LAPD in the late 1990s and started a Boys & Girls Club in a small town north of L.A.

Laura Peterson, who took time off from her career to help me realize my vision of expanding this club, went back into the private sector after helping me raise the money for our capital campaign, but she soon found that she missed the sense of purpose and satisfaction derived from helping others. In 1998, she quit her job and co-founded Hollywood CPR, a nonprofit training program for at-risk youths and young adults that's specifically designed to teach the skills needed to get well-paying union jobs in the entertainment industry.

When I talked so many years ago about the energy of the sun nourishing the roots of a tree to create strong branches, I was thinking of that first group of boys, grown and giving back to their community—I certainly didn't have people like Laura and Bruce in mind.

As strong as my vision for the club has always been, there was a lot I didn't see coming. I knew I wanted to have fun with the kids in my community and make a difference in their lives. What I didn't count on was that my "neighborhood" would grow and grow as the needs of our community grew and grew. I'm just thankful I've been able to do my part to have a positive impact, like my mother and cousin did with me.

Part of what's kept me going is that I truly enjoy what I do. I love seeing kids' faces light up when they realize their good behavior has earned them a trip to Magic Mountain or Disneyland. I love hearing parents—from those who bring their kids to me as a last resort to those who are looking for exactly the kind of enrichment the club offers—talk about the positive changes they've seen. I get to enjoy the satisfaction that comes from knowing that in some small way, I've done something to help the children no one else pays attention to. The kids have fun, the community loves it, and I love this community. That's why I'm here.

Bibliography

Books and Manuscripts

Burby, Lisa N. *The Watts Riot*. San Diego: Lucent Books, 1997.

Cannon, Lou. *Official Negligence: How Rodney King and the Riots Changed Los Angeles and the LAPD*. Boulder, CO: Westview Press, 1999.

Cohen, Jerry, and William S. Murphy. *Burn, Baby, Burn! The Los Angeles Race Riot, August, 1965*. New York: E. P. Dutton & Co., 1966.

Jah, Yusuf, and Sister Shah'Keyah. *Uprising: Crips and Bloods Tell the Story of America's Youth in the Crossfire*. New York: Touchstone (Simon & Schuster), 1997.

Articles and Documents

Bandele, Asha. "Everyone's Favorite Leading Man Turns His Talent to Directing a Powerful New Film." *Essence*, November, 2002.

Connell, Rich, David Ferrell, Jesse Katz, and John L. Mitchell. "The Real Cost of Crack: How a Decade of Addiction Has Changed Los Angeles." *Los Angeles Times*, December 18–21, 1994.

Foote, Donna, and Andrew Murr. "Back on the Block: Ten Years Later, a Street Corner in South-Central Still Smolders." *Newsweek*, May 6, 2002.

McCone Commission on the Los Angeles Riots, 1965.

PBS. "Frontline: Inside the Teenage Brain." February, 2002.

Public Papers of President George H. W. Bush. Remarks to Community Leaders in Los Angeles, May 8, 1992.

Stolberg, Sheryl. "King Case Aftermath: A City in Crisis; Anger Smolders along Vermont Avenue." *Los Angeles Times*, May 2, 1992.

United Way of Greater Los Angeles. SPA 6-Databook, South, 1999.

Index